*Semantic Incorporation
and Indefinite Descriptions*

DISSERTATIONS IN LINGUISTICS

A series edited by
Joan Bresnan, Sharon Inkelas, William J. Poser, and Peter Sells

The aim of this series is to make work of substantial empirical breadth and theoretical interest available to a wide audience.

Semantic Incorporation and Indefinite Descriptions

Semantic and Syntactic Aspects of Noun Incorporation in West Greenlandic

VEERLE VAN GEENHOVEN

CSLI Publications
Center for the Study of Language and Information
Stanford, California

Copyright ©1998
CSLI Publications
Center for the Study of Language and Information
Leland Stanford Junior University
Printed in the United States
02 01 00 99 98   5 4 3 2 1

Library of Congress Cataloging-in-Publication Data

Van Geenhoven, Veerle 1965–
    Semantic incorporation and indefinite descriptions : semantic and
syntactic aspects of noun incorporation in West Greenlandic / Veerle
Van Geenhoven.
        p.   cm.
    Includes examples in German and Kalâtdlisut.
    Includes bibliographical references.
    ISBN 1–57586–133–X (cloth : alk. paper). — ISBN 1–57586–132-1
(paper : alk. paper)
    1. Grammar, Comparative and general—Syntax. 2. Semantics.
    3. Grammar, Comparative and general—Noun. 4. Definiteness (Linguistics)
    5. Kalâtdlisut dialect—Syntax. I. Title.
    P291.V356   1998
    415—dc21   98–12973
                                                                    CIP

The drawing on the cover of the paperback edition of this book is by Maurice-Pillard
Verneuil from his *Étude de la Plante: Son application aux industries d'art* (1903, Paris:
Librairie centrale des beaux-arts). Courtesy Richard Manuck.

♾The acid-free paper used in this book meets the minimum requirements of the
American National Standard for Information Sciences—Permanence of Paper for Printed
Library Materials, ANSI Z39.48-1984.

aan mijn ouders, Marieke Huysmans en Guido Van Geenhoven

Contents

3 Setting the Semantic Scene

Preface

This book is a revision of my 1996 dissertation submitted to the Eberhard-Karls-Universität in Tübingen. It presents an analysis of the (discourse) semantic properties of noun incorporation in West Greenlandic. My interest in a semantic analysis of this construction originates from an interest in the more general questions of how and to what extent morphology delivers relevant information for the construction of semantic representations. In West Greenlandic, noun incorporation turns out to be an outstanding morphological mirror of a semantic process that applies to phrasal nominal constituents as well. Like most other "narrow" indefinites, a West Greenlandic incorporated noun and its external modifiers are interpreted as predicates. The latter are "absorbed" by a semantically incorporating verb as the restrictions of this verb's internal argument. This semantic process called "semantic incorporation" sheds new light on the notion of "weak NP", as well as on the task of introducing a discourse referent.

Semantic incorporation deals with the interpretation of a subset of indefinites only, namely the predicative indefinites. Next to these, I distinguish free variable indefinites, which undergo accommodation as a pre-interpretive step. This process deals with the "specific", wide, intermediate and partitive interpretations of indefinites. Also the accommodation of indefinites sheds new light on the way discourse referents are introduced.

Although this study mainly focuses on the semantic properties of noun incorporating constructions, it addresses its morphosyntactic aspects as well. I defend the view that West Greenlandic noun incorporation is a case of syntactic word formation, that is, noun incorporating configurations are base generated in the syntax.

Without the help of Miriam Butt, Jürgen Pafel, Udo Pletat, Peter Stadler, Rob van der Sandt and Ede Zimmermann the predecessor of this book would still be an intensional object. They each provided me with different but equally important kinds of support needed for writing and — most importantly — finishing a dissertation. I thank them for everything.

I also wish to thank my advisors Hans Kamp and Arnim von Stechow. Arnim's linguistic presence in Tübingen was the reason I joined the Graduiertenkolleg Integriertes Linguistikstudium. Hans' interest in this Greenlandic adventure was the reason I never really left Stuttgart. Having these two outstanding semanticists as my teachers has been a challenging experience in many respects. I felt myself mentally doing the splits more than once but these extra mental exercises have certainly been worth it.

I am indebted to Dorit Abusch, Nicholas Asher, Sigrid Beck, Franz Beil, Maria Bittner, Gennaro Chierchia, Molly Diesing, Regine Eckardt, Fritz Hamm, Jack Hoeksema, Birgit Kaiser, Inga Kohlhof, Peter Krause, Bill Ladusaw, Uwe Mönnich, Renate Musan, Mats Rooth, Jerry Sadock, Mary Swift, Hanneke van Hoof, Klaus von Heusinger, and Karina Wilkinson. They are only some of the various people I have had discussions with about the (earlier stages of the) work presented here and about many other (non)linguistic issues as well. I wish to recognize Graham Katz, Wolfgang Klein, Manfred Krifka, Louise McNally, two anonymous reviewers, and, once more, my two advisors for their careful comments on prefinal versions and Tony Gee and Ann Kelly for their help with the publication of this book.

Over the past three years, there have been many occasions to present parts of my work. I am grateful to the audiences I met at the Universiteit van Amsterdam, the RijksUniversiteit Groningen, the University of Texas at Austin, the University of California at Santa Cruz, Stanford University, the Heinrich-Heine Universität in Düsseldorf, Cornell University, the University of Oregon at Eugene, and the Max Planck Institute for Psycholinguistics in Nijmegen for their many comments and questions.

I extend my thanks to my friends, colleagues and informants at Ilisimatusarfik, the University of Greenland in Nuuk. I appreciate very much the effort of Karen Langgård from the Department of Greenlandic to make my stay in Nuuk possible. For their patience in answering my many questions, I am grateful to Ester Jensen, Birgit Kleist Pedersen, Arne Mølgaard, Kistâra M. Vahl, Robert Pedersen, Arnajaraq Sommer, Sofie Schultz Risenger and, in particular, Pia Rosing Heilmann from Ilisimatusarfik, as well as Nuka Elisasen and Angunguaq Berthelsen from Kujalliit J, the dorm where I stayed. For their help with analyzing the West Greenlandic data, I am thankful to Maria Bittner, Pia Rosing Heilmann and Jerry Sadock.

Finally, I thank Sandro for talking about everything but linguistics.

Abbreviations

ABL	ablative case
ABS	absolutive case
ACC	accusative case
ALL	allative case
AP	antipassive morpheme
CAUS	causative
DAT	dative case
e	empty category
DPST	dependent past mood
EQU	equative case
ERG	ergative case
FUT	future tense
GEN	genitive case
GER	gerund
HAB	habitual aspect
IND	indicative
INF	infinitive
INTER	interrogative
INST	instrumental case
LOC	locative case
NEG	negation
NOM	nominative case
PL	plural number
PERF	perfective aspect
PSV	possessivizer
PROX	proximate
PRT	participle
REL	relativizing morpheme
SG	singular number
[-tr]	intransitive
[+tr]	transitive
VIAL	vialis case

1

Introduction

0 Introduction

The empirical point of departure of this book is noun incorporation in West Greenlandic, the configuration illustrated in the following examples.[1]

(1) Kaage-liur-p-u-t.   [fw]

cake-make-IND-[-tr]-3PL

"They made cake/a cake/cakes."

(2) Nillataartarfim-mi   tallima-nik   manne-qar-p-u-q.   [fw]

fridge-LOC   five-INST.PL   egg-have-IND-[-tr]-3SG

"There are five eggs in the fridge."

Like any other linguistic phenomenon noun incorporation can be studied from (at least) two perspectives. One perspective is to look at the *structural* aspects of noun incorporation. Most of the literature studies noun incorporation exactly (and only) from this perspective [Sadock (1980; 1991), Di Sciullo and Williams (1987), Baker (1988), Rosen (1989), Anderson (1992), et al.].[2] The second perspective is its *meaning*. The primary goal of the present study is to gain more insight into the meaning of noun incorporation. More particularly, I investigate how the semantics of incorporated nouns can be embedded into a general theory of indefinite descriptions.

However, from the fact that we can study a linguistic phenomenon from these two perspectives it does not follow that these perspectives are

---

[1] West Greenlandic, Kalaallit oqaasii, is the official language of Greenland. It is the Inuit dialect spoken by the majority of the Greenlandic population. The West Greenlandic data presented in this study are partly adopted from the literature, partly the result of my own fieldwork (abbreviated as [fw]). Except for some of the case terminology, I gloss the West Greenlandic examples as in Bittner (1994).

[2] The reason that I use the term *structural* rather than *syntactic* is to preclude terminological ambiguity. In the literature, *syntactic* noun incorporation is often synonymous with a Bakerian, that is, a head movement approach to noun incorporation [Baker (1988)]. The latter's opponent is known as *lexical* noun incorporation [Di Sciullo and Williams (1987)]. What I call a *structural* analysis of noun incorporation is a cover term for both a head movement, a lexicalist and any other approach to the structural aspects of noun incorporation one can think of.

unrelated or that they give rise to unrelated insights. On the contrary. An appropriate structural representation of a linguistic configuration is a crucial basis for the representation of its semantics. And, vice versa, our intuitions about the meaning of a particular linguistic phenomenon often give useful insights about its structural representation. Particular meaning aspects of a sentence are already visible at its S-structural level, or they will be made transparent at the syntactic level of Logical Form [LF; von Stechow (1993)]. These aspects include the interpretation position of genuine quantifiers and of those indefinites that I call *predicative* indefinites. Other meaning aspects of a sentence require yet another syntactic level of representation, namely, the level of a discourse representation structure [DRS; Kamp and Reyle (1993)]. These aspects include the resolution of anaphoric expressions and the interpretation of what I call *free variable* indefinites.

With this in mind, my second goal is to show how particular meaning aspects of noun incorporating configurations are transparent in their syntactic representation. Given the variety of existing structural analyses of noun incorporation [see fn. 2], it is an important subtask of this study to find out which analysis is the most appropriate one for this purpose. Bittner (1994) has argued that from a Montagovian semantic perspective a transformational analysis of noun incorporation does a good job. I will argue that from a semantic perspective that allows differentiation between meanings of nominal expressions, a syntactically base generated analysis of noun incorporation does a better job.

1 The field of inquiry

Noun incorporation is found in a wide array of typologically unrelated languages [Mithun (1984), Baker (1988)]. I will focus my attention on noun incorporation in West Greenlandic. The meaning aspects that I will concentrate on are the scope behaviour of West Greenlandic incorporated nouns, their external modification, their lack of presuppositional force and of partitivity, and, last but not least, their ability of anteceding an anaphoric expression. I basically look at those verbal predicates which morphologically incorporate their Direct Object.[3] Obviously, the results of this semantic study cannot be blindly applied to other noun incorporating languages. Since it is challenging to ask what the common semantic denominator of noun incorporation in typologically different languages is, I see my results as a guideline for those that are interested in the semantics of other noun incorporating languages than the one on which I have concentrated.

---

[3] In this study, I capitalize the names of grammatical relations, that is "Subject" stands for the subject relation, "(Direct) Object" for the direct object relation, etc.

2 Seeking semantic counterparts

It is clear that before one can make the meaning of noun incorporating configurations transparent in their syntactic representations, one has to grasp what semantically noun incorporation in West Greenlandic is about. It is therefore useful to ask whether (some of) its meaning aspects remind us of the characteristics of particular configurations in languages that we are more familiar with. If we do find such "nonexotic" counterparts, we can check whether we can use our knowledge about these counterparts for a semantic analysis of the less familiar cases. In this study, I am mainly interested in finding *semantic* counterparts of noun incorporating configurations.[4]

2.1 Incorporated nouns and English bare plurals

In my search for semantic counterparts, I started from Bittner's (1994) observation that West Greenlandic incorporated nouns tend to take narrow scope. Example (3) illustrates the narrow scope behaviour of a nonmodified incorporated noun with respect to negation realized as the affix *-nngi(t)-*.[5]

(3)   Juuna Kaali-mit   allagar-si-nngi-l-a-q.   [Bittner (1994): 118]

     J.ABS K.-ABL   letter-get-NEG-IND-[-tr]-3SG

    i.   "It is not the case that Juuna got a letter / letters from Kaali."

    ii.   # "There is/are a letter / letters from Kaali that Juuna didn't get."

Moreover, Bittner observes that a West Greenlandic incorporated noun cannot be interpreted as definite. This amounts to saying that it cannot be interpreted as carrying a presupposition, that is, as an expression linked to some salient object [Heim (1982), van der Sandt (1992)]. This inability is illustrated in (4): the incorporated noun *puurtugar* ("parcel") in the second sentence of this piece of discourse cannot be set equal to the parcel mentioned in the first sentence.

(4)   Qaammatit qassit   matuma siurnagut Juuna   puurtukka-nik

    months   several of.this   before   J.ABS   parcel-INST

    allakka-nil-lu nassip-p-a-ra.

    letter-INST-and send-IND-[+tr]-1SG.3SG

    "Several months ago I sent Juuna a parcel$_i$ and some letters. ...

---

[4] *Structural* counterparts of noun incorporation often cited in the literature are synthetic compounding and derivation in English and typologically related languages.

[5] The # sign in front of an English paraphrase indicates that a particular sentence cannot have this paraphrase as its reading.

Ullumi aatsaat *puurtugar*-si-v-u-q, ...   [Bittner (p.c.)]

today first parcel-get-IND-[-tr]-3SG

Only today he got a parcel$_i$, ..."

This (discourse) semantic behaviour reminds one very much of the English bare plural construction [Carlson (1977)]. (5) shows that a bare plural Object takes narrow scope with respect to negation. (6) illustrates that a bare plural cannot pick up a salient referent.

(5)   John didn't see spots on the floor.   [Carlson (1977): 19]

    i.   "It is not the case that John saw spots on the floor."

    ii.   # "There were spots on the floor such that John didn't see them."

(6)   Jeremy's mother has sent him two letters$_i$ last week.

    # He got letters$_i$ today.

It is for that reason — and other reasons discussed in chapter 2 — that I have taken the West Germanic bare plural Object as a semantic counterpart of a West Greenlandic incorporated noun.[6]

2.2 Modified incorporated nouns and German split topics

In the same spirit, the meaning constraints on a particular noun incorporating configuration in West Greenlandic, namely, the one in which an incorporated noun is modified by some external modifier, reminded me of the meaning constraints on split topicalization in German [van Riemsdijk (1987), Fanselow (1988; 1993), Kratzer (1988), Diesing (1992)]. I have two constraints in mind.

The first constraint has to do with *specificity*. In German, only indefinite NPs which are located to the left of a negation marker can get a wide scope or a "specific" reading. This is illustrated in the following contrastive pair of examples.

(7)   Die   Studenten haben   zwei   Hausaufgaben nicht   mal   gelesen.

    the   students   have   two   home.tasks   not   even   read

    "There are two homework sets that the students didn't even read."

(8)   Die   Studenten haben   nicht   mal   zwei   Hausaufgaben gelesen.

    the   students   have   not   even   two   home.tasks   read

    "It is not the case that the students read even two homework sets."

---

[6] I use "West Germanic" as a cover term for English, German and Dutch.

Notably, "specific" NPs are the ones that cannot undergo split topicalization, whereas NPs that are in the scope of negation can.[7] This is shown in (9) and (10), respectively.

(9)   * Hausaufgaben haben   die Studenten zwei   nicht mal   gelesen.

       home.tasks   have   the students two   not   even read

(10)   Hausaufgaben haben die Studenten nicht mal   zwei   gelesen.

       home.tasks   have the students not   even two   read

       "As for homework sets it is not the case that the students read even two."

Interestingly, this specificity constraint also holds for another case of nominal discontinuity, namely, the case in which a West Greenlandic incorporated noun is modified by an external INSTRUMENTAL numeral. This is illustrated in the following example.[8]

(11)   Juuna Kaali-mit ataatsi-mik   allagar-si-nngi-l-a-q.

       J.ABS K.-ABL   one-INST.SG   letter-get-NEG-IND-[-tr]-3SG

       i.   "It is not the case that Juuna got one letter from Kaali."

       ii. # "There is one letter from Kaali that Juuna did not get."

The second constraint has to do with *partitivity*.[9] When a particular context is presupposed, an indefinite NP can get a partitive reading. One such context is set up in (12), in which a set of ten questions is introduced by some speaker A.

(12)   A: Bei der Prüfung mußten   die   Studenten zehn   Fragen

          at the exam   must   the   students ten   questions

          beantworten.

          answer

       "During the exam the students had to answer ten questions."

---

[7] See Diesing (1992) for a similar observation.

[8] This example is taken from Bittner (1994) except for the choice of the external modifier.

[9] In the literature, "specificity" and partitivity are often treated on a par as if they were one and the same phenomenon [Enç (1991), Diesing (1992)]. I clearly distinguish between these two semantic phenomena for reasons that will be outlined in chapter 3, and explained in chapter 6.

> B: Wieviele   von den Fragen   hat Johann richtig
>   how.many of   the questions   has J.   correctly
>   beantwortet?
>   answered

"How many of the questions did Johann answer correctly?"

(13) is a possible answer to the question of B: the indefinite NP *sieben Fragen* is understood as the partitive "seven of the questions." This means that we can link the seven questions in (13) to the presupposed set of ten questions in (12).

(13) Johann hat sieben Fragen   richtig   beantwortet.

   J.   has seven   questions correctly answered

   "John has answered seven of the questions correctly."

Its split counterpart in (14) is not an appropriate answer to B's question. That is, it cannot be understood as a partitive NP.

(14) Fragen   hat Johann sieben richtig   beantwortet.

   questions has J.   seven correctly answered

   i.   "As for questions John has answered seven correctly."

   ii. # "Of the questions John has answered seven correctly."

Again, externally modified incorporated nouns in West Greenlandic are subject to the same constraint.[10] Suppose we have the following piece of discourse:

(15) A: Nillataartitsivim-mi tallima-nik   manne-qar-p-u-q.   [fw]

      fridge-LOC   five-INST.PL   egg-have-IND-[-tr]-3SG

   "There are five eggs in the fridge."

   B: Jensi-p uku-nannga   qassi-t

      J.-ERG those-ABL.PL   how.many-ABS.PL

      neri-ssa-v-a-i?

      eat-FUT-INTER-[+tr]-3SG.3PL

   "How many from those will Jensi eat?"

---

[10] Bittner (1994) is silent about the absence of partitive readings for West Greenlandic noun incorporating configurations.

(16) in which the incorporated *mannik* ("egg") is modified by the INSTRUMENTAL numeral *marlunnik* ("two"), is not an appropriate answer to B's question under (15).

(16) Jensi marlun-nik manni-tu-ssa-a-q. [fw]

    J.ABS two-INST.PL egg-eat-FUT-IND.[-tr]-3SG

    i. "Jensi will eat two eggs."

    ii. # "Jensi will eat two of the eggs."

The numeral can only be understood as a cardinality marker and the incorporated eggs are not related to the set of eggs introduced by A in (15).

2.3 Summary

In sum, the idea to relate West Greenlandic incorporated nouns to the West Germanic bare plural and German split topicalization is promising because we can make use of our knowledge about the semantics of these nonexotic counterparts to gain more insight into the largely unexplored field of the semantics of noun incorporation. Vice versa, particular semantic and syntactic characteristics of noun incorporation in West Greenlandic may give us answers to questions about the semantics and syntax of the English and German bare plural and German split topics. Aspects of phenomena that look rather different on the surface and that have been studied separately so far can — to a large extent — be reduced to the same semantic (and syntactic) denominator.

3 A common semantic denominator: Predicative indefinites

The central task of the present study is to clarify the nature of this common semantic denominator. My approach generalizes on the insight of Williams (1983) and Partee (1987) that NPs can be interpreted predicatively. I claim that in existential contexts West Greenlandic incorporated nouns as well as English (and German) bare plurals are indefinite descriptions which denote a predicate only. This predicate is absorbed or, as I will call it, *semantically incorporated* by a verb as the predicate of that verb's internal argument. It is thus the verbal predicate, which is the semantic head of a noun incorporating configuration.[11] It is also the verb which contributes the existential quantifier binding its internal argument's variable. This feature of semantic incorporation has been adopted from Carlson's (1977) analysis of the English bare plural. Interestingly, Carlson's idea that the existential interpretation of the bare plural comes from an external source, namely the

---

[11] In this respect, I argue against the view that an incorporated noun is the semantic head in a noun incorporating configuration, and that an incorporated noun is interpreted as a predicate modifier, that is, as an expression of type $<<e,t>,<e,t>>$ [de Hoop (1992), Bittner (1994)].

verb, anticipates the Kamp-Heim view that indefinite descriptions are nonquantificational expressions [Heim (1982), Kamp (1981)].[12] Moreover, as Carlson pointed out, it follows from the lexicalized existential interpretation of the bare plural that the latter necessarily receives a narrow scope interpretation when other scope taking operators are involved.[13] I argue that this explanation of the scope effects of the bare plural can be regarded as a general explanation of the narrow scope effect of a West Greenlandic incorporated noun, a West Germanic bare plural, a German split topic — in short: of any "narrowest" indefinite.

Semantic incorporation is a subtheory of a more global approach to indefinites. That is, with semantic incorporation we have a good answer to the question of *why* particular indefinites do *not* reach non-narrow scope positions. Other questions that a theory of indefinite descriptions has to answer are *how* indefinites reach wide and intermediate scope positions, and *why* some indefinites receive a partitive interpretation while others don't. My answers to these questions are based on a distinction between predicative and free variable indefinites.[14] Whereas predicative indefinite descriptions introduce the restriction of a variable only, free variable indefinites translate into a free variable and a restriction over this variable. As such, they contain a component that cannot be incorporated, and they can combine with semantically nonincorporating verbs only. I argue that a free variable indefinite undergoes *accommodation* as a necessary pre-interpretive step. As a consequence of my approach to indefinites, the task of introducing a variable which in a Kamp-Heim approach has always been associated with the indefinite itself, is now being associated either with a semantically incorporating verb or with accommodation.

4 On the discourse behaviour of predicative indefinites

The discourse semantic aspects of predicative indefinite descriptions that I consider are their lack of an anaphoric reading [see (4) and (6)], their lack of a partitive reading [see (16) and (14)] and their discourse transparency, illustrated in the following examples.[15]

---

[12] I do not follow Carlson's (1977) claim that the English bare plural unambiguously denotes a kind individual. In chapter 3, I revisit some problems of Carlson's approach.

[13] This aspect of Carlson's theory has been rejected by different authors. In chapter 3, I argue against these rejections.

[14] In Diesing (1992), we find a distinction between different meanings for indefinite descriptions as well. According to her, we need Kamp-Heim indefinites as well as quantifier denoting indefinites. In chapter 3, I revisit some problems of Diesing's distinction.

[15] Sadock (1980) was the first who described the discourse transparency of West Greenlandic incorporated nouns.

(17) Aani   qimmi-qar-p-u-q.

     A.ABS   dog-have-IND-[-tr]-3SG

     Miki-mik   ati-qar-p-u-q.   [Bittner (1994): 67]

     M.-INST   name-have-IND-[-tr]-3SG

     "Aani has a dog$_i$. Its$_i$ name is Miki."

(18) Johann hat   Blumen gepflückt.

     J.   has   flowers   picked

     Jetzt stehen sie   in einer Vase auf dem   Tisch.

     Now   stand   they   in a   vase   on   the   table

     "Johann has picked flowers$_i$. Now, they$_i$ are in a vase on the table."

The fact that the internal argument of an incorporating verb gets its existential interpretation in the lexicon does not prevent pronominal reference to it. The discourse transparency of the incorporated noun in (17) and of the bare plural in (18) require that we investigate the exact nature of the pronoun–antecedent relation. I show how the lexicalized interpretation of predicative indefinites can be integrated into a Kamp-Heim style semantics. This means that unlike Carlson's approach, the existential quantifier introduced by an incorporating verb has *dynamic* force.

With respect to the discourse transparency of West Greenlandic incorporated nouns, I finally discuss why these nouns do not behave as anaphoric islands, whereas nominal expressions that are part of a compound in Germanic languages often do [Postal (1969), Ward, Sproat and McKoon (1991)].

(19) John is a donkey farmer and he often beats it.

     # "John is a donkey$_i$ farmer and he often beats it$_i$."

5 The syntactic visibility of semantically incorporated indefinites

The next question I will address is whether particular morphosyntactic aspects of an incorporating configuration indicate that its nominal components are semantically incorporated predicates of a lexically bound variable. I propose that the semantic distinction between incorporating and nonincorporating verbs is mirrored in a syntactic distinction between VPs. Adopting de Hoop's (1992) distinction between *weak* and *strong* Case, I argue that in addition to this distinction we need a Case-less Object position in a weak VP as the slot for syntactically base generated incorporated nouns.[16] Morphosyntactic aspects indicating that a particular nominal expression is the Object of a weak VP are: morphological adjacency [e.g. the position of a West Greenlandic incorporated noun], weak Case [e.g. the INSTRUMENTAL case of an incorporated noun's modifier in West Greenlandic], the lack of Object agreement [e.g. the intransitive agreement suffix on a noun incorporating verb in West Greenlandic] and the presence of a particular morpheme [e.g. the antipassive morpheme in West Greenlandic].

Moreover, I defend the view that a West Greenlandic incorporated noun is *base generated* in its verb adjacent position. In this respect, I argue against Baker (1988) who proposes that such a noun reaches this position through head movement.[17] From a natural language semantic perspective it makes a lot of sense to have a natural language syntax which is not restricted to productive *phrasal* syntax only, but one which embodies productive *word* syntax as well.[18] This does not mean that word-level syntax has to be "phrasalized", a trend which became very popular in generative grammar since Baker (1988) and Pollock (1989). I believe that the integration of morphology into phrasal syntax should not be at the expense of morphology. A semantically incorporated indefinite can thus be realized either as a syntactic *morpheme* [e.g. a West Greenlandic incorporated noun] or as a syntactic *phrase* [e.g. a West Germanic bare plural or a West Greenlandic INSTRUMENTAL constituent].

Finally, can a structural representation of a noun incorporating configuration tell us anything about the discourse behaviour of the semantically incorporated indefinite involved? Against Baker (1988), I show that the discourse transparency of a West Greenlandic incorporated noun is not an argument in favour of a transformational analysis of noun incorporation. The minimal condition for an incorporated noun to be discourse semantically visible is that the discourse referent restricted by this noun is an accessible antecedent. In order to meet this requirement it need not be analyzed as a D-structural phrase.

6 The way in which this book has been organized

Apart from this introductory chapter, the reader will find six more chapters.

Chapter 2 presents the empirical basis for why we need semantic incorporation. Apart from the West Greenlandic data, two semantic

---

[16] I will not follow de Hoop's semantics. De Hoop argues that strong Case NPs are generalized quantifiers whereas weak Case NPs are either individual denoting expressions or predicate modifiers.

[17] Bittner (1994) presents a semantic analysis of West Greenlandic noun incorporation which assumes that noun incorporation is the result of head movement and which deals with the lack of a specific and of a definite reading of West Greenlandic incorporated nouns. In chapter 5, I point out some shortcomings of Bittner's account.

[18] See Dowty (1979) and Bach (1983) for an elaboration of this view from a categorial syntactic perspective.

counterparts of a West Greenlandic incorporated noun play a crucial role: West Germanic bare plurals and German split topics. Section 1 illustrates some *structural* characteristics of West Greenlandic noun incorporation. Section 2 is devoted to some *semantic* aspects of West Greenlandic incorporated nouns. The first semantic issue that I address is the meaning of those verbal affixes, which incorporate a noun. Next, I get to some semantic properties of incorporated nouns: their narrow scope, nonspecific and de dicto behaviour. The *discourse semantic* properties discussed in section 3 are the impossibility for a West Greenlandic incorporated noun and a West Germanic bare plural of getting a definite or a partitive interpretation, on the one hand, and their ability of being the antecedent of a definite pronoun, on the other.

In chapter 3, I set the semantic scene within which I will move around. In section 1, I give a short review of the Kamp-Heim approach in which indefinite NPs are regarded as variables that are bound by an external quantificational source. Next, I move to the question of whether there are different types of indefinite descriptions. In section 2, I discuss Diesing's (1992) affirmative answer to this question. According to her, the scope behaviour of indefinites requires that one distinguishes between nonquantificational and quantificational indefinites, a distinction which is argued to be syntactically visible. In section 3, I show that Abusch (1994) rejects a Diesingian view: given that indefinites can escape scope islands and genuine quantifiers cannot, the scope position of an indefinite is not determined by means of QUANTIFIER RAISING. What is interesting about Abusch's contribution is that for the interpretation of indefinites she shifts the attention from the variable aspect of an indefinite to the latter's descriptive content without dropping the idea that indefinites are *always* nonquantificational. In section 4, I move to an aspect that both Diesing and Abusch fail to account for, namely, the fact that particular indefinites lack a non-narrow reading. In preparing for my account of this fact, I revisit Carlson's (1977) theory of the English bare plural and some (apparent) problems of this theory. In section 5, I first recapitulate the pros of the theories discussed in chapter 3 in order to find out the features of the ideal theory of indefinite descriptions. Next, I sketch my approach to indefinites, in which I basically distinguish predicative from free variable indefinites.

The central question addressed in chapter 4 is whether and to what extent the semantic aspects of West Greenlandic incorporated nouns and their semantic counterparts are visible in the syntax. As a first step towards this answer, I discuss two mainstream approaches in the morphosyntactic literature on noun incorporation, the lexicalist and the transformational approach. One of the questions addressed is whether these approaches deliver appropriate inputs for the semantic interpretation. In section 2, I present the view that noun incorporating configurations are syntactically base generated constructions as a third approach to the structure of noun incorporation. I relate my proposal to a similar proposal of Dowty (1979) and integrate it into de Hoop's (1992) theory of the VP. Finally, section 3 shows that in German syntactic adjacency of the incorporatee with respect to its verbal incorporator often makes semantic incorporation visible in bare plural configurations.

Chapter 5 is devoted to semantic incorporation. In section 1, I start with an outline of the theory and contrast it with Carlson's (1977) theory of the English bare plural. In light of the West Greenlandic constructions discussed in chapter 2, section 2 illustrates semantic incorporation and shows how a semantic incorporation analysis of these data is compatible with the possibility of modifying incorporated nouns. Sections 3, 4 and 5 discuss how semantic incorporation accounts for the "narrow scope" and de dicto effects of predicative indefinites in West Greenlandic and West Germanic. Section 6 compares the semantic incorporation approach with Bittner's (1994) predicate modifier analysis of West Greenlandic noun incorporation. I close chapter 5 with a section on why, and under which circumstances a semantically incorporated indefinite can antecede a definite pronoun, and which words are anaphoric islands.

Chapter 6 widens the perspective and presents semantic incorporation as a subtheory of a theory of indefinite descriptions. Starting from a distinction between predicative and free variable indefinites, I propose in section 1 that free variable indefinites undergo accommodation as a pre-interpretive mechanism. In section 2, I revisit the role of accommodation in van der Sandt's (1992) theory of presupposition projection. In section 3, I outline interesting similarities in the projection properties of presuppositions and the "scope" properties of free variable indefinites. I conclude that accommodation is a useful tool for capturing these similarities. Section 4 comes up with a proposal for why predicative indefinites, even when they are modified by a numeral determiner, cannot get a partitive interpretation.

Chapter 7 summarizes the contributions made in this book and the questions it has left open.

Aspects of Noun Incorporation in
West Greenlandic

0 Introduction

In this chapter, I present data which illustrate particular characteristics of the structure and of the (discourse) meaning of West Greenlandic noun incorporating configurations. In particular, I show that many of these properties are reminiscent of the (discourse) semantic characteristics of West Germanic bare plural NPs and of German split topicalization. This common semantic behaviour will serve as the basis for a uniform semantic analysis of West Greenlandic incorporated nouns, on the one hand, and of West Germanic bare plurals and German split topics, on the other.

The first section of this chapter concentrates on some structural characteristics of West Greenlandic noun incorporation. The second and the third sections are about the word-, sentence- and discourse-level meaning aspects of this phenomenon.

One part of the data presented here has been adopted from various sources in the literature. The other part has been collected from about ten informants during my stay in Nuuk, the capital of Greenland. For each example, I have mentioned its source.

1 Some structural aspects

West Greenlandic Inuit is a language with ERGATIVE–ABSOLUTIVE morphology. The Subject of an intransitive construction bears the same case as the Object of a transitive configuration, namely, the ABSOLUTIVE case. The Subject of a transitive structure bears ERGATIVE case. These configurations are illustrated in (1) and (2) below.

(1) Angunguaq tikip-p-u-q.   [fw]

   A.ABS   arrive-IND-[-tr]-3SG

   "Angunguaq arrived."

(2) Angunguu-p aalisagaq neri-v-a-a.   [fw]

   A.-ERG   fish.ABS eat-IND-[+tr]-3SG.3SG

   "Angunguaq ate the/a particular fish."

In (2), the transitivity of *neri-* ("to eat") is not only made visible through the ABSOLUTIVE case assigned to its Object but also through the Object agreement inflection on the verb itself. Note that (2) means that Angunguaq ate a *specific* object.[1]

It is possible to "intransitivize" a transitive construction such as the one under (2). Intuitively, intransitivizing a transitive sentence comes down to either not mentioning the Direct Object of the transitive verb or combining the transitive verb with a nonspecific Object in the INSTRUMENTAL case. (3) and (4) illustrate these two possibilities.

(3)   Angunguaq neri-v-u-q.   [fw]

      A.ABS   eat-IND-[-tr]-3SG

      "Angunguaq was eating (something)."

(4)   Angunguaq aalisakka-mik   neri-v-u-q.   [fw]

      A.ABS   fish-INST.SG   eat-IND-[-tr]-3SG

      "Angunguaq ate fish."

When we compare the inflection on the verb in (3) and (4) with the inflection on the intransitive verb in (1), it is clear that we are dealing with an intransitive configuration: the agreement morpheme lacks information about the Object. Even though the verb *neri-* ("to eat") is intransitivized in (4), it is still possible to realize its Direct Object in the INSTRUMENTAL case. This is the famous antipassive construction whereby the thematic role constituent of a transitive verb is suppressed.[2] Jumping ahead, I will argue that in West Greenlandic an INSTRUMENTAL Object and the absence of Object agreement are linguistic markers of what I will call "semantic incorporation."

1.1 Morphological incorporation

The fact that the West Greenlandic language has a very rich word-level syntax is not only shown in its agreement and case morphology. Another phenomenon that illustrates this richness is noun incorporation. Below, we have an example in which the verb *to eat* is realized as the morpheme *-tur-*

---

[1] The observation that a correlation between case and meaning exists is not new. See Bittner (1988), (1994) for West Greenlandic, Butt (1993) for Hindi/Urdu, Enç (1991) for Turkish, and de Hoop (1992) and Bittner (1994) for a general discussion.

[2] See Bittner (1988) for a detailed discussion of the antipassive in West Greenlandic. Following Baker (1988), Bittner (1994) treats the antipassive as yet another instance of transformational noun incorporation. In chapter 5, I discuss how my semantic analysis of noun incorporation could be extended so that it covers the antipassive as well.

which is attached to a noun stem that expresses its Direct Object. Note that the verbal inflection lacks Object agreement.[3]

(5) Arnajaraq *eqalut*-tur-p-u-q.   [fw]

    A.ABS   salmon-eat-IND-[-tr]-3SG

    "Arnajaraq ate salmon."

The main characteristics of the incorporated noun *eqalut-* ("salmon") are its lack of morphological case, its indeterminacy with respect to number and the strict adjacency to the incorporating verb.

1.1.1 Adjectives, numerals, *wh*-words, names and verbs

Although noun incorporation is a very widespread and common incorporating configuration in West Greenlandic, morphological incorporation is not restricted to the incorporation of nouns. Other expressions that can be combined with incorporating verbal affixes are adjectives, numerals, *wh*-words, names and even verbs as illustrated in (6), (7), (8), (9) and (10) below.

(6) Illu *angi*-v-u-q.   [fw]

    house.ABS big.be-IND-[-tr]-3SG

    "The house is big."

(7) Angut *marlu*-raar-p-u-q.   [Sadock (1991): 94]

    man.ABS two-catch-IND-[-tr]-3SG

    "The man caught two."

(8) *Su*-tur-p-i-t.   [Sadock (1991): 96]

    what-drink/eat-INTER-[-tr]-2SG

    "What did you drink/eat?"

(9) Uanga *Tuumasi*-u-v-u-nga.   [Fortescue (1984): 82]

    I.ABS Tuumasi-be-IND-[-tr]-1SG

    "I am Tuumasi."

---

[3] In West Greenlandic we also find noun incorporating verbs that bear transitive inflection, some of which I discuss in Van Geenhoven (1997) and (1998). In this book I concentrate on the intransitive cases.

(10)   Aani-p miiqqa-t   Juuna-mut

    A.-ERG children-ABS.PL J.-DAT

       paari-sur(i-v)-a-i.   [Bittner (1994): 18]

       look.after-think-IND-[+tr]-3SG.3PL

    "Aani thinks that Juuna is looking after the children."

In this study, I will pay attention to these other cases of morphological incorporation only to a limited degree. It will be argued that what nominal and adjectival incorporated expressions have in common is that they denote properties.

1.1.2 Incorporation and adjacency

The most common link drawn in the literature between noun incorporation in an "exotic" language to less exotic counterparts is a link on the structural level, more particularly, on the morphological level. In this sense, noun incorporation in a language like West Greenlandic is usually compared with compounding and derivation in West Germanic languages. Although from a purely morphological perspective this may be a very obvious way to go, I believe that from a broader structural — and semantic — perspective it does not do justice to noun incorporation.

    Consider again adjacency as a very straightforward structural aspect of a West Greenlandic noun incorporating configuration. An incorporated noun is strictly adjacent to the verbal affix with which it is combined. A German construction which correlates most closely with the West Greenlandic one is a verb combining with a bare plural in Object position. From the perspective of adjacency, the German bare plural may be established as a structural counterpart of a West Greenlandic incorporated noun. The following two sets of German examples show that the DATIVE goal argument of a three-place verb cannot show up between the ACCUSATIVE theme argument and this verb when this ACCUSATIVE is a bare plural. In contrast, it can when the ACCUSATIVE is a singular indefinite.

(11)   a.   Daß Bart seinem Freund *Briefe*   geschickt hat, ...

              that B.   his.DAT friend   letters.ACC sent   has

              "That Bart sent a friend letters ..."

      b.   * Daß Bart *Briefe*   seinem Freund geschickt hat, ...

              that B.   letters.ACC   his.DAT friend sent   has

      c.   Daß Bart *einen Brief* seinem Freund geschickt hat, ...

              that B.   a.ACC letter   his.DAT friend   sent   has

              "That Bart sent his friend a letter ..."

(12) a. Daß Hans der Frau *Kartoffeln* verkauft hat, ...

  that H. the.DAT woman potatoes.ACC sold has

  "That Hans sold the woman potatoes ..."

  b. * Daß Hans *Kartoffeln* der Frau verkauft hat, ...

  that H. potatoes.ACC the.DAT woman sold has

  c. Daß Hans *eine Kartoffel* der Frau verkauft hat, ...

  that H. a.ACC potato the.DAT woman sold has

  "That Hans sold the woman a potato ..."

From a structural perspective, I do not focus on the derivational aspect of noun incorporation, but rather on a configurational aspect, namely, on the position of a nominal constituent with respect to its verbal incorporator. Whereas in some cases the German bare plural underlies the constraint of phrasal adjacency, a West Greenlandic incorporated noun underlies the constraint of what I call morphological adjacency. Still, the adjacency requirement is not as strict as it is for incorporated nouns. Von Stechow (p.c.) points out that it is possible to have verbal adjuncts between a bare plural Object and a verb. One of his examples is (13).

(13) Ich habe heute Kartoffeln *in den Keller* gebracht.

  I have today potatoes in the cellar brought

  "Today, I brought potatoes into the cellar."

I do not intend to examine the exact nature of the adjacency requirement in the examples (11) and (12). Rather, I regard phrasal adjacency in German as a possible structural reflex of semantic incorporation.

1.2 External modification

One important characteristic of noun incorporation in West Greenlandic is the fact that an incorporated noun can be modified by one or more verb external constituents. These can be adjectives, numerals, *wh*-words, nouns or relative clauses. In a way, one could look at an incorporated noun and its external modifier as a discontinuous nominal constituent. In the following, I will link the presentation of modified West Greenlandic incorporated nouns to the presentation of yet another case of nominal discontinuity, namely, German split topicalization [van Riemsdijk (1987), Fanselow (1988), (1993), Diesing (1992)].

From a semantic perspective, these discontinuity data give rise to the question of how their representation can capture the fact that the adjectival modifier and the nominal part of these discontinuous constituents are predicates of one and the same variable. A second question that arises in this respect is whether an appropriate semantic representation of these data requires particular manipulations in their syntactic representations. I will answer these questions in chapters 4 and 5. Here, we first take a look at the relevant data.

1.2.1 Adjectives

A West Greenlandic incorporated noun can be modified by means of an adjective. The latter bears INSTRUMENTAL case, not surprisingly given the fact that a noun incorporating configuration is intransitive.[4]

(14) Esta   *nutaa-mik*   aalisagar-si-v-u-q.   [fw]

E.-ABS   fresh-INST.SG   fish-get-IND-[-tr]-3SG

"Ester got (a) fresh fish."

(15) Esta   *nutaa-nik*   aalisagar-si-v-u-q.   [fw]

E.-ABS   fresh-INST.PL   fish-get-IND-[-tr]-3SG

"Ester got (more than one) fresh fish."

In (14), the incorporated *aalisagaq* ("fish") is modified by the external INSTRUMENTAL modifier *nutaamik* ("fresh"). In (15), the plurality marker on the same external modifier indicates that the incorporated noun has to be understood as a plural object.

The most obvious reaction to the above West Greenlandic data is that the adjectival modifier and the incorporated noun establish a discontinuous constituent. Some syntacticians have argued that an incorporated noun and its modifier form one constituent at D-structure [Baker (1988)]. In chapter 4, I revisit this proposal, discuss its deficiencies, and propose an alternative nontransformational syntactic analysis of the above discontinuity.

---

[4] Apart from INSTRUMENTAL modifiers, we sometimes find ERGATIVE modifiers in noun incorporating configurations. Bittner (1994) argues that these are exceptions. Sadock (1991) claims that they are not. Here are some examples.

(i)   *Kunngi-p*   panik-passua-qar-p-u-q.   [Sadock (1991): 96]
      king-ERG   daughter-many-have-IND-[-tr]-3SG
      "There are many king's daughters (i.e., princesses).

(ii) Hansi-p   *qimmi-p*   ame-qar-tip-p-a-a.   [Sadock (1991): 97]
      H.-ERG   dog-ERG   skin-have-CAUSE-IND-[+tr]-3SG.3SG
      "Hans let him have a dog's skin."

(iii) *Sisimiut   sissa-p*   naalaga-qar-p-u-q.   [Rischel (1971): 234]
      S.ABS   shore-ERG   chief-have-IND-[-tr]-3SG
      "Sisimiut had a chief of the shore."

Note that what the incorporated nouns in these examples have in common is that they are relational nouns, that is, that they are interpreted as binary predicates. The ERGATIVE constituents represent the internal arguments of these predicates. In Van Geenhoven (1997), I present an analysis of these external possessors in which the ERGATIVE modifiers are treated as parts of a lexical compound.

In German, there is also a possibility of realizing the Object argument of a verb as a discontinuous constituent. This phenomenon is known as split topicalization.[5]

(16) *Torten*   hat   Jana   bis   jetzt nur   *frische*   verkauft.

     cakes   has   J.   until   now only   fresh   sold

     "As for cakes, Jana has only sold fresh ones so far."

The topicalized nominal expression *Torten* ("cakes") in (16) is modified by means of the adjective *frische* ("fresh"). Again, syntacticians have claimed that the topicalized bare plural forms one constituent with the adjectival "remnant" [van Riemsdijk (1987)]. In chapter 4, I defend the view that the topicalized bare plural and the "remnant" NP are separately base generated constituents. I present a syntactic analysis of German split topicalization, which is much in line with my analysis of West Greenlandic noun incorporation.

1.2.2 Numerals

A numeral in the INSTRUMENTAL case can make the number of an incorporated noun's referent explicit. This is what *marlunnik* ("two") does in (17) and (18):

(17) *Marlun-nik*   ammassat-tur-p-u-nga.   [Sadock (1991): 94]

     two-INST.PL   sardine-eat-IND-[-tr]-1SG

     "I ate two sardines."

(18) Juuna Kaali-mit   *marlun-nik*   allagar-si-v-u-q.   [Bittner (1994): 72]

     J.ABS   K.-ABL   two-INST.PL   letter-get-IND-[-tr]-3SG

     "Juuna got two letters from Kaali."

Again, the number of a topicalized nominal constituent in German can be made explicit by means of a numeral as well.

(19) Briefe   hat   Julius   *zwei*   gekriegt.

     letters has   J.   two   got

     "As for letters, Julius got two of them."

---

[5] Most of the literature has focused on split topics in German V2 sentences where part of a verbal argument is topicalized. Gisbert Fanselow (p.c.) provided the following example illustrating that split topicalization shows up in V-final sentences as well.

(i)   weil   man *Bücher* damals   in den Osten *keine*   mitnehmen   durfte.
     because one books   in.the.past   in the east   no   with.take   be.allowed
     "... because in the past it was not allowed to take books to East Germany."

In section 2.2 and 3.2, we will see that from a (discourse) semantic perspective numeral modifiers of West Greenlandic incorporated nouns and numeral modifiers of topicalized nominal expressions in German have very much in common as well.

1.2.3 *Wh*-words

In section 1.1.1, we saw that it is possible to incorporate *wh*-words. Here, I illustrate how *wh*-words can modify West Greenlandic incorporated nouns.

First, it is possible to ask for the *kind* of an incorporated noun.

(20) *Qanuq-it-tu-mik*   qimmi-qar-p-i-t?   [fw]

   how-be-REL.[-tr]-INST.SG   dog-have-INTER-[-tr]-2SG

   "What kind of dog do you have?"

Also the *number* of an incorporated noun can be questioned:

(21) *Qassi-nik*   qimmi-qar-p-i-t?   [fw]

   how.many-INST.PL   dog-have-INTER-[-tr]-2SG

   "How many dogs do you have?"

(22) *Qassi-nik*   aalisaga-tur-p-i-t?   [fw]

   how.many-INST.PL   fish-eat-INTER-[-tr]-2SG

   "How many fish did you eat?"

In German, the number of a topicalized nominal constituent can be asked for as well.

(23) *Fische*   habt Ihr   *wieviele*   gegessen?

   fish   have you.PL how.many eaten

   "As for fish, how many did you eat?"

One case of German split that needs to be mentioned in the present context is the *was-für* split, a *wh*-configuration that asks for a kind.

(24) *Was für Wale*   habt Ihr   gesehen?

   what for whales have you.PL seen

   "What kind of whales did you see?"

(25) *Was* habt Ihr   *für Wale*   gesehen?

   what have you.PL for whales seen

   "What kind of whales did you see?"

The fact that we can ask a question about an incorporated noun gives rise to the semantically interesting question of whether one can ask a question about the kind or the number only. That is, is it only possible to ask questions that do not presuppose a particular set of objects? I postpone my answer to this question until section 3.2.

1.2.4 Nouns

We saw before that some West Greenlandic verbal affixes allow the incorporation of numerals. The latter can be modified by means of an external noun.

(26) *Natser-nik*   sisama-raar-p-u-q.   [Fortescue (1984): 308]

ringed.seal-INST.PL   four-catch-IND-[-tr]-3SG

"He caught four ringed seals."

In this respect, German split differs from the modification of West Greenlandic incorporated nouns: the topicalized constituent must be a nominal. If not, we get something like (27) which is ungrammatical and therefore rather hard to understand.

(27)   *   *Zwei* hat Julius Briefe   gekriegt.

          two   has J.   letters got

#? "As for two things, Julius has got letters."

1.2.5 Relative clauses

In West Greenlandic, it is possible to use a relative clause to modify an incorporated noun. A relative clause in this language is a nominalized verbal construction.

(28)   Juuna kalaalli-sut   oqalus-sinnaa-su-mik

      J.ABS Greenlander-EQU   speak-can-REL.[-tr]-INST.SG

      ilinniartitsisu-siur-p-u-q.   [Bittner (1994): 70]

      teacher-seek-IND-[-tr]-3SG

"Juuna is looking for a teacher who can speak West Greenlandic."

(29)   Arne qatanngute-qar-p-u-q   *Canada-mi*

      A.ABS sister-have-IND-[-tr]-3SG   C.-LOC

      najuga-lim-mik.   [fw]

      dwelling.place-have.REL.[-tr]-INST.SG

"Arne has a sister who lives in Canada."

In German, it is possible to modify a sentence initial nominal expression by means of a relative clause as well. However, the examples below illustrate that such a relative clause needs to be syntactically "anchored" to a (numeral) determiner.

(30) Lehrer   braucht die Schule [*zwei* t$_i$], [*die Latein lehren können*]$_i$

teachers needs   the school two   who Latin teach can

"As for teachers, the school needs two who can teach Latin."

(31) * Lehrer   braucht die   Schule,   *die Latein lehren können.*

teachers needs   the   school   who Latin teach can

(32) Belgier hat es   schon immer [*viele* t$_i$] gegeben,

Belgians has there already always many   given

[*die mehrsprachig sind*]$_i$

who multilingual are

"As for Belgians, there have always been many who are multilingual."

(33) * Belgier   hat   es   schon immer gegeben,

Belgians has there already always given

die mehrsprachig sind.

who multilingual are

1.3 Summary

In this descriptive section on the structure of noun incorporation, I have pointed out three main issues.[6] First of all, in West Greenlandic we are dealing with *morphological* incorporation. *Adjacency* of an incorporated noun with respect to its verbal incorporator is thus ensured. Secondly, incorporated nouns can be modified by means of one or more external INSTRUMENTAL modifiers: these can be adjectives, numerals, *wh*-words, nouns and relative clauses. Thirdly, in many cases a West Greenlandic noun incorporating configuration, on the one hand, and a German bare plural and split Object, on the other, are structurally very much alike. In the remainder of this chapter, I will show how this structural similarity is also reflected in the semantics. The German bare plural and a German split topic are presented as semantic counterparts of West Greenlandic noun incorporation.

---

[6] Many theory-laden questions concerning the structure of West Greenlandic noun incorporation will be raised and answered in chapter 4. One question (too) often raised in this respect is whether noun incorporation is a lexical or a syntactic phenomenon. Another, and I believe a more important question is whether noun incorporation is a base generated configuration or whether it is the result of a transformation, namely, of head movement.

2 Semantic aspects of West Greenlandic noun incorporation

In this section, I focus on some word- and sentence-level semantic aspects of West Greenlandic noun incorporation. I start out with an overview of the meanings of some verbal affixes that incorporate nominal stems. Then, I move up to some sentence-level semantic properties of incorporated nouns, that is, their behaviour with respect to negation and distribution.

2.1 Incorporating verbs

In Fortescue (1984), we find an exhaustive list of derivational verbal affixes that combine with a noun stem to build an incorporating configuration. I do not intend to just repeat this list nor do I adopt his semantic classification of these affixes. Rather, I have picked out those affixes that have been used rather often by my informants.[7] These affixes typically mean: to make, eat, drink, get, buy, sell, have, lose, etc. Also, I will pay special attention to two verbal affixes that are particularly interesting from a semantic perspective. The first one is the verbal affix *-qar-* ("to have") which is also used as the verbal component of the West Greenlandic existential construction. The other one is the intensional verbal affix *-siur-* ("to seek").

2.1.1 *Make* and *eat*

• Make

The affixal verb of creation *-liur-* ("to make") is very often used: one can make just about anything.[8]

(34) Kaage-*liur*-p-u-t.   [fw]

cake-make-IND-[-tr]-3PL

"They made cake/a cake/cakes."

(35) Vittu mamorto-mik nerisass-*iur*-tar-p-u-q.   [fw]

V.ABS good-INST   food-made-HAB-IND-[-tr]-3SG

"Usually, Vittus makes good food."

Notice that the number of the incorporated noun *kaage-* ("cake") can be either plural or singular. In addition, an incorporated count noun can be interpreted as a mass noun. In chapter 5, I elaborate the view that an

---

[7] Many of the affixes described in Fortescue (1984) have meanings that are related to the life of a hunter. Most of my informants were students which were not familiar with hunting vocabulary.

[8] In this book, I largely ignore temporal and aspectual meaning. In West Greenlandic, temporal and aspectual marking are contributed through optional affixes on the verb, the lexical meaning of the verb and temporal (affixal) modifiers.

incorporated noun usually denotes a property which is absorbed by an incorporating verb as the *predicate* of its internal argument's variable.

• *Eat* and *drink*

The "consumption" affix *-tur-* can be used for drinking and for eating. The incorporated noun clarifies its actual meaning.

(36)   Tii-*tur*-p-u-nga.   [fw]

  tea-drink-IND-[-tr]-1SG

  "I am drinking tea."

(37)   Ivviar-*tur*-p-u-gut.   [Fortescue (1984): 323]

  rye.bread-eat-IND-[-tr]-1PL

  "We are eating ryebread."

2.1.2 *Sell*, *get* and *buy*

• *Sell*

A very common way to say that one is selling something is by means of the verbal affix *-rniar-* ("to sell").

(38)   Kaageeraa-*rniar*-p-u-gut.   [fw]

  cooky-sell-IND-[-tr]-1PL

  "We are selling cookies."

The affix *-rniar-* shows up in the name of about any kind of Greenlandic store: *pinnguaa-rniar-fik* ("toy store"), *skuue-rniar-fik* ("shoe store"), *neqaa-rniar-fik* ("meat store, butcher"), *atuagaa-rniar-fik* ("book store"), etc. These store names are composed according to the schema "place where one sells *x*."

• *Get* and *buy*

The examples below show that the Greenlandic affix *-si-* has more than one straightforward meaning. Roughly, it is translated as *to get* [see example (18)]. In particular contexts, it can mean *to buy* or *to find*.

(39)   Niviarsiagga-t mamaluiguttu-*si*-pp-u-t.   [fw]

  girl-ABS.PL   candy-buy-IND-[-tr]-3PL

  "The girls bought candy."

(40)   Ilinniartitsisu-t   nutaa-mik allattarfi-*si*-pp-u-t.   [fw]

  teacher-ABS.PL   new-INST   blackboard-buy-IND-[-tr]-3PL

  "The teachers bought a new blackboard."

(41) Kaali nutaa-nik tumi-*si*-v-u-q.   [Bittner (1994): 71]

K.ABS new-INST.PL track-find-IND-[-tr]-3SG

"Kaali found fresh tracks."

2.1.3 *Have*

West Greenlandic has an affix -*qar*- which expresses the relational predicate *TO HAVE*.

(42) Arne qatanngute-*qar*-p-u-q   Canada-mi

A.ABS sister-have-IND-[-tr]-3SG   C.-LOC

najuga-lim-mik.   [fw]

dwelling.place-have.REL.[-tr]-INST

"Arne has a sister who lives in Canada."

(43) Angut   taanna   atur-sinnaa-nngit-su-nik

man.ABS that.ABS be.used-can-NEG-REL.[-tr]-INST.PL

qimmi-*qar*-p-u-q.   [Fortescue (1984): 117]

dog-have-IND-[-tr]-3SG

"That man has useless dogs."

The reason that I call the meaning expressed by -*qar*- in (42) and (43) relational *TO HAVE* is to distinguish it from possessive *TO HAVE*. The latter denotes a relation between an owner and an ownee, and this is exactly not what -*qar*- — and often neither the English verb *to have* — denotes. Rather, -*qar*- requires that the noun it incorporates is relational in the wider sense of "belonging to the family, belonging to a person." When -*qar*- incorporates a nonrelational noun, the morpheme -*ute*- has to be incorporated as well.

(44) a. * Tuttu-qar-p-u-q.   [Sadock (p.c.)]

reindeer-have-IND-[-tr]-3SG

b. Tuttu-*ute*-qar-p-u-q.   [Sadock (p.c.)]

reindeer-PSV-have-IND-[-tr]-3SG

"He/she has a reindeer (to eat)."

(45) a. Illu-qar-p-u-q.   [fw]

house-have-IND-[-tr]-3SG

"He/she has a house."

b.   Illu-*ute*-qar-p-u-q.   [fw]

house-have-PSV-IND-[-tr]-3SG

"He/she has a house."

(44a) is bad because one cannot have a reindeer as a pet. (45a) means that someone has a house in which he lives himself, (45b) simply means that someone owns a house. Jumping ahead, I will argue that West Greenlandic -*qar*- is a typically semantically incorporating verb. This means that the existential interpretation of the internal argument is part of such a verb's lexical meaning.[9]

Moreover, I claim that also in English we need to distinguish between the relational meaning of the verb *to have* and its possessive meaning. With this distinction we cannot only explain why (46) and (47) are ungrammatical, but also why (48) is grammatical. Assuming that the relational predicate *TO HAVE* is inherently incorporating, the quantified expression *every sister* in (46) and the definite description *the brother* in (47) do not denote the meaning required by this incorporating verb, namely that of a predicate of a "novel" variable.

(46)   * John has every sister.

(47)   * Julia has the brother.[10]

As opposed to (47), (48) is well-formed because in the latter *to have* is interpreted as possessive *TO HAVE* which is not necessarily incorporating.

(48)   John has the key.

---

[9] In West Greenlandic, there is yet another noun incorporating affix -*gi*- which means *TO HAVE AS*. It always comes with transitive agreement inflection.

(i)   Nuka-p   Ester   anaana-g-a-a.   [fw]
      N.-ERG   E.ABS   mother-have.as-IND.[+tr]-3SG.3SG
      "Ester is Nuka's mother (lit. Nuka has Ester as his mother)."

The noun incorporated by transitive -*gi*- describes the relation in which the external ABSOLUTIVE Object stands to the ERGATIVE Subject. In (i), this is motherhood. The incorporated noun has to be analyzed in the way one analyzes the *as*-phrases in the following English examples.

(ii)   The German soccer team has Berti Vogts as its trainer.
(iii) Jimmy has Mr. Jones as his math teacher.

In chapter 5, I discuss the meaning differences between relational *TO HAVE* and *TO HAVE AS*.

[10] A counterexample was pointed out by Wolfgang Klein (p.c.).

(i)   John has the brother he deserves.
(ii) What kind of brother does John have?

I consider this an apparent counterexample because *the brother he deserves* does not refer to a particular person who is John's brother but to the kind of brother John has. That is, (i) is a felicitous answer to the question under (ii).

In West Greenlandic, possessive *TO HAVE* is realized as the verb *pigi-*. The distinction between relational and possessive *TO HAVE* is thus lexicalized in West Greenlandic.

(49) Juuna-p illu-t marluk *pigi*-v-a-i. [fw]

J.-ERG house-ABS.PL two.ABS have-IND-[+tr]-3SG.3PL

"Juuna owns (the) two houses."

2.1.4 The existential construction

The verbal affix *-qar-* does not only denote the relational predicate *TO HAVE*. It is also the verbal part of the West Greenlandic existential construction.

(50) Nillataartarfim-mi tallima-nik manne-*qar*-p-u-q. [fw]

fridge-LOC five-INST.PL egg-have-IND-[-tr]-3SG

"There are five eggs in the fridge."

(51) Festi-mi qallunaar-passua-*qar*-p-u-q. [fw]

party-LOC white.man-many-have-IND-[-tr]-3SG

"There were many Danes (lit. white men) at the party."

It is not only in West Greenlandic that one and the same lexeme is used to express the relational predicate *TO HAVE* and the existential predicate. A similar situation we find in some South German dialects.

(52) Julia hat einen Bruder.

J. has a brother

"Julia has a brother."

(53) Es hat heute nur Milch.

there has today only milk

"There is only milk today."

Assuming that the existential predicate is inherently semantically incorporating, I will argue in chapter 5 that the violation of the definiteness restriction [Milsark (1974)] in (54) and (55) has the same semantic source as the ungrammaticality of our above examples (46) and (47).

(54) * There is every donkey in the garden.

(55) * There is the donkey in the garden.

Neither *every donkey* in (54) nor *the donkey* in (55) denotes the meaning required by this incorporating verb, namely, that of a predicate of a novel variable. This means that I give an explanation that is very similar to the one given in McNally (1992).

2.1.5 Intensional affixes

Although there surely are other intensional affixal verbs in West Greenlandic, I focus my attention to *-siur-* ("to seek").[11]

(56) Vittu cykili-ssar-*siur*-p-u-q.　　　　　　　　　　[fw]

　　 V.ABS bike-FUT-seek-IND-[-tr]-3SG

　　 i. "Vittus is looking for an arbitrary bike/bikes."

　　 ii. # "There is/are a specific bike/bikes such that Vittus is looking for it/them."

The English paraphrases of this sentence show that it has a de dicto reading only. It is not possible to understand the incorporated noun as a specific object.[12] This is supported by the fact that the FUTURE morpheme *-ssar-* has to follow the noun incorporated by *-siur-* ("to seek").[13] That *-siur-* has an intensional meaning only is also supported by the observation that we get nonsense if we modify its incorporated noun with a relative clause that requires that the object described by the incorporated noun be a familiar one. Here are two examples.

(57) Ullumi　 Esta　　 ilinniartitsisu-ssar-siur-p-u-q　 ippassaq

　　 today　　 E.ABS　　 teacher-FUT-seek-IND-[-tr]-3SG　 yesterday

　　 naapi-ta-ni-mik.　　　　　　　　　　　　　　　　　[fw]

　　 meet-REL.[-tr]-3SG.PROX-INST.SG

　　 # "Today Ester was looking for a teacher who she had met yesterday."

(58) Ullumi　 Ole　　 qimmi-ssar-siur-p-u-q　　　　 ippassaq

　　 today　　 O.ABS　 dog-FUT-seek-IND-[-tr]-3SG　　 yesterday

　　 tammaa-sima-su-mi-nik.　　　　　　　　　　　　　[fw]

　　 lose.sight.of-PERF-REL.[-tr]-3SG.PROX-INST.PL

　　 # "Today Ole was looking for some arbitrary dogs that someone lost sight of yesterday."

---

[11] Two more intensional affixes are illustrated in (i) and (ii):

(i)　　 Cykili-si-taar-*niar*-p-u-nga.　　　　　　　　　　[fw]
　　　 bike-get-new-want-IND-[-tr]-1SG
　　　 "I want a new bike."

(ii)　　 Aalisegaq　 una　　 qilaluga-*nnga*-v-u-q.　　　　[fw]
　　　 fish.ABS　　 this.ABS　 beluga-look.like-IND-[-tr]-3SG
　　　 "This fish looks like a beluga."

[12] I thank Maria Bittner for pointing out the lack of a de re reading for incorporating verbs.

[13] All my informants rejected examples with *-siur-* that lacked the future morpheme.

It doesn't make sense to specify a teacher one doesn't know as a teacher one has met the day before. It is also senseless to look for your future dogs as if they were the dogs that someone lost the day before. When you wish to express that you are looking for a teacher that you have met the day before, or for dogs that took off, you must use a transitive structure.

(59) Esta-p ilinniartitsisoq ippassaq naapi-ta-ni

      E.-ERG teacher.ABS   yesterday meet-REL.[-tr]-3SG.PROX.ABS

      ullumi ujar-p-a-a.   [fw]

      today look.for-IND-[+tr]-3SG.3SG

      "Today Ester was looking for a/the teacher who she met yesterday."

(60) Ole-p qimmi-t ippassaq

      O.-ERG dog-ABS.PL yesterday

      tammaa-sima-s-ai

      lose.sight.of-PERF-REL.[-tr]-3SG.PROX.ABS.PL

      ullumi ujar-p-a-i.   [fw]

      today look.for-IND-[+tr]-3SG.3PL

      "Today Ole was looking for some/the dogs that took off yesterday."

Relating my view that an incorporated noun denotes a property to Zimmermann's (1993) view that the intensional predicate *TO SEEK* denotes a relation between an individual and a property, it does not come as a surprise that an incorporated noun gets a de dicto reading only. Moreover, the observation that a noun incorporated by an intensional predicate gets a de dicto reading only looks very similar to Carlson's (1977) observation that, if an English bare plural NP appears in an attitude context, this NP has the de dicto reading only. The same holds for the German bare plural.

(61) Miles wants to meet policemen.   [Carlson (1977): 16]

    i. "Miles wants to meet some arbitrary policemen."

    ii. # "There are policemen that Miles wants to meet."

(62) Peter hat Polizisten gesucht.

     P.   has policemen looked.for

    i. "Peter has been looking for an arbitrary set of policemen."

    ii. # "There is a specific set of policemen that Peter has been looking for."

Carlson's explanation of his observation can be roughly summarized as follows. A bare plural NP introduces a kind, and it is the verbal predicate of which this bare plural is an argument that introduces instances, i.e., "stages" of this kind together with an existential interpretation of these instances. The narrow scope effect of a bare plural with respect to any other operator in a sentence follows because the existential quantifier introduced by the verb cannot take scope over any other quantifier. However, Kratzer (1980) presents the following example as a counterexample to Carlson's observation:

(63) Otto wollte Tollkirschen   in den Obstsalat   tun, weil

      O.   wanted belladonna.berries in the fruit.salad put, because

         er   sie   mit richtigen Kirschen verwechselte.

         he   them   with real   cherries changed

      "Otto wanted to put belladonna berries in the fruitsalad because he took them for real cherries."

She argues that if *Tollkirschen* ("belladonna berries") were understood de dicto, that is, within the scope of the modal operator *wollte* ("wanted"), it could not act as an antecedent to the pronoun *sie* ("them"), which is arguably outside the scope of *wollte*. In chapter 3, I show that Kratzer's point is not a counterexample to Carlson's claim but rather that it points out a gap in Carlson's theory. Despite this gap, the analysis of her example is compatible with his idea of a lexicalized existential interpretation.

2.1.6 Copulae

Copulae in West Greenlandic are realized as incorporating affixes.

(64) Kamma-*gii*-pp-u-t.   [Fortescue (1984): 321]

      friend-be-IND-[-tr]-3PL

      "They are friends."

(65) Vittu tuniriaas-*unngu*-ssamaar-p-u-q.   [fw]

      V.ABS salesman-become-intend-IND-[-tr]-3SG

      "Vittus intends to become a salesman."

Because the incorporated nouns in these examples are predicates par excellence, they support my claim that these nouns denote properties in the most obvious way.

2.1.7 Summary

As I have said in the beginning of this section, this list of West Greenlandic incorporating verbal affixes is not exhaustive.[14] Still, it has served its purpose. That is, it gives an impression of what kind of meanings the most commonly used affixes have. Another important part of this presentation was the discussion of West Greenlandic nouns combined with intensional verbal affixes and of their incorporation into the West Greenlandic existential construction.

2.2 Incorporated nouns and their "scope" behaviour

In this section, I shift my attention from the verbal to the nominal component of a West Greenlandic noun incorporating configuration, in particular, to the scope behaviour of that nominal part with respect to scope taking elements, namely, negation and distribution. I start with some examples illustrating a "narrow scope" effect of West Greenlandic nouns with respect to negation [Bittner (1994)]. I relate this to a similar effect arising with the West Germanic bare plural as observed by Carlson (1977). Next, I move to collective and distributive readings of West Greenlandic incorporated nouns. Again, I will illustrate the collective–distributive behaviour of the West Germanic bare plural in parallel.

2.2.1 Negation

Bittner (1994) illustrates the narrow scope behaviour of West Greenlandic incorporated nouns in the light of negation realized as the affix *-nngi(t)-*.

(66) Arnajaraq aalisaga-si-*nngi*-l-a-q.   [fw]

     A.ABS   fish-buy-NEG-IND-[-tr]-3SG

     i.   "It is not the case that Arnajaraq bought (a/more than one) fish."

     ii. # "There is/are (a) fish that Arnajaraq didn't buy."

(67) Juuna Kaali-mit marlun-nik allagar-si-*nngi*-l-a-q. [Bittner (1994): 118]

     J.ABS   K.-ABL   two-INST.PL   letter-get-NEG-IND-[-tr]-3SG

     i.   "It is not the case that Juuna got two letters from Kaali."

     ii. # "There are a two letters from Kaali that Juuna didn't get."

---

[14] Yet another class of noun incorporating verbal affixes are some affixes that incorporate a directional adjunct, as illustrated in (i).

(i)   Qaqurtu-*liar*-p-u-q.   [Fortescue (1984): 322]
     Qaqortoq-go.to-IND-[-tr]-3SG
     "He went to Qaqortoq."

Bittner's observation immediately reminds one of the observation made by Carlson (1977) that the English bare plural always takes narrow scope with respect to negation.

(68) John didn't see spots on the floor.   [Carlson (1977): 19]

    i. "It is not the case that John saw spots on the floor."

    ii. # "There were spots on the floor that John didn't see."

The explanation he gives for this narrow scope effect is the same as the one given for the de dicto effect discussed in section 2.1.5: the existential interpretation of the bare plural *spots* in (68) is contributed by the lexical semantics of the extensional verb *to see*. Any operator which takes the verb in its scope will take the lexically bound arguments in its scope as well. Rooth (1989) has brought up (69) as a counterexample to Carlson's observation.

(69) The Dean failed to act on petitions submitted to his office.

[Rooth (1989): 282]

According to this author, it is possible to assign the bare plural *petitions submitted to his office* in (69) a specific interpretation. In chapter 3, I show that Rooth's example is not a real counterexample to Carlson's observation.

Still, even if one succeeds in putting new life into Carlson's original proposal in such a way that it also covers the scope behaviour of West Greenlandic incorporated nouns, it has to be done in such a way that it also covers *modified* "bare" plurals. Carlson's observation is about *bare* plurals whereas Bittner's observation is not only about bare, but about modified incorporated nouns as well [see (67)]. What we need is a theory which covers both bare and modified narrow scope nominals.

At this point, I return to German split topicalization, which I introduced as a structural counterpart of West Greenlandic noun incorporation in section 1.2. Also German split can be shown to be a semantic counterpart of West Greenlandic noun incorporation. The interaction of negation and indefinite NPs in German shows that only those nominals that are in the scope of negation can split. This is very reminiscent of Bittner's example (67). Let us first look at two German examples with unsplit Objects.

(70) Lisa hat im   Keller keine schwarzen Spinnen gesehen.

    L.   has in.the cellar no   black   spiders seen.

    "It is not the case that Lisa saw black spiders in the cellar."

(71) Lisa hat im   Keller einige schwarze Spinnen nicht

    L.   has in.the cellar some black   spiders   not

gesehen.

seen

"There are some black spiders that Lisa didn't see in the cellar."

In (70), black spiders are in the scope of negation which is linguistically realized on the negative polarity item *keine* ("no"). In (71), some black spiders are outside the scope of the negation operator, now realized as *nicht* ("not"). The following two examples illustrate that only the indefinite Object in the former but not the one in the latter can split.[15]

(72) Schwarze Spinnen hat Lisa im   Keller keine gesehen.

      black   spiders has L.   in.the cellar no   seen

"As for black spiders, it is not the case that Lisa saw some in the cellar."

(73) * Schwarze Spinnen hat Lisa im Keller einige nicht gesehen.

Apparently, the syntactic discontinuity of a nominal expression in German *and* in West Greenlandic gives rise to particular semantic constraints on the meaning of these expressions. With respect to similar data in German, Diesing (1992) and Schwarz (1992) point out that only "weak" quantifiers can split. Diesing's explanation for this semantic constraint on Split is a syntactic one which is based on Huang's (1982) CONDITION ON EXTRACTION DOMAIN [CED]. She assumes that split topicalization is the result of a syntactic transformation which moves the topicalized material out of a D-structural NP. To get a wide scope reading of this split NP, its remnant must raise at LF. This, however, gives rise to a violation of the CED: it is not possible to extract material from an ungoverned position. Interestingly, Bittner (1994) gives a syntactic account for the narrow scope constraint on West Greenlandic incorporated nouns as well. She assumes with Baker (1988) that noun incorporation is the result of a syntactic transformation which moves a noun from its head-position in a D-structural NP and adjoins it to a verb. A wide scope reading of an incorporated noun is out because the remnant NP containing the trace of this noun cannot raise: it would lead to a violation of the EMPTY CATEGORY PRINCIPLE [ECP, Chomsky (1981)]. However, my fieldwork has shown that the above West Greenlandic

---

[15] To some German speaking readers, my decision to call (73) ungrammatical may seem too strong. In contrastive contexts, it seems possible to create "wide scope" split topics. The following example is a well-formed sentence when uttered in a context where different kinds of mistakes which didn't strike someone are being discussed.

(i) Orthographische Fehler waren ihm sogar drei nicht aufgefallen. [Kamp (p.c)]
    orthographical mistakes were   him   even three not   struck
"As for spelling mistakes, there were even three that he didn't recognize."

A wide reading of a split topic is only possible in such a contrastive context.

examples (66) and (67) do not only lack wide scope readings. They also lack the following narrow partitive readings [see section 3.2 below]:

(66)   iii. # "It is not the case that Arnajaraq bought one of the fish."

(67)   iii. # "It is not the case that Juuna got two of the letters from Kaali."

Bittner (1994) is silent about the nonexistence of these readings, and it is unclear how her syntactic approach could account for this. Another deficiency with her ECP account is that it cannot explain the narrow scope effects of the West Germanic bare plural, since it would require the stipulation of the existence of some empty category in a bare plural configuration. Moreover, in the next chapter I show that Diesing's (1992) syntactic account cannot capture partitive interpretations of NPs in an appropriate way either.

As an alternative to these syntactic accounts, I propose a uniform semantic explanation covering the narrow scope effects of West Germanic bare plurals, German split topics and West Greenlandic incorporated nouns. The central idea is that these nominal expressions belong to the class of predicative indefinite descriptions. These indefinites get their existential interpretation from the verb by which they are semantically incorporated. The scope effects are then the result of this semantic process. This is essentially the same explanation as the one Carlson (1977) gives for the narrow scope behaviour of the English bare plural. Two important differences between Carlson's theory and mine are that in nongeneric contexts I regard the bare plural as a property denoting expression, and that my approach is an overall theory of "narrow" indefinites.

2.2.2 Distributivity

The next issue to be considered is the interpretation of a West Greenlandic incorporated noun with respect to a distribution operator. In his study on one of its semantic counterparts, namely the English bare plural, Carlson (1977) has claimed that the latter always takes narrow scope with respect to the universal quantifier *everyone*. According to Carlson this distinguishes a bare plural from a singular indefinite NP as illustrated in the following pair of examples.

(74)   Everyone read books on giraffes.   [Carlson (1977): 20]

    i. "Every person was reading (different) books on giraffes."

    ii. # "There were books on giraffes that everyone was reading."

(75)   Everyone read a book on giraffes.

    i. "Every person was reading a book on giraffes."

    ii. "There is a book on giraffes that everyone was reading."

Carlson claims that the narrow scope of the bare plural *books on giraffes* with respect to *everyone* in (74) follows because this plural receives its existential interpretation from the verb *to read*, which is in the scope of this universal quantifier. That the singular indefinite in (54) receives two readings follows because this singular is an existential quantifier that can stay in or leave the scope of the universal quantifier *everyone*.

Having in mind that we took the West Germanic bare plural as a semantic counterpart of the West Greenlandic incorporated noun, we can now ask the question of whether this observation about the distribution of the English bare plural carries over to West Greenlandic when an incorporated noun is involved. West Greenlandic does not have a direct counterpart of the distributive determiner *every*. The following sentence with the universal determiner *tamarmik* ("all") and the incorporated noun *tuttu-* ("caribou") can be interpreted in a distributive or in a collective way.

(76) Pinartu-t   *tamarmik* tuttu-raar-p-u-t.   [fw]

      hunter-ABS.PL   all   caribou-catch-IND-[-tr]-3PL

      i.   "All the hunters caught a caribou/caribous together."

      ii.   "All the hunters caught a caribou/caribous by themselves."

This vagueness disappears when one inserts the adverbs *immikut* ("by.self") and *ataatsimut* ("together"), respectively:

(77) Pinartu-t   tamarmik *immikut* tuttu-raar-p-u-t.   [fw]

      hunter-ABS.PL   all   by.self   caribou-catch-IND-[-tr]-3PL

      "All the hunters caught a caribou/caribous by themselves."

(78) Pinartu-t   tamarmik *ataatsimut*   tuttu-raar-p-u-t.   [fw]

      hunter-ABS.PL   all   together   caribou-catch-IND-[-tr]-3PL

      "All the hunters caught a caribou/caribous together."

This shows that it is not the presence of *tamarmik* ("all") which forces a distributive reading, but rather the presence of the adverb *immikut* ("by.self"). Moreover, against Carlson (1977) and following Kamp and Reyle (1993) I will not regard the collective–distributive ambiguity of (76) as a matter of "taking scope." In addition to its collective reading, it is possible to interpret (76) in a distributive way. For the representation of this distributive reading, we only need to add a (silent) distributive operator to the representation of the collective reading.

The ambiguity of Carlson's example (75) will not be explained as a scope ambiguity either. Rather, I argue that the narrow scope reading of the singular indefinite in this example has the same source as the narrow reading of the bare plural in (74). Both are interpreted as predicates that are absorbed by the incorporating verb *to read*. The additional wide reading of the singular indefinite in (75) follows from the possibility of assigning this NP a secondary interpretation, namely that of a free variable expression. In chapter 6, I argue that free variable indefinites reach their wide position through a repair mechanism, namely, accommodation. A bare plural lacks a wide reading since it can be interpreted as a predicative indefinite only.

2.3 Summary

The list of verbal affixes given in section 2.1 and the data illustrating the "scope" of incorporated nouns given in section 2.2 showed us quite a bit about the semantic behaviour of West Greenlandic noun incorporating configurations. Moreover, we saw that many of the empirical issues discussed in this section have parallels in West Germanic languages. I intend to elaborate a common semantic explanation which holds for the West Greenlandic and the West Germanic facts. My point of departure is the view adopted from Abusch (1994) that indefinite descriptions remain *in situ* at the syntactic level of Logical Form. In addition, I draw a semantic distinction between predicative and free variable indefinites. The former receive their inherent narrow scope interpretation through semantic incorporation.

3 Discourse aspects of West Greenlandic noun incorporation

Now, I move from the sentence-level semantic aspects of incorporated nouns to their semantic behaviour in a larger piece of discourse. I have picked out three empirical issues that I think are relevant in this respect.

First, it has been observed by Bittner (1994) that a West Greenlandic incorporated noun lacks a definite reading. From the perspective that definite expressions are anaphoric expressions [Heim (1982)], one can reformulate Bittner's observation and say that a West Greenlandic incorporated noun never presupposes its descriptive content. Looking at its semantic counterpart, the West Germanic bare plural, we will see that the latter lacks an anaphoric interpretation as well.

Secondly, my own fieldwork has led to the observation that a West Greenlandic incorporated noun which is modified by an external numeral cannot be given a partitive interpretation. Again, we will see that its semantic counterpart, the German split topic, lacks this discourse semantic feature as well.

Finally, it has been often brought up in the literature on noun incorporation that West Greenlandic incorporated nouns are "discourse transparent" [Sadock (1980; 1991), Baker (1988), Bittner (1994)]. What this means is that when they are located in a semantically nonsubordinating position, these nouns seem to be able to antecede a definite pronoun. Again, West Germanic indefinites often display the same discourse behaviour.

3.1 Presuppositional force

Bittner (1994) observes that an incorporated noun cannot get a definite interpretation.

(79)   Juuna allagar-si-v-u-q.   [Bittner (1994): 119]

    J.ABS   letter-get-IND-[-tr]-3SG

    i.   "Juuna got a letter/letters."

    ii.   # "Juuna got the letter(s)."

In other words, an incorporated noun cannot anaphorically refer to a familiar object as we would expect if it could be interpreted as a definite description. This is exemplified in the following two pieces of discourse.

(80)   a.   Qaammatit   qassiit   matuma   siortinagut   Juuna

        months   several   of.this   before   J.ABS

        puurtukka-nik   allakka-nil-lu   nassip-p-a-ra.

        parcel-INST   letter-INST.PL-and   send-IND-[+tr]-1SG.3SG

        "Several months ago, I sent Juuna a parcel$_i$ and some letters."

    b.   Ullumi   aatsaat   puurtugar-si-v-u-q, ...   [Bittner (p.c.)]

        today   first   parcel-get-IND-[-tr]-3SG

        i.   "Only today he got a parcel, ..."

        ii.   # "Only today he got the parcel$_i$, ..."

(81)   a.   Ippassaq   kaage-liur-p-u-gut.

        yesterday   cake-make-IND-[-tr]-1PL

        "Yesterday, we made cake$_i$."

    b.   Ullumi   kaage-rniar-p-u-gut.   [fw]

        Today   cake-sell-IND-[-tr]-1PL

        i.   "Today, we are selling cake."

        ii.   # "Today, we are selling the cake$_i$."

If one wants to use a nominal expression to pick up the parcel mentioned in (80a), for instance, one has to use an NP in a transitive, that is, a nonincorporating configuration.[16]

---

[16] *puurtukkat* is always plural.

(80)   c.   Ullumi   aatsaat   *puurtukka-t*   tiq-u-a-i.   [fw]

today   only   parcel-ABS.PL   get-IND-[+tr]-3SG.3PL

"Only today he got the parcel$_i$, ..."

A German bare plural cannot be used as an anaphoric expression either.

(82)   a.   Johanns Mutter   hat ihm   letzte Woche   zwei Briefe   geschickt.

J.'s mother   has him   last week   two letters   sent

"Last week, John's mother sent him two letters$_i$."

b.   Heute   hat   er   Briefe   gekriegt.

today   has   he   letters   got

i.   "Today, he got letters."

ii.   # "Today, he got the letters$_i$."

What about those verbal affixes that presuppose the existence of their internal argument? One example is the affix *-irsir-* ("to lose").[17]

(83)   Qilalukka-mut   ali-irsir-p-u-q   [Fortescue (1984): 83]

beluga-ALL   harpoon.line-lose-IND-[-tr]-3SG

"He lost a harpoonline for a beluga."

Even though it may follow from the lexical semantics of *to lose* that there is something which someone does not have anymore, this does not trigger an anaphoric interpretation of its incorporated argument. Similarly, if some person utters (84), namely, that she lost keys, it is understood that she lost her own keys.

(84)   Matuasaata-rser-p-u-nga.   [fw]

key-lose-IND-[-tr]-1SG

"I have lost a key/keys (= my key(s))."

Apparently, the incorporated *key* is interpreted as definite. However, this "definite" interpretation is not computed from the parts of this sentence. It follows from the sentence's pragmatics. The following example illustrates that it is not possible to understand the incorporated *key* as some other person's key.

(85)   * Johni-p   matuersaata-rser-p-u-nga.   [fw] [18]

J.-ERG   key-lose-IND-[-tr]-1SG

---

[17] Note that this example has an ALLATIVE external modifier.

[18] In West Greenlandic, the ERGATIVE case is not only the case of the Subject in a transitive configuration, but it is also the counterpart of what we know as the GENITIVE case.

Again, one needs a transitive construction to express that one has lost some specific key(s).

(86) Johni-p   matuersaata-a   tammar-p-a-ra.   [fw]

     J.-ERG   key-3SG.ABS   lose-IND-[+tr]-1SG.3SG

     "I have lost John's keys."

Another affix which somehow presupposes the existence of the referent standing for its internal argument is *-ir-* ("to remove"): it is only possible to remove something that is present.[19]

(87) Nuka-p   puisi-p   ami-a   panerse-rusuk-ka-mi-uk

     N.-ERG   seal-ERG   skin-3SG.ABS   dry-want-DPST-3SG.PROX-3SG

     puisi   ami-ir-p-a-a.   [fw]

     seal.ABS   skin-remove-IND-[+tr]-3SG.3SG

     "Because he wanted to dry the skin of the seal, Nuka removed the skin from the seal (lit. skinned the seal)."

The second occurrence of *ami-* ("skin"), namely, as an incorporated noun, is not to be understood as anaphoric to its first occurrence. This type of nonanaphoric "definite" incorporated noun is comparable with the complex verbal predicates we find in the following German sentences:

(88) a. weil   Nuka   dem Seehund   die Haut   entfernen   wollte.

        because   N.   the.DAT seal   the.ACC skin   remove   wanted

        "because Nuka wanted to remove the seal's skin."

     b. weil   Nuka   den Seehund   häuten   wollte.

        because   N.   the.ACC seal   skin   wanted

        "because Nuka wanted to skin the seal."

(89) a. daß   der Koch   dem Fisch   den Kopf   abschneidet.

        that   the cook   the.DAT fish   the.ACC head   cuts

        "that the cook cuts the fish's head."

---

[19] I regard this affix as a 3-place predicate, which can be papaphrased as "*x* removes *z*'s *y* from *z*." The transitive inflection agrees with the constituents refering to *x* and *z*. See Van Geenhoven (1997) for a semantic analysis of this possessor raising construction in which the ABSOLUTIVE possessor is analyzed as a full-fledged argument of the verb.

    b.   daß   der Koch den Fisch   köpft.

         that the cook the.ACC fish   beheads

         "that the cook beheads the fish."

In the a-examples the verbs *entfernen* ("remove") and *abschneiden* ("cut") are combined with a definite NP. These definites denote inalienable body parts that build a semantic unit with the verb. This is supported by the fact that the a-examples and the b-examples in which the body part is verbalized have exactly the same meaning. It is also supported by the ungrammaticality of (90) and (91), where the definite expressions are not adjacent to their respective incorporating predicates.

(90)   * weil Nuka die Haut dem Seehund entfernen wollte.

(91)   * daß der Koch den Kopf dem Fisch abschneidet.

Moreover, from a semantic perspective definite "body part" NPs can only be interpreted in a relational way. As pointed out by von Stechow (p.c.), the following example shows that such a definite NP cannot escape negation, a crucial property of presuppositional expressions.

(92)   daß   der Koch   keinem Fisch den Kopf   abschneidet.

        that   the cook   no.DAT fish   the.ACC head cuts

    i.   "It is not the case that there is a fish f such that the cook cuts f's head."

    ii. # "There is a head h such that it is not the case that there is a fish such that the cook cuts h."

The existential presupposition triggered by the use of a definite NP expressing inalienable possession is a dependent one. It can only be interpreted in the scope of the body it is a part of. In other words, *die Haut* in (88a) is interpreted as *seine Haut* ("its skin") and *den Kopf* in (89a) as *seinen Kopf* ("its head") and the possessive pronouns in these paraphrases are coreferential with *dem Seehund* ("the seal") and *dem Fish* ("the fish"), respectively.

3.2 Partitivity

Partitivity is a discourse semantic property of particular nominal expressions. Intuitively, partitivity indicates the membership relation between a discourse referent and a familiar set of discourse referents.[20] On the one hand, we have overt partitive NPs such as *one of the books*, *most of the students*. On the other hand, in particular contexts an NP can be

---

[20] In what follows I do not consider group partitives (e.g. *a member of our party*) and measure phrases (e.g. *a bottle of wine*).

understood in a partitive way: *one book* can be interpreted as an element of a familiar set of books.

In this section, I address two issues. First, I illustrate how overt West Greenlandic partitive expressions are constructed and how nominal expressions can get partitive readings. Next, I show that a West Greenlandic incorporated nominal together with its INSTRUMENTAL modifier cannot get a partitive reading. The modifiers that are interesting in this investigation are the numerals and the *wh*-words [see sections 1.2.2 and 1.2.3]. Simultaneously, I check whether German split topics can get partitive readings.

3.2.1 Overt and covert partitives

What does an overt partitive expression in West Greenlandic look like? Again, I borrow two examples from Bittner (1994).

(93)   *Atuartu-t*   *ila-an-nik*

      student-ERG.PL   part-3PL.SG-INST.PL

        ikiu-i-sariaqar-p-u-nga.   [Bittner (1994): 138]

        help-AP-must-IND-[-tr]-1SG

    "I must help one of the students (lit. students one part of them), any will do."

(94)   *Atuartu-t*   *ila-a-t*

      student-ERG.PL   part-3PL.SG-ABS.PL

        ikiur-tariaqar-p-a-ra.   [Bittner (1994): 138]

        help-must-IND-[+tr]-1SG.3SG

    "There is one of the students that I must help."

The part denoting the element that is related to this familiar set *ila-* ("part"), bears INSTRUMENTAL case, if it is the Object of a verb with intransitive morphology, or ABSOLUTIVE case, if it is the Object of a verb with transitive morphology. This case distinction correlates — roughly speaking — with a specificity distinction: the INSTRUMENTAL Object *ilaannik* in (93) is interpreted nonspecifically, the ABSOLUTIVE Object *ilaat* in (94) specifically.[21]

---

[21] Note that *atuartut* ("students"), which realizes the familiar part of a West Greenlandic partitive construction, bears the ERGATIVE case. In a determiner-free language such as West Greenlandic the presence of strong Case in a partitive construction could be regarded as a variation on the definiteness requirement in Jackendoff's PARTITIVE CONSTRAINT [Jackendoff (1977)].

Apart from the possibility of expressing partitivity by means of the *ila*-construction, it is also possible to understand full indefinite NPs in a partitive way. The following piece of discourse is a case in point.

(95) a.   Angunnguu-p   qamuti-t   quli-nik   qimmi-lli-t

      A.-ERG   sledge-ABS   ten-INST   dog-have.REL.[-tr]-ABS

      tak-u-a-i.   [fw]

      see-IND-[+tr]-3SG.3PL

      "Angunguaq saw a sledge with ten dogs."

    b.   Qimmi-t   ila-a-t   nissu-mi-gut

      dog-ERG.PL   part-3PL.SG-ABS.PL   leg-3SG.PROX-VIAL

      mila-qar-p-u-q.   [fw]

      spot-have-IND-[-tr]-3SG

      "One of the dogs had a spot on its leg."

    c.   Qimmeq ataaseq   nissu-mi-gut   mila-qar-p-u-q.   [fw]

      dog.ABS   one.ABS   leg-3SG.PROX-VIAL   spot-have-IND-[-tr]-3SG

      "One (of the) dogs had a spot on its leg."

In (95b), the overt partitive *qimmit ilaat* picks out one of the dogs mentioned in (95a). The indefinite *qimmeq ataaseq* ("one dog") in (95c) can do the same job. This ABSOLUTIVE constituent is thus a covert partitive.

3.2.2 Numerals

As to the second question: can an incorporated noun together with its INSTRUMENTAL numeral modifier function as a covert partitive, that is, can it receive a partitive interpretation? As I show in this section, the answer to this question is no. Before I get to the Greenlandic data, I first investigate whether a German split topic receives a partitive reading. This is done by checking whether a German split topic can be the answer to the partitive question "how many of the ... ."

(96)   A: Bei der Prüfung   mußten   die Studenten   zehn   Fragen

         at   the   exam   have.to   the students   ten   questions

         beantworten.

         answer

         "During the exam the students had to answer ten questions."

B: Wieviele   von   den   Fragen   hat   Johann   richtig

how.many   of   the   questions has   J.   correctly

beantwortet?

answered

"How many of the questions did Johann answer correctly?"

In (96), speaker B raises the partitive question "how many of the ..." to which (97) is a possible answer: the indefinite NP *sieben Fragen* ("seven questions") is then understood as the partitive *sieben von den Fragen* ("seven of the questions"). This means that we can link the descriptive content of the indefinite NP in (97) to the set of questions in (96).

(97)   Johann   hat   sieben   Fragen   richtig   beantwortet.

J.   has   seven   questions correctly   answered

"John has answered seven (of the) questions correctly."

However (98), the split counterpart of (97), is not an appropriate answer to B's question. It cannot be understood as a partitive.

(98)   Fragen   hat   Johann sieben   richtig   beantwortet.

questions has   J.   seven   correctly   answered

i.   "As for questions, John has answered seven correctly."

ii.   # "Of the questions, John has answered seven correctly."

(98) can only be the appropriate answer to the cardinality question "how many ..." which does not presuppose an existing set of questions. In other words, the topicalized *Fragen* ("questions") in (98) is nonpresuppositional, that is, it can not be anaphorically related to a set of familiar questions.

Now that we have a way of testing whether a nominal expression can be understood as a partitive expression, namely by asking the "how many of the" question, I return to externally modified incorporated nouns in West Greenlandic. Suppose we have the following piece of discourse:

(99)   A: Nillataartitsivim-mi   tallima-nik   manne-qar-p-u-q.   [fw]

fridge-LOC   five-INST.PL   egg-have-IND-[-tr]-3SG

"There are five eggs in the fridge."

B: Jensi-p uku-nannga   qassi-t

J.-ERG   those-ABL.PL   how.many-ABS.PL

neri-ssa-v-a-i?   [fw]

eat-FUT-INTER-[+tr]-3SG.3PL

"How many from those will Jensi eat?"

(100), in which *mannik* ("egg") is incorporated and modified by the INSTRUMENTAL numeral *marlunnik* ("two"), is not an appropriate answer to B's question under (99).

(100) Jensi marlun-nik manni-tu-ssa-a-q.   [fw]

    J.ABS two-INST.PL egg-eat-FUT-IND.[-tr]-3SG

    i.   "Jensi will eat two eggs."

    ii. # "Jensi will eat two of the eggs."

The numeral can only be understood as a cardinality marker and the incorporated eggs are not anaphorically relatable to the set of eggs introduced by A in (99). A possible answer to B's question is the following transitive configuration:

(101) Jensi-p marluk neri-ssa-v-a-i.   [fw]

    J.-ERG two.ABS eat-FUT-IND-[+tr]-3SG.3PL

    "Jensi will eat two (of the eggs)."

Again, we have a reason to believe that the structural discontinuity realized by German split topicalization and the one realized by the modification of West Greenlandic incorporated nouns have similar semantic constraints. The numeral modifiers used in these configurations have a predicative function only [Klein (1980), Hoeksema (1983a)].

3.2.3 Quantifiers

From the fact that incorporated nouns modified with an INSTRUMENTAL numeral do not get a partitive reading, one expects that genuine quantifiers, which presuppose their domain, cannot modify such nouns. For the same reason, one expects that in German a quantificational NP cannot split. The following example illustrates that this prediction comes out true for German: splitting a quantifier results in ungrammaticality.

(102) a. Karl hat die meisten Birnen einzeln verpackt.

        K. has the most pears separately packed

      "Karl has packed most pears separately."

    b. * Birnen hat Karl die meisten einzeln verpackt.

For its interpretation, the determiner *most* requires a familiar set of objects in the background. The descriptive content in the unsplit NP in the a-example can deliver this background set. However, when this descriptive material is realized as a topicalized bare plural, this requirement cannot be met. Schwarz (1992) points out that it is possible to split a genuine quantifier if we are dealing with quantification over kinds rather than over objects. He is thinking about examples such as the following.

(103) Johann hat alle Früchte schon mal gegessen.

     J.   has all fruits already once eaten

    i.   # "John has eaten all the pieces of fruit already once."

    ii. "John has eaten all kinds of fruit already once."

Given the presence of the adverbial *schon mal* ("already once"), the quantifier *alle* in (103) cannot be understood as quantifying over familiar objects but only as quantifying over kinds. It is possible to split the quantificational NP *alle Früchte* ("all fruits"):

(104) Früchte hat Johann alle schon mal gegessen.

    fruit.PL has J.   all already once eaten

    "Johann has eaten all kinds of fruit already once."

Bittner (p.c.) suggests that (105) illustrates the same point for West Greenlandic:

(105) Juuna tama-nik atuagar-si-v-u-q.   [Bittner (p.c.)]

    J.ABS all-INST.PL book-get-IND-[-tr]-3SG

    i.   # "Juuna got all the books."

    ii. "Juuna got all kinds of books (i.e., novels, comics, dictionaries)."

However, I had a hard time with my informants to make them accept (105) at all. This was not because this sentence was ungrammatical but because it was nearly impossible for them — and for me — to set up a situation in which (105) could be uttered felicitously.

3.2.4 *Wh*-modifiers

Among the *wh*-elements, we can distinguish between partitive and nonpartitive ones as well, namely, between those that presuppose a set of objects and those that do not presuppose such a set. The English *wh*-determiner *how many* is ambiguous in this respect:

(106) How many houses did you buy?

    i.   "How many of the houses did you buy?"

    ii. "How many houses did you buy?"

It is now interesting to check whether the same ambiguity arises when an incorporated noun is modified by means of a *wh*-word [see section 1.2.3]. When (107) provides the context, it is only possible to use the transitive construction in (108) if we want to ask for the number of the eggs mentioned in (107).

(107) Nillataartitsivim-mi   tallima-nik   manni-qar-p-u-q.   [fw]

fridge-LOC   five-INST.PL   egg-have-IND-[-tr]-3SG

"There are five eggs in the fridge."

(108) Jensi-p   mannii-t   qassi-t   neri-v-a-i?   [fw]

J.-ERG   egg-ABS.PL   how.many-ABS.PL   eat-INTER-[+tr]-3SG.3PL

"How many (of the) eggs did Jensi eat?"

With (107) in the background, it is not possible to ask a similar question by using an incorporating construction: (109) can only be used as a purely nonpartitive cardinality question.

(109) Jensi *qassi-nik*   manni-tu-v-a?   [fw]

J.ABS   how.many-INST.PL   egg-eat-INTER-[-tr]-3SG

i.   # "How many of the eggs did Jensi eat?"

ii. "How many eggs did Jensi eat?

Another interesting *wh*-element in this respect is English *which*. As Heim (1987) points out, *which* can only be understood in a partitive manner. The *which*-phrase in (110) can either ask a question about the membership of a particular house with respect to a larger set of houses, or it can question the membership of a particular house kind with respect to a presupposed set of house kinds (e.g. in a brochure of a building-contractor). In other words, it can be understood in a partitive way only.

(110) Which house did you buy?

i.   "Which of the houses did you buy?"

ii. "What kind of house of the kinds available did you buy?"

The West Greenlandic correspondent of English *which* is *sorleq*. The two paraphrases below the English example each have their own West Greenlandic translation. The object-partitive question (110i) is realized as a transitive configuration and the kind-partitive question (110ii) as an intransitive incorporating one.

(111) Illu   *sorleq*   pisiari-v-iuk?   [fw]

house.ABS which.ABS   buy-INTER-[+tr].2SG.3SG

i.   "Which of the houses did you buy?"

ii. # "What kind of house did you buy?"

(112) *Sorlem-mik*   illu-si-p-i-t?   [fw]

which-INST   house-buy-INTER-[-tr]-2SG

i.   # "Which of the houses did you buy?"

ii. "What kind of house did you buy?"

Before we mentioned that another way of asking for the property denoted by the incorporated noun is by means of the *wh*-element *qanuqittu-* ("what kind of").

(113) *Qanuq-it-tu-mik*   qimme-qar-p-i-t?   [fw]

how-be-REL.[-tr]-INST.SG   dog-have-INTER-[-tr]-2SG

"What kind of dog do you have?"

A German split configuration which comes to mind in this respect is the famous *was für* split, which can be considered to be a special case of split topicalization.

(114) Was für einen Hund habt Ihr?

what for a dog have you.PL

"What kind of dog do you have?"

(115) Was habt Ihr für einen Hund?

what have you.PL for a dog

"What kind of dog do you have?"

Both questions are not presuppositional, that is, they do not require that a set of objects is presupposed.

3.2.5 Summary

The data presented in this section indicate that a West Greenlandic incorporated noun modified by a numeral or a *wh*-element cannot be interpreted in an object-partitive way. The same holds of German split topics. This nonpartitivity follows from the analysis of incorporated indefinites that I will propose in this study, namely that an incorporated indefinite denotes a predicate. As such it does not meet the requirement that a partitively interpreted expression always translates into a variable which triggers the membership relation. We will return to this requirement in chapter 6.

3.3 Anaphoric potential

3.3.1 Incorporated antecedents

Although West Greenlandic incorporated nouns cannot themselves be understood as anaphoric expressions, Sadock (1980) observed that these nouns can antecede a definite pronoun. The following examples illustrate this anaphoric potential:[22]

---

[22] Note that a pronoun in West Greenlandic is realized as a part of the verbal inflection.

(116) Suulut   timmisartu-liur-p-u-q.

Søren.ABS airplane-made-IND-[-tr]-3SG

Suluusa-qar-p-u-q   aquute-qar-llu-ni-lu.   [Sadock (1980): 311]

wing-have-IND-[-tr]-3SG rudder-have-INF-3SG.PROX-and

"Søren made an airplane_i. It_i has wings and it_i has a rudder."

(117) Erneq-taar-p-u-t   atser-lu-gu-lu

son-get.a.new-IND-[-tr]-3PL   name-INF-3SG-and

Mala-mik.   [Sadock (1986): 23]

Mala-INST

"They had a son_i and they called him_i Maala."

(118) Aani   qimmi-qar-p-u-q.

A.ABS dog-have-IND-[-tr]-3SG

Miki-mik ati-qar-p-u-q.   [Bittner (1994): 67]

M.-INST   name-have-IND-[-tr]-3SG

"Aani has a dog_i. It_i is called Miki."

Clearly, the incorporated nouns in these West Greenlandic examples behave very much like indefinite NPs in English.

(119) Frederik has a horse. It is a very nice one.

(120) Mark was eating potato chips. He bought them at the supermarket.

The fact that the indefinites *a horse* in (119) and *potato chips* in (120) are discourse transparent was one of the reasons for many semanticists [Heim (1982), Kamp (1981)] to believe that indefinite descriptions are not quantificational expressions, but rather expressions that get a propositional interpretation. The idea is that an indefinite NP introduces a variable together with a condition that holds of this variable. If the indefinite is not part of the restrictor of a quantificational expression, it gets an existential interpretation. The meaning of (119) and (120) is captured by the truth conditions under (119a) and (120a) respectively:

(119) a. $\exists x$ [horse(x) & have(frederik, x) & very-nice(x)]

(120) a. $\exists X$ [chips(X) & eat(mark, X) & buy(mark, X, at-the-superm.)]

This semantic binding strategy to capture the discourse transparency of indefinites is an alternative to what is known as the E-type approach to syntactically unbound variables [Evans (1980), Heim (1990), Neale (1990)]. In this approach, syntactically unbound variables stand for a pragmatically derived description.

(119) b. Frederik has a horse. *The horse that Frederik has* is a very nice one.

(120) b. Mark is eating potato chips. He bought *the potato chips he was eating* at the supermarket.

This book is not the locus where I want to decide which of these approaches captures the discourse transparency of West Greenlandic incorporated nouns in the most appropriate way. In chapter 5, I favour a Kamp-Heim style approach.

At the beginning of my presentation of the West Greenlandic data, I pointed out that the number of an incorporated noun is undetermined: it can either be understood as singular or as plural expression. In the examples (116), (117), and (118), the use of a singular anaphor — which is part of the inflectional morphology on the verb — fixes the number denoted by the respective incorporated nouns. When a plural pronominal suffix is used, the number of the incorporated noun is fixed as "more than one." This is illustrated in the following piece of discourse.

(121) Aani   qimmi-qar-p-u-q.   Kusana-q-a-a-t.   [fw]

A.ABS dog-have-IND-[-tr]-3SG. nice.very-be-IND-[-tr]-3PL

"Aani has dogs$_i$. They$_i$ are very nice."

This is a situation which does not arise in a West Germanic language: the indefinite antecedents in (119) and (120) determine their number themselves.

3.3.2 Are words anaphoric islands?

In the literature on the structural aspects of noun incorporation, it is often argued that the fact that an incorporated noun can antecede a definite pronoun supports the view that at some level of syntactic representation it must be the head of a phrasal constituent [Baker (1988)]. The idea behind this argument is that West Greenlandic incorporating configurations cannot be parts of words at every level of structural representation since words are "anaphoric islands" [Postal (1969)]: a definite pronoun is not supposed to pick up a word that is part of a compound.[23]

(122) Johann ist Buchhändler. Es ist im Angebot.

"John is a book$_i$ dealer. # It$_i$ (= the book) is on sale."

(123) Carol bought cat food. It turned out soon that it didn't like it.

"Carol bought cat$_i$ food. # It turned out soon that it$_i$ (= the cat) didn't like it."

---

[23] Ward, Sproat and McKoon (1991) have argued that in English words are not always anaphoric islands either. See chapter 5 for a discussion of some of their data.

In a transformational account of noun incorporation, the distinction between the discourse transparency of West Greenlandic incorporated nouns, on the one hand, and the nontransparency of the nouns embedded into English compounds, on the other, is captured by the idea that the former are syntactic phrases, whereas the latter are parts of lexical compounds.

However, I doubt whether the stipulation that an incorporated noun is the head of a D-structural phrase has anything to do with the discourse transparency of such a noun. Otherwise, why would a noun incorporated into a negated verbal affix lose its transparency?

(124) Aani   qimmi-qa-nngi-l-a-q.

A.ABS dog-have-NEG-IND-[-tr]-3SG.

Miki-mik   ati-qar-p-u-q.   [fw]

M.-INST   name-have-IND-[-tr]-3SG

"Aani doesn't have a dog$_i$. # It$_i$ is called Miki."

An apparently easy answer to this question is that an incorporated noun loses its discourse transparency when embedded under negation because the NP *a dog* in the English paraphrase of (124) loses its transparency as well. However, in contrast to incorporated nouns indefinite NPs do not necessarily lose their ability of anteceding a definite pronoun. (125) illustrates a case in point:

(125) David didn't eat an apple. It is still in his lunch box.

"David didn't eat an apple$_i$. It$_i$ is still in his lunch box."

3.3.3 Questions

I readdress Sadock's observation that a West Greenlandic incorporated noun can antecede a pronoun with respect to the following two questions.

First, how can we capture the discourse transparency of a (incorporated) nominal expression as a case of semantic binding? The answer to this question will lead us to integrating semantic incorporation into a Kamp-Heim semantic approach to discourse. The major novelty that I introduce in this respect is that verbs can introduce discourse referents.

The second question is whether the discourse transparency of a nominal expression puts any *structural* requirement on this expression. I will conclude that there is no reason to believe that the discourse transparency of incorporated nouns is a valid argument *pro* a transformational account. Rather, the transparency of these nouns is directly related to whether or not they are semantically embedded. Furthermore, I readdress Postal's observation and contrast his kind of data with data showing that nouns in English compounds can antecede a kind anaphor [Ward, Sproat and McKoon (1991)].

(126) John is a book dealer. He sells *them* for several publishers.

(127) Carol always buys high quality cat food. She thinks it is good for *their* health.

I will explain the fact that nouns in English compounds cannot antecede a nonkind anaphoric expression whereas an incorporated noun can as the consequence of the fact that only the latter receive a "dynamic" existential interpretation. This does not block the former's ability of establishing a kind antecedent.

3.4 Summary

Summarizing this section about the discourse semantic aspects of West Greenlandic incorporated nouns and their West Germanic counterparts we can say the following. Neither a West Greenlandic incorporated noun nor a West Germanic bare plural can be interpreted as carrying a presupposition. With respect to other data presented in this chapter, more particularly the data illustrating the existential construction in section 2.1, this should not be a big surprise. Neither a West Greenlandic modified incorporated noun nor a German split topic can receive a partitive interpretation. Unlike parts of West Germanic compounds, West Greenlandic incorporated nouns can antecede a pronominal expression.

4 Chapter summary

A wide variety of semantic properties of West Greenlandic noun incorporating configurations have been discussed in this chapter. In parallel, I presented West Germanic bare plural constructions and German split topics as semantic counterparts of West Greenlandic noun incorporation. In what follows, I argue that West Greenlandic incorporated nouns as well as these counterparts are indefinite descriptions of a special sort, namely, *predicative* indefinites. What we need is a general explanation for why predicative indefinites always have narrow scope interpretations, why they lack a presuppositional reading, and why they do not receive a partitive interpretation. On top of that, we want to figure out under which circumstances they can be the antecedent of an anaphoric expression. In addition to these (discourse) semantic questions, we have to ask the questions of whether and how the predicative meaning of an incorporated noun and of its semantic counterparts is visible in their structural representation.

3

Setting the Semantic Scene

0 Introduction

The many questions that have been raised by the West Greenlandic and the West Germanic examples in chapter 2 call for an explanation. The basis for the explanation I will offer is the assumption that West Greenlandic incorporated nouns, West Germanic bare plurals and German split topics are indefinite descriptions of a particular sort. They belong to the class of *predicative* indefinites. In other words, the semantic analysis of the West Greenlandic and West Germanic nominal expressions illustrated in chapter 2 forms part of a theory of indefinites sketched at the end of this chapter and outlined in more detail in chapter 5 and chapter 6.

A theory about indefinite descriptions has to explain *how* indefinites get into particular scope positions, *why* particular indefinites receive a partitive interpretation and — most importantly — *why* particular indefinites do *not* get into particular scope positions and *why* they do *not* get a partitive reading. In addition, a theory about indefinites has to capture their generic interpretations as well. Fortunately, many authors have thought about indefinite descriptions before I found myself trapped in it, and I elaborate my ideas about indefinites against the background of their ideas. One of the basic assumptions I adopt from the literature is that indefinite descriptions are not quantificational expressions. Against the Montagovian spirit in formal semantics at that time, Kamp (1981) and Heim (1982) independently elaborated the idea that indefinites introduce a variable that is bound by an external quantificational source together with a restriction of this variable. Still, Kamp and Heim have little to say about how indefinites get into particular scope positions, why particular indefinites do not get into particular scope positions and why particular indefinites receive a partitive interpretation whereas others don't.

In the literature, we can distinguish (at least) two different kinds of answers to the scope question. The first one is based on the assumption that indefinite descriptions denote different semantic types [Partee (1987)] and representative for this approach is Diesing (1992). Diesing clearly abandons the Kamp-Heim view that all indefinites are nonquantificational expressions. According to her, the distinct scope and partitivity behaviour of indefinites correlates with a semantic type distinction. Moreover, she argues that this distinction is syntactically transparent. Wide scope positions of indefinite descriptions are argued to be the result of syntactic QUANTIFIER RAISING. Partitive interpretations of indefinites are the result of QUANTIFIER RAISING as well. A second kind of answer to the scope question we find in Abusch (1994). Sticking to the original Kamp-Heim view that indefinites are not quantifiers, Abusch proposes that indefinites reach their scope position by means of an interpretive storage mechanism. However, neither Diesing nor Abusch gives a satisfactory answer to the narrow scope question. Although both authors offer mechanisms accounting for how an indefinite can reach a particular scope position, they lack an account for why particular indefinite descriptions in nongeneric contexts — more particularly West Greenlandic incorporated nouns and West Germanic bare plurals — necessarily take narrow scope with respect to other operators.

To find an interesting answer to the narrow scope question one has to go back to Carlson (1977) who gives a semantic explanation for the narrow scope effects of the English bare plural. According to Carlson, the narrow scope effect of a bare plural in a nongeneric context is the direct consequence of the idea that a bare plural gets its existential interpretation from the verbal head of which it is an argument. Although many objections have been raised against this part of Carlson's theory, I will combine it with the Kamp-Heim idea that indefinites are nonquantificational expressions. This combination allows us to give a more finegrained realization of the Kamp-Heim idea, namely, it allows us to draw a distinction between *predicative* and *free variable* indefinite descriptions. This distinction lays the foundation of my explanation for *why* particular indefinites do and others do *not* get into particular scope positions, and *why* particular indefinites do and others do not get a partitive interpretation. Whereas predicative indefinites are said to receive their existential interpretation from the verb by which they are semantically incorporated, the interpretation of free variable indefinites is determined through the accommodation of their descriptive content.

The first section of this chapter starts with a presentation of Kamp's (1981) Discourse Representation Theory [DRT], more particularly, its further elaboration in Kamp and Reyle (1993) to which I refer as DRT-93.[1] In addition to this representational framework, I present Heim's syntactic treatment of the interpretation of indefinites [Heim (1982, chapter 2)]. Then, I move to some examples showing that indefinite descriptions can get different scope interpretations, that some indefinites do not reach scope positions that others do, and that some indefinites lack partitive readings that others have. In the second section, I discuss Diesing's (1992) proposal to deal with the scope question and — to some extent — the partitivity question. In the third section, I present data from Abusch (1994) showing that the scope position of an indefinite NP is not syntactically determined.

---

[1] The term DRT has been used by different authors and for different purposes. To preclude terminological ambiguities, I give this version of DRT its own name: DRT-93.

The fourth section revisits Carlson's (1977) treatment of the English bare plural. In the fifth section, I propose a novel distinction between predicative and free variable indefinite descriptions. The intuitive idea is that the differences with respect to scope and partitivity in the class of indefinites are a direct consequence of which interpretive mechanism applies to an indefinite's descriptive content.

1 Indefinite descriptions aren't quantificational

The standard interpretation of indefinite descriptions in formal semantics is to regard them as existential quantifiers [Montague (1974), Barwise and Cooper (1981)]. Since the early eighties, this view shares the company with the Kamp-Heim view that indefinites are not existential quantifiers: they introduce a variable which is bound by an external quantificational source. One of the advantages of this view is that it is able to treat intersentential binding phenomena. Another advantage is that it provides us with a semantic treatment of donkey pronouns.

1.1 DRT-93: A representational discourse semantic framework

1.1.1 Intersentential binding

Following Kamp (1981), Kamp and Reyle (1993) defend the idea that the existential interpretation of an indefinite description results from the formulation of the truth conditions of its discourse representation structure [DRS]. In light of example (1), I give a short overview of how DRT-93 accounts for the anaphoric relation between the pronoun *it* in (1b) and the indefinite NP *a horse* in (1a).

(1) a. Frederik has a horse.

     b. It is very nice.

The syntactic representation of (1a) delivers the structural triggers required to construct an appropriate DRS for this sentence in an incremental way. This means that the syntactic tree (2) will be transformed into a DRS step by step.

(2)

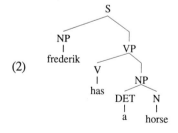

First, we substitute a discourse referent x for the Subject NP *frederik* and place this referent into the discourse universe of the DRS in preparation. The name *frederik* will be stored as a DRS condition which holds for its referent.

(3)

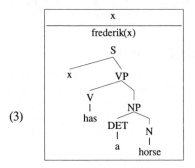

Next, we substitute another discourse referent for the indefinite Object NP *a horse*. The descriptive content of the indefinite is added to the set of DRS conditions.

(4)

The DRS (5) is a shorthand of (4):

(5)

To this we add the syntactic tree of the next piece of discourse, namely, of (1b).

(6)

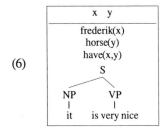

The presence of the pronoun in this tree triggers the introduction of a new referent and the identification of this referent with its antecedent. The result is (7).

(7)

$$
\begin{array}{|l|}
\hline
x \quad y \quad z \\
\hline
frederik(x) \\
horse(y) \\
have(x,y) \\
z = y \\
be\text{--}very\text{--}nice(z) \\
\hline
\end{array}
$$

The truth conditions of (7) are defined according to the idea that

> a DRS is true provided we can find individuals for each of the discourse referents in its universe in such a way that the conditions which the DRS contains for particular discourse referents are satisfied by the corresponding individuals [Kamp and Reyle (1993): 73].

In other words, (7) is true iff

(8)   There are individuals a and b such that a is frederik and b is a horse and a has b and b is very nice.

At this final stage, we see that the existential interpretation of the indefinite object NP *a horse* is built into the formulation of the truth conditions of the DRS to which it contributes its variable and its descriptive content.

1.1.2 Negation

The discourse binding of a pronoun is blocked if its antecedent is embedded under negation. That is, the horse mentioned in (9a) cannot be the antecedent of the pronoun in (9b) because it is not accessible as such.

(9)   a.   Frederik doesn't have a horse.

        b.   # It is very nice.

In DRT-93, this inaccessibility is visualized in the following way.

(10)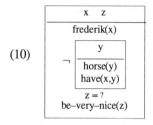

Ignoring the way in which (10) has been obtained from (9), we can say that (10) is true iff

(11)   There are individuals *a* and *c* such that *a* is frederik and *c* is ? and *c* is very nice and *it is not the case that* there is an individual *b* such that *b* is a horse and *a* has *b*.

(11) makes clear that although the indefinite *a horse* gets an existential interpretation, this existential interpretation is embedded under negation. Hence, it cannot provide an antecedent for those pronouns that are not embedded under this operator.

1.1.3 Donkey pronouns

Apart from the pronoun–antecedent relations in a sentence like (1), the discourse transparency of indefinites embedded in the restrictor of a quantifier was yet another reason to believe that indefinites are not existentially quantified expressions. These cases are usually called donkey sentences [Geach (1962)].

(12)   Every farmer who has a donkey beats it.

(13)   Every man who has a dime in his pocket puts it into the meter.

Inspired by Lewis (1975), the original work of Kamp and Heim defended the view that the quantifiers in these sentences bind the free variable introduced by the respective indefinites. The following boxes represent the Kamp-Heim semantics of (12).

(14)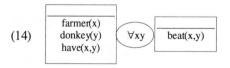

This DRS says that for every *x* who is a farmer and for every donkey *y* who is *x*'s donkey it is the case that *x* beats *y*. The universal quantifier binds the farmers and the donkeys in pairs.

The Kamp-Heim treatment of donkey sentences was a reaction against the E-type account to deal with the interpretation of donkey pronouns [Evans (1980)]. In this approach, indefinites are regarded as existential quantifiers, and as such they are semantically inaccessible for anaphoric reference. Donkey pronouns are interpreted as descriptions which are pragmatically derived from the context. (15) illustrates a case in point.

(15)   Every farmer who has a donkey, beats *the donkey he has.*

The problem with the original E-type approach is that these descriptions give rise to a uniqueness presupposition which does not fit with the way these sentences are interpreted intuitively. Since the Kamp-Heim treatment of donkey sentences, many other authors have extended and discussed the pros and cons of both approaches from various perspectives and with more or less persuasive force and I do not want to repeat all of that here.[2] The only issue that I want to address here in passing is that the original Kamp-Heim treatment does not do justice to the fact that donkey sentences may have a "strong", that is, a universal, or a "weak", that is, an existential interpretation. Whereas (12) is a typically universal donkey sentence, (13) became a standard example illustrating the existential interpretation of a donkey pronoun. (13) requires that its donkey pronoun is interpreted in an existential rather than in a universal way since no man would put every dime he has in his pocket into one and the same parking meter. Do we have to conclude from this observation that donkey pronouns are E-type pronouns? No, we don't. And fortunately Kamp and Reyle (1993) indirectly offer a solution to this problem. To deal with the famous proportion problem, these authors revise the original Kamp-Heim view that an indefinite in the antecedent of a donkey sentence is unselectively bound.[3] They suggest that instead such an indefinite could be given an existential interpretation.

---

[2] See Chierchia (1995) for a recent overview.

[3] The standard DRT treatment can only account for sentences with a universal quantifier: in (14) we are quantifying over farmer-donkey pairs. If we assign similar truth conditions to donkey sentences with other quantifiers this gives rise to the proportion problem [Kadmon (1987)]. For instance, if we interpret (i) as (ii), it is easy to imagine a situation in which these truth conditions are wrong.

(i)   Most farmers who own a donkey, beat it.
(ii)   MOST x y [farmer(x) $\land$ donkey(y) $\land$ have(x,y)] [beat(x,y)]

(i) is true if most of the farmer-donkey pairs that satisfy the antecedent, satisfy the consequent. That is, if in a village there are three farmers with one donkey each who do not beat their donkeys and there is one farmer with ten donkeys who does beat his animals, (ii) would — against our intuitions — come out true.

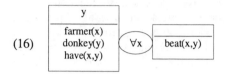

(16)

For its interpretation, the verification of this DRS in a model is defined in such a way that although the indefinite gets an existential interpretation, it can widen its scope and, hence, bind the donkey pronoun.[4]

1.2 Heim's (1982) syntactic treatment

Heim (1982, chapter 2) elaborates a system in which, first, syntactic trees of English expressions are associated with syntactic Logical Forms (LFs) and, secondly, these LFs are assigned truth conditions.[5] I sketch the first part of her system which consists of the transformation of S-structure trees into LFs. This transformation is directed by the following rules of construal together with a set of wellformedness conditions.

NP-INDEXING   [Heim (1982): 132]

Assign every NP a referential index

NP-PREFIXING   [Heim (1982): 132]

Adjoin every nonpronominal NP to S

EXISTENTIAL CLOSURE – SUBRULE 2 [6]   [Heim (1982): 140]

Adjoin the quantifier ∃ to T (where T is a sequence of sentences)

QUANTIFIER INDEXING   [Heim (1982): 146]

Copy the referential index of every NP as a selection index onto the
      lowest c-commanding quantifier

In light of our example (1), I illustrate how these rules apply. We start from (17) as the S-structure of (1).

---

[4] Kamp and Reyle (1993) still favour the universal interpretation of donkey sentences. For more details, see Kamp and Reyle (1993): 420-425.

[5] This is only one of Heim's (1982) realizations of the indefinites-are-variables idea. I present her syntactic approach here, because it will be relevant for my discussion of Diesing's (1992) and Abusch's (1994) approaches to this idea [see section 2 and section 3 below]. In chapter 5, I make use of Rooth's (1987) version of Heim's semantic approach.

[6] The construal rule EXISTENTIAL CLOSURE comes with two subrules. Here, I only mention the second one, which applies to indefinites in an unembedded position. The first one applies to indefinite NPs that are embedded in quantificational and negative contexts [see section 2].

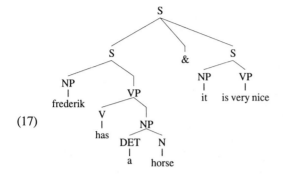

(17)

According to the rule of NP-INDEXING, we first assign every NP a referential index. This gives us (18).

(18)   [$_S$ [$_S$ [$_{NP_1}$ Frederik] [$_{VP}$ has [$_{NP_2}$ a horse]]] & [$_S$ [$_{NP_2}$ it] [$_{VP}$ is very nice]]]

Note that the pronoun *it* bears the same index as the indefinite *a horse*. This is possible since the definite comes after the indefinite. If things were the other way round, namely, if the indefinite had been mentioned after the definite pronoun, the NOVELTY CONDITION would have prohibited that they bear the same index.

NOVELTY CONDITION   [Heim (1982): 151]

An indefinite NP must not have the same index as an NP to its left.

Secondly, the nonpronominal NPs are prefixed as in (19).

(19)   [$_S$ [$_S$ [$_{NP_1}$ Frederik] [$_S$ [$_{NP_2}$ a horse] [$_S$ e$_1$ [$_{VP}$ has e$_2$]]]] & [$_S$ [$_{NP_2}$ it] [$_{VP}$ is very nice]]]

Finally, in (20) the index of NP$_2$ is bound through EXISTENTIAL CLOSURE at text level.

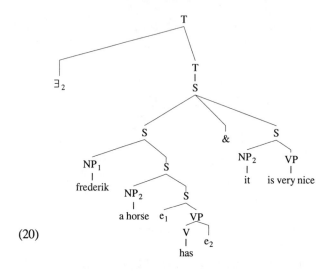

(20)

According to the interpretation mechanism proposed in Heim (1982), (20) is true iff

(21)   There are individuals a and b such that a is frederik and b is a horse and a has b and b is very nice.

That is, the LF under (20) is assigned exactly the same truth conditions as our above DRS (7).

The main difference between Heim's (1982) syntactic picture of the indefinites-are-variables idea and its representational picture in DRT-93 is that in the latter approach there is space for a representational treatment of the projection of presuppositions and — as I show in chapter 6 — of the determination of wide and intermediate readings of indefinite descriptions. In Heim's syntactic approach, where the meaning is fully transparent at the syntactic level of LF, one has to stipulate that the interpretation of wide and intermediate indefinite descriptions and of presuppositions is derived by means of syntactic rules. With respect to the scope properties of indefinites, Abusch (1994) has shown that this stipulation is not compatible with the facts [see section 3 below].

1.3 Are there different types of indefinites?

One of the nice aspects of DRT-93 and of Heim (1982) is that both approaches are able to treat intersentential and donkey pronouns in a semantic way, something that classical syntax and classical predicate logic have not been able to. Another interesting pay-off of the indefinite-as-variable approach is that it suggests an obvious way to treat generic indefinites. Heim (1982) uses the following example to illustrate this use.

(22)   A cat that has been exposed to 2,4-D goes blind.   [Heim(1982): 191]

The NP *a cat* translates into a restriction over a variable which lands in the restrictor of an invisible generic operator. The latter unselectively binds this variable, as illustrated in (23):[7]

(23) GEN_x [cat(x) $\land$ exposed-to-2,4-D(x)] [go-blind(x)]

However, the Kamp-Heim frameworks do not provide us with a satisfactory treatment of different existential readings of indefinite descriptions. In Kamp and Reyle's example (24), the indefinite NP *a girl who Mary doesn't know* can be either interpreted as a "specific" girl who Mary doesn't know or as a "nonspecific" girl.

(24)   Every boy in Mary's class fancies a girl who Mary doesn't know.

[Kamp and Reyle (1993): 288]

   i.   "There is a girl g who Mary doesn't know and every boy fancies g."

   ii.   "For every boy b there is a girl g who Mary doesn't know and b fancies g."

Moreover, Carlson (1977) was one of the first who observed that, whenever we replace the singular NP with its bare plural counterpart, the "specific" reading vanishes.

(25)   Every boy in Mary's class fancies girls who Mary doesn't know.

   i.   # "There are girls g who Mary doesn't know and every boy fancies g."

   ii.   "For every boy b there are girls g who Mary doesn't know and b fancies g."

An appropriate theory of indefinite descriptions should not only explain which mechanism makes indefinites reach particular scope positions, but also why this mechanism does not operate on particular indefinites, such as the bare plural in English. Clearly, with this second question we also touch upon the narrow scope effects of the West Greenlandic incorporated nouns and their semantic counterparts that we were dealing with in the previous chapter.

---

[7] This kind of analysis of generic indefinites has become very popular if not standard in the linguistic literature on generics [Krifka et al. (1995), Carlson and Pelletier (1995)]. I return to it in my discussion of Carlson (1977) in section 4.

An appropiate theory of indefinites should also explain why particular indefinites do not get a partitive interpretation. In chapter 2, I showed that German split topics are indefinite descriptions that — as opposed to their nonsplit counterparts — cannot receive a partitive reading. I repeat the data here.

(26) a. Johann   hat   *sieben Fragen*   richtig   beantwortet.

            J.   has   seven questions correctly answered

            i.   "John has answered seven questions correctly."

            ii.   "John has answered seven of the questions correctly."

    b. *Fragen*   hat   Johann *sieben* richtig   beantwortet.

        questions has J.   seven   correctly answered

          i.   "As for questions, John has answered seven correctly."

         ii.   # "Of the questions, John has answered seven correctly."

The reading differences between the pair of examples (24) and (25), and the pair (26a) and (26b) may give rise to the impression that these reading differences can be made visible at LF by means of QUANTIFIER RAISING. If this is the case, it means that we have to give up the Kamp-Heim view that indefinites are *always* nonquantificational expressions. This is exactly what Diesing (1992) proposes: the different readings of indefinites correspond with different types of indefinite descriptions, namely, variable introducing indefinites versus existential quantifiers. Moreover, she claims that this type distinction is directly mirrored in the syntax and that syntactic principles are responsible if particular indefinites lack a "strong" reading.[8] In section 2, I revisit Diesing's proposal and I give some arguments against it. One of them is that Diesing does not give a principled answer to the question of why the bare plural in (25) lacks the wide reading, which its singular counterpart in (24) easily gets. Yet another argument against Diesing is brought up in Abusch (1994). This author clearly shows that from a syntactic perspective indefinite descriptions cannot be regarded as quantificational expressions: it would leave unexplained why indefinites can escape syntactic scope islands whereas genuine quantifiers cannot.

When the interpretation differences in the class of indefinites descriptions are not a matter of syntactic scope differences, one can argue that the differences correspond with differences of interpretive processing principles. If this is the case, it means that we do not have to give up the

---

[8] Diesing uses Milsark's (1977) distinction between "weak" and "strong" NPs. In Diesing's theory, the "weak" ones get a variable interpretation, whereas the "strong" ones are interpreted as quantifiers. Note that "strong" is a cover term for specific, generic, presuppositional, quantificational and partitive. Against Diesing, I argue in chapter 6 that partitive NPs are not necessarily "strong." See McNally and Van Geenhoven (1997) for a novel cross-linguistic definition of the weak–strong distinction.

Kamp-Heim view that indefinites are always nonquantificational expressions. It is along this line that Abusch (1994) develops an interpretive storage mechanism to determine the scope position of indefinite descriptions. However, also Abusch's proposal lacks an answer to the question of why the bare plural in (25) lacks a "specific" reading.

In the remainder of this chapter, I first present Diesing's syntactic proposal to deal with the scope of indefinites, then Abusch's semantic proposal and finally, Carlson's treatment of the narrow scope behaviour of English bare plurals. I close this chapter with a sketch of my answers to the questions of why particular indefinites fail to have readings which others have and how indefinites reach their "scope" position.

2 The scope of indefinites: A syntactic proposal

Some semanticists were only partly convinced that an indefinite's meaning is that of introducing a variable. Partee (1987) argues that the variable introducing meaning is only one of three potential interpretations an indefinite can get. Apart from its variable interpretation, an indefinite can denote an existential quantifier or a predicate. Following this line of thought, Diesing (1992) proposes that the wide versus narrow scope of an indefinite corresponds with a semantic type distinction, namely, the quantifier–variable distinction. Moreover, this distinction is argued to be transparent in the syntactic representation of the configuration in which the indefinite occurs.

2.1 Diesing (1992)

According to Diesing, the reading of an indefinite is either directly visible from its S-structural syntactic position or determined by means of QUANTIFIER RAISING at the syntactic level of LF. She assumes that we need two types of indefinite descriptions, those without and those with quantificational force. Indefinite NPs without quantificational force, which are the variable introducing indefinites, are (to be) located in the VP of a sentence. Indefinites that are existential quantifiers are obligatorily located outside the VP and they form a restrictive clause. The purpose of this process called "tree splitting" is to establish a syntactic representation which displays a quantificational tripartite structure.

(27)   MAPPING HYPOTHESIS   [Diesing (1992): 15]

      Material from VP is mapped into the nuclear scope;

      Material from IP is mapped into a restrictive clause.

In light of example (28), Diesing illustrates how different syntactic derivations deliver three different readings for this sentence.

(28)   Every cellist played some variations.   [Diesing (1992): 65]

   a.   EVERY x [cellist(x)] [SOME y [variations(y)] [x played y]]

   b.   EVERY x [cellist(x)] [$\exists$y [variations(y) $\land$ x played y]]

   c.   SOME y [variations(y)] [EVERY x [cellist(x)] [x played y]]

I start with the derivation of the wide scope reading in (28c). A situation that is compatible with this reading is a competition situation in which there is a fixed set of variations that each cellist played. To derive this reading, Diesing first raises the quantificational Subject NP *every cellist* at LF. She furthermore interprets the indefinite Object *some variations* as a quantificational expression so that this NP raises at LF as well. It is adjoined to the left of the Subject NP.

(29)   [$_{IP}$ some variations$_y$ [$_{IP}$ every cellist$_x$ [$_{VP}$ t$_x$ played t$_y$]]]

This LF is the input for tree splitting. According to the MAPPING HYPOTHESIS in (27), this means that the first IP layer builds a restrictive clause:

(29)   a.   SOME y [variations(y)] [$_{IP}$ every cellist$_x$ [$_{VP}$ t$_x$ played y]]

Then, the second IP layer produces another restrictive clause, which is embedded below the first one.

(29)   b.   SOME y [variations(y)] [EVERY x [cellist(x)] [$_{VP}$ x played y]]

Finally, the VP is mapped into a nuclear scope and the traces are interpreted as bound variables. The result of this first derivation is the above "wide" reading under (28c).

(28)   c.   SOME y [variations(y)] [EVERY x [cellist(x)] [x played y]]

Next, (28b) represents the cardinal reading of the indefinite *some variations*. This time the latter is interpreted as a variable introducer. The LF input is (30):

(30)   [$_{IP}$ every cellist$_x$ [$_{VP}$ t$_x$ played some variations$_y$]]]

Because the nonquantificational indefinite remains in the VP, tree splitting only applies to the subject NP *every cellist*. The variable introduced by *some variations* is bound through EXISTENTIAL CLOSURE.[9] The result is (28b):

(28)   b.   EVERY x [cellist(x)] [$\exists$y [variations(y) $\land$ x played y]]

Finally, (28a) represents what Diesing calls a "narrow presuppositional" reading, namely, the reading in which *some variations* is to be understood as *some of the variations*. We receive this reading when each cellist

---

[9] Diesing makes use of Heim's EXISTENTIAL CLOSURE construal rule that applies to indefinites in the scope of some operator [see fn. 6].

EXISTENTIAL CLOSURE — SUBRULE 1   [Heim (1982): 139]
Adjoin a quantifier $\exists$ to the nuclear scope of every operator.

chooses a different subset out of a given list of optional variations. (28a) is the result of the following syntactic derivation. First, we raise the indefinite *some variations* which is interpreted as a quantifier out of the VP and we adjoin it to IP. This step is triggered by the presuppositional component of the indefinite. Then, the quantificational Subject *every cellist* is adjoined left to the Object NP.

(31)   [$_{IP}$ every cellist$_x$ [$_{IP}$ some variations$_y$ [$_{VP}$ t$_x$ played t$_y$]]]

Next, tree splitting applies to the Subject NP. It builds a restrictive clause.

(31)   a.   EVERY x [cellist(x)] [$_{IP}$ some variations$_y$ [$_{VP}$ x played t$_y$]]

In the following step, the IP layer into which the Object NP has been moved builds a restrictive clause that is located below the first one.

(31)   b.   EVERY x [cellist(x)] [SOME y [variations(y)] [$_{VP}$ x played y]]

Finally, the VP is mapped into a nuclear scope. The result of this derivation is (28a).

(28)   a.   EVERY x [cellist(x)] [SOME y [variations(y)] [x played y]]

2.2 Why German split topics lack strong readings

Before I get to some problems that arise in a Diesingian framework, I outline her syntactic account for why German split topics cannot get "strong" readings. In chapter 2, I presented the data illustrating that only narrow scope indefinites can split. I repeat these data here.

(32)   a.   Lisa   hat   im   Keller   keine   schwarzen   Spinnen   gesehen.

             L.   has   in.the cellar   no   black   spiders   seen

             "It is not the case that Lisa saw black spiders in the cellar."

       b.   Schwarze   Spinnen   hat   Lisa   im   Keller   keine   gesehen.

             black   spiders   has   L.   in.the cellar   no   seen

             "As for black spiders, it is not the case that Lisa saw any in the cellar."

(33)   a.   Lisa   hat   im   Keller   einige   schwarze   Spinnen

             L.   has   in.the cellar   some   black   spiders

             nicht   gesehen.

             not   seen

             "There are some black spiders that Lisa didn't see in the cellar."

       b.   * Schwarze Spinnen hat Lisa im Keller einige nicht gesehen.

In example (32a), *keine schwarzen Spinnen* is in the scope of negation which is linguistically realized on the determiner *keine* ("no"). In example (33a), *einige schwarzen Spinnen* is outside the scope of the negation operator which is realized as *nicht* ("not"). (32b) illustrates that the narrow indefinite Object NP can split, whereas (33b) shows that its wide counterpart cannot. According to Diesing,

> the overall generalization seems to be that extraction is only possible from a nonscrambled (VP-internal) object NP. ... extraction from NP is not compatible with the QR (quantificational) reading of the NP [Diesing (1992): 120].

Her answer to the question of why extraction and interpretation are related in such a way is the REVISED EXTRACTION CONSTRAINT.

(34)   REVISED EXTRACTION CONSTRAINT   [Diesing (1992): 128]

   Extraction cannot take place out of an NP that must raise out of VP before tree splitting.

In other words, it is only possible to split material that is in the VP. Assuming that in German all the relevant movement occurs at S-structure, Diesing claims that NPs with a variable interpretation remain in the VP — as in (35) — and that NPs with a quantificational interpretation are scrambled out of VP at S-structure — as in (36).

(35)   L. hat im Keller [$_{VP}$ keine schwarzen Spinnen gesehen]

(36)   L. hat im Keller [$_{NP}$ einige schw. Spinnen]$_i$ [$_{VP}$ t$_i$ nicht gesehen]

Furthermore, she adopts Huang's (1982) CONSTRAINT ON EXTRACTION DOMAIN [CED] which says that one cannot extract from an ungoverned position. Hence, (38) is ungrammatical because splitting a raised indefinite gives rise to a CED violation. (37) does not violate the CED: the D-structural position of the topicalized material is properly governed.

(37)   Schwarze Spinnen$_i$ hat L. im Keller [$_{VP}$ keine t$_i$ gesehen]

(38)   * Schwarze Spinnen$_k$ hat L. im Keller [$_{NP}$ einige t$_k$]$_i$ [$_{VP}$ t$_i$ nicht gesehen]

Summarizing, the semantic constraint on German split topics, that is, their lack of a strong reading, is argued to be the direct consequence of a syntactic constraint.

2.3 Problems for Diesing

In this section, I argue against the assumption that an indefinite with a partitive reading has to be interpreted as a quantifier. This assumption is a central part of Diesing's proposal. On top of that, I point out that Diesing's proposal lacks a principled answer to the question of why bare plurals in nongeneric contexts never raise.

2.3.1 Are partitive NPs necessarily quantifiers?

Diesing's MAPPING HYPOTHESIS in (27) is based on the view that any expression which bears presuppositional content is a quantifier. Moreover, such an expression finds its LF position through QUANTIFIER RAISING. I argue that this view is wrong. From the insight that a quantifier presupposes its domain, we should not conclude that every expression that contains a presuppositional component is a quantifier.

First, Diesing argues that the LF in (28a) and the one in (28b) are assigned different truth conditions. In particular, she claims that (28a) captures the narrow presuppositional reading of the indefinite in (28), that is, the reading where *some variations* is inderstood as *some of the variations* and remains in the scope of the *EVERY* quantifier. (28b) captures the cardinal reading of *some variations*. I repeat the example and both LFs.

(28) Every cellist played some variations.   [Diesing (1992): 65]

    a. EVERY x [cellist(x)] [SOME y [variations(y)] [x played y]]

    b. EVERY x [cellist(x)] [$\exists$y [variations(y) $\land$ x played y]]

As a first step in my argument, I use a more fine-grained representation of the cardinal reading of *some variations* in the sense of Kamp and Reyle (1993). The nuclear scope of the *EVERY* quantifier in (28b) is then replaced by (28b') where Σ is the summation operator:

(28) b'. $\exists Y [Y = \Sigma y' : (\text{variations}(y') \land x \text{ played } y') \land \text{some } (|Y|)]$

(28b') says that there is a set which is the sum of the variations played and whose cardinality satisfies the predicate *some*. As a second step, I take a closer look at the nuclear scope of the *EVERY* quantifier in (28a), repeated here as (28a').

(28) a'. SOME y [variations(y)] [x played y]

(28a') is true if the quantifier *SOME* holds between the set defined by its first argument and the set defined by its first and its second argument taken together. This relation holds if the latter set has the cardinality "some", which is precisely the truth condition associated with (28b').[10] In other words, there is no truth conditional difference between (28a) and (28b). Hence, they fail to capture the difference between the narrow presuppositional reading of *some variations*, on the one hand, and its cardinal reading, on the other.

Secondly, if (28a) is supposed to capture the narrow presuppositional (= partitive) reading of *some variations*, the question arises how Diesing would capture its wide presuppositional (= partitive) reading paraphrased in (39).

(39) "Some of the variations, every cellist played."

---

[10] For a similar line of thought, see Kamp and Reyle (1993): 457-458.

The only answer that I can offer is that the LF of this wide reading is equal to the LF representation of the wide reading under (28c).

(28)   c.   SOME y [variations(y)] [EVERY x [cellist(x)] [x played y]]

By treating "specific" and partitive indefinites on a par, an idea introduced by Enç (1991), one does not only lose the difference between wide and narrow partitive expressions but the semantic contribution of partitivity as well. In none of her representations, Diesing mentions that for an NP to get a partitive reading means that this NP triggers the membership relation between some variable and a familiar set. That is, in no way Diesing's analysis contributes to the phenomenon of partitivity itself. If we want to capture the presuppositional component of a partitive NP, we have to find an antecedent for this component.[11] This step does not interact with the determination of the scope position of this NP. With respect to the partitive interpretation of *some variations* as *some of the variations*, this means that we look for an antecedent for the definite NP *the variations*. Independently of this process of anaphora resolution, the indefinite *some of the variations* receives a narrow or wide scope reading with respect to the *EVERY* quantifier.

   Thirdly, as I will discuss in section 3 below Abusch (1994) rejects the assumption that the scope of indefinites is syntactically determined by QUANTIFIER RAISING. Abusch shows that indefinite NPs and genuine quantificational NPs exhibit different scope properties. She argues that if indefinite descriptions behaved at LF like genuine quantifiers do, we would have no explanation for why indefinites can escape syntactic scope islands and genuine quantifiers cannot. Similarly, I believe that if we interpret every NP with a partitive interpretation as a quantifier, it remains unexplained why partitive indefinites can escape scope islands whereas genuine quantifiers cannot.

(40)   Every professor rewarded every student who read *one of the books* he
           had recommended.

(41)   Every professor rewarded every student who read *each of the books* he
           had recommended.

For (40) but not for (41), we can think of an intermediate reading [Abusch (1994)] that can be paraphrased as follows:

(40)   INTERM   "For every professor p there is one b' of the books that
                       p had recommended such that p rewarded every student
                       who read b'."

---

[11] I adopt van der Sandt's (1992) view that presuppositions are anaphoric expressions.

An approach that interprets *one of the books* in (40) as a quantifier fails to explain why this "quantifier" can escape a syntactic island whereas the quantifier *each of the books* in (41) cannot.

Finally, the following examples show that partitive NPs can be interpreted as a property.

(42)   Jim is one of the boys who made the cake.

(43)   To open this beer bottle, I need one of your keys.

(42) says that Jim has the property of being a member of a familiar set of boys who made a cake. Under the view that intensional verbs denote a relation between an individual and a property [Zimmermann (1993)], (43) says that I am looking for the property of being a member of a set of familiar keys. To open my beer bottle, I will be happy with any of the keys mentioned.

2.3.2 Why do bare plurals never raise?

A theory that deals with the scope of indefinite descriptions should not only explain which mechanism makes indefinites reach particular scope positions, but also why this mechanism does not operate on particular indefinites. Diesing does not offer an explanation for why in nongeneric contexts bare plurals can only get narrow, nonpartitive interpretations. The following example illustrates a case in point:

(44)   John didn't play variations.

      i.   "It is not the case that John played variations."

      ii.   # "There are variations that John didn't play."

In the previous section, I sketched Diesing's syntactic explanation for why German split topics lack strong readings which is based on the REVISED EXTRACTION CONSTRAINT under (34). Since it applies to extraction cases only, it is clear that this explanation cannot be used to explain why the English bare plural lacks a strong reading as well. Although in a Diesingian approach one expects to get a syntactic explanation for the semantic constraint in (44), the only solution Diesing could offer to explain why (44) lacks a wide reading, is to stipulate that bare plurals in a nongeneric context get a variable introducing interpretation only. Obviously, it remains puzzling why this should be the case.

2.4 Summary

In this section, I discussed Diesing's proposal that the scope of an indefinite is fully determined in the syntax. I then questioned Diesing's assumption that indefinites are quantifiers. More particularly, I pointed out that the resolution of the presuppositional component of an indefinite with a partitive interpretation, on the one hand, and the determination of such an indefinite's scope, on the other, are two separate issues. Finally, I pointed out that Diesing does not offer an account for why bare plurals in nongeneric contexts lack wide readings.

3 The scope of indefinites: A semantic proposal

Abusch (1994) argues that the fact that indefinite NPs can escape syntactic scope islands provides us with additional support for the Kamp-Heim view that indefinite NPs are not quantificational per se. In other words, the scope position of indefinite descriptions is not computed by means of QUANTIFIER RAISING. Focusing on intermediate readings of indefinite descriptions, Abusch proposes that the correct scope position of an indefinite is reached by means of a interpretive mechanism storing both the indefinite's variable and its restriction until the former is bound.

3.1 Indefinites receive intermediate readings

Abusch's central observation is that only indefinite NPs can escape scope islands whereas genuine quantifiers cannot.[12] (45) and (46) illustrate this contrast.

(45)   Each author in this room despises every publisher who would not publish a book that was deemed pornographic.

(46)   Each author in this room despises every publisher who would not publish each book that was deemed pornographic.

According to Abusch

> sentence [(45)] seems to have an intermediate reading in addition to the narrow and wide scope ones, namely the reading where for each author there is a possibly different book satisfying the stated condition [Abusch (1994): 88].

The indefinite NP *a book that was deemed pornographic* thus escapes the relative clause island into which it is syntactically embedded. In contrast, the quantifier *each book that was deemed pornographic* in sentence (46) cannot escape the relative clause and gets an *in situ* interpretation only. Abusch successfully shows that the intermediate reading of (45) is a genuine reading rather than a pragmatic widening of the narrow reading or a narrowing of the maximal one. For reasons of space, I will not go through her argumentation here.

Some further examples borrowed from Abusch supporting her claim that indefinite NPs can escape a scope island are shown in (47) through (51).

---

[12] The same observation has been made in Farkas (1981) and Ruys (1992).

(47)   Every professor rewarded every student who read a book he had recommended.

(48)   Each choreographer believes that it would be damaging for a dancer of his to quit the company.

(49)   Every gambler will be surprised, if one horse wins.[13]

(50)   Every purported miracle attributed to Moses would have been less impressive, if a now uncontroversial scientific theory had been known at the time.

(51)   Every professor got a headache whenever a student he hated was in class.

The indefinite in (47) is embedded into a relative clause island, the one in (48) into a *that*-clause island, those in (49) and (50) into an *if*-clause island, and, finally, the one in (51) into a *whenever*-clause. For each of them, there is an independent intermediate reading.

3.2 Why not a Heimian account?

With the help of example (49), Abusch further illustrates why a Heimian account cannot capture the intermediate reading of the above examples correctly.

(49)   Every gambler will be surprised, if one horse wins.

A Heim style LF that gets closest to the intermediate reading of this example looks as follows: [14]

---

[13] Abusch observes that for this example a narrow scope reading is pragmatically strange because it suggests a contrast between "if one horse wins" with the clause "if two (or more) horses win." See Abusch (1994): 94.

[14] In addition to the rules given in section 1.2 and the rule mentioned in fn. 9, we need to know one more of Heim's rules to capture the construction of this LF.

QUANTIFIER CONSTRUAL   [Heim (1982): 133]
Attach every quantifier as a leftmost immediate constituent of S.

This rule applies to quantificational determiners and to adverbial quantifiers.

(52)

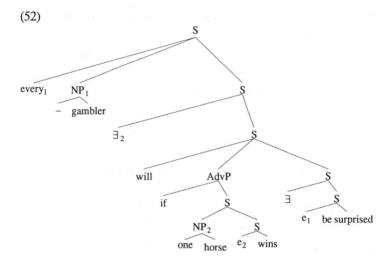

First, Abusch shows that this LF does not represent the intermediate reading of the indefinite *one horse* in (49). The truth conditions corresponding to this LF are:

(53)   For every gambler x there is a y such that for every accessible future world w such that if <u>y is a horse in w</u> and y wins in w then x is surprised in w.

These truth conditions are too weak. When the underlined *if*-clause which is the restrictor of the WILL operator is made false — for instance by choosing a y which is not a horse in w —, the implication as a whole is vacuously true. Moreover, in (52) the indefinite NP *one horse* is coindexed with the quantifier $\exists_2$, which is not its lowest c-commanding quantifier and which therefore violates Heim's rule of QUANTIFIER INDEXING [see section 1.2]. To avoid this, one could move the indefinite *one horse* out of the *if*-clause and adjoin it to the same S-node to which the existential quantifier $\exists_2$ has been adjoined. This syntactic movement, however, is a violation of an island constraint: an NP cannot escape a syntactic scope island.

3.3 Abusch (1994)

Abusch starts from the insight that at LF an indefinite NP cannot escape a syntactic scope island by means of syntactic movement. Whereas the scope of a quantificational NP is syntactically transparent at LF by means of QUANTIFIER RAISING, an indefinite NP always remains *in situ* at that level of syntactic representation. She furthermore suggests that the scope position of an indefinite NP is the result of a semantic mechanism, that is, it is fixed during the interpretation process of the LF.

Abusch's semantic account of the scope of indefinite NPs relies on two crucial insights. First, she adopts the Kamp-Heim view that an indefinite NP comes with a variable and a restriction of this variable. She does not adopt their view that the indefinite simultaneously introduces a discourse referent in a discourse universe. Rather, its variable remains free at LF. Secondly, Abusch shows that the above problem with the truth conditions of (49) arises from the common assumption that the restriction of an indefinite becomes a conjunct in the interpretation of the phrase in which it immediately occurs. For example: the restriction *horse* in (49) becomes a conjunct of the clause *wins* in the *if*-clause. The problem is that it has to remain in this fixed position regardless of whether the variable of which it holds is interpreted in this position or not. Therefore, Abusch goes on,

> we would like a mechanism which "automatically" preserves the restrictions on free variables corresponding to indefinites, instead of conjoining them at the level of an in situ indefinite [Abusch (1994): 108].

The key idea of Abusch's account is that the scope of an indefinite has to be computed for the indefinite's free variable *together* with the indefinite's restriction. In her semantic metalanguage, the free variable and the restriction of an indefinite NP are gathered in the U-set, which is a set of pairs consisting of a free variable and a restriction. For instance, the sentence

(54)   One horse wins.

is translated into the following "$\phi : U$" notation:

(55) $win(x_2) : \{<x_2, \ horse(x_2)>\}$

Two functions, "1" and "2', take care of picking out the formula ϕ and the U-set from the form "$\phi: U$", respectively.

(56) $1(\phi : U) = \phi$

      $2(\phi : U) = U$

Variable binding rules have two functions. On the one hand, they remove variables they bind from the U-set. On the other, they are explicit about what happens with the restrictions in the U-set. A case in point is the rule of EXISTENTIAL CLOSURE:

(57)   EXISTENTIAL CLOSURE RULE

Configuration: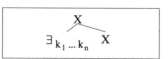

Where $\langle x_{k1}, \phi_1 \rangle, ..., \langle x_{kn}, \phi_n \rangle \in 2(X')$, the interpretation is:

$\exists x_{k1} ... \exists x_{kn} [\phi_1 \wedge ... \wedge \phi_n \wedge 1(X')] : 2(X') - \{\langle x_{k1}, \phi_1 \rangle, ... , \langle x_{kn}, \phi_n \rangle \}$

As an illustration, I show how the semantics of (54) is computed. First, we apply (56) to (55).

$X' = win(x_2) : \{\langle x_2, horse(x_2) \rangle\}$

$1(X') = win(x_2)$

$2(X') = \{\langle x_2, horse(x_2) \rangle\}$

Then, we apply the rule of Existential Closure and the interpretation is:

$\exists x_2[horse(x_2) \wedge win(x_2)]: \{\langle x_2, horse(x_2) \rangle\} - \{\langle x_2, horse(x_2) \rangle\} =$

$\exists x_2[horse(x_2) \wedge win(x_2)]$

The restriction *horse(x_2)* is taken into the formula ϕ at the same position where the variable x_2 is existentially bound.

In the remainder of this section, I go through the gambler example (49) to illustrate how the U-set mechanism captures the ability of an indefinite NP to escape a scope island.

(49)   Every gambler will be surprised, if one horse wins.

The input LF for the interpretation of (49) is the following one:

(58)

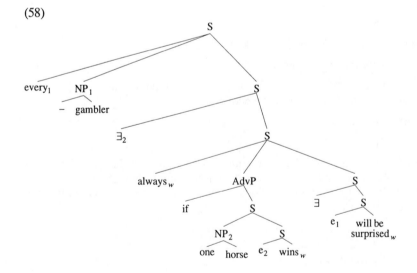

The NP *one horse* is still in its original syntactic position: there is no escape possible by means of syntactic movement. That it has been coindexed with the existential quantifier indicates its desired intermediate reading. Note that I do not adopt Abusch's proposal that the future tense triggers the presence of a quantifier *WILL* as in her Heim style LF (52). Rather, I assume the presence of a silent quantificational adverb *always* and leave the future tense unanalyzed.[15] Furthermore, the verbal predicates have been assigned an additional world argument. In order to interpret the LF under (58), we need one more variable binding rule, the EVERY RULE:[16]

(59)   EVERY RULE

Configuration:
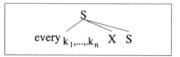

Where $<x_{k1}, \phi_1>, ..., <x_{kn}, \phi_n> \in 2(X')$, the interpretation is:

$$\forall x_{k1} ... \forall x_{kn} [[\phi_1 \wedge ... \wedge \phi_n \wedge 1(X')] \rightarrow [1(S')]] : [[2(X') - \{<x_{k1}, \phi_1>, ..., <x_{kn}, \phi_n>\}] \cup 2(S')]$$

Once a variable that is an element of the U-set is bound by the universal quantifier, the pair consisting of that variable and the latter's restriction is taken from the U-set. The restriction becomes a conjunct in the restriction of that quantifier.

With the EVERY RULE (59) and the EXISTENTIAL CLOSURE RULE (57), the interpretation of (58) is set up as follows. First, we distinguish the U-set of the restrictor and of the scope of the deepest embedded quantifier from the form ϕ, respectively. This gives us:

$1(X') = win_w(x_2)$

$2(X') = \{<x_2, horse(x_2)>\}$

and

$1(S') = will\text{-}be\text{-}surprised_w(x_1)$

$2(S') = \{ \}$

Then, we apply the EVERY RULE to *always*$_w$ yielding

$\forall w [win_w(x_2) \rightarrow will\text{-}be\text{-}surprised_w(x_1)] : \{<x_2, horse(x_2)>\} \cup \{ \}$

---

[15] I assume that the future tense should be analyzed as the indefinite "a time t after t_0", which is existentially closed in the scope of the implicit quantificational adverb.

[16] The configuration in this EVERY RULE slightly differs from the one proposed by Abusch (1994) because I want it to capture both universal quantification over individuals restricted by an NP and over worlds restricted by an adverbial clause.

Note that nothing has been subtracted from the U-set of the restrictor, $2(X')$, since the universal quantifier does not bind any variable which is an element of that set.

Next, we move one step higher, and again we distinguish the U-set from the form ϕ of the existential quantifier $\exists_2$.

$1(X') = \forall w[\text{win}_w(x_2) \rightarrow \text{will-be-surprised}_w(x_1)]$

$2(X') = \{<x_2, \text{horse}(x_2)>\}$

We apply the rule of EXISTENTIAL CLOSURE and we get

$\exists x_2[\text{horse}(x_2) \wedge \forall w[\text{win}_w(x_2) \rightarrow \text{will-be-surprised}_w(x_1)]] : \{<x_2,$
$\text{horse}(x_2)>\} - \{<x_2, \text{horse}(x_2)>\} =$

$\exists x_2[\text{horse}(x_2) \wedge \forall w[\text{win}_w(x_2) \rightarrow \text{will-be-surprised}_w(x_1)]] : \{ \}$

The restriction *horse(x2)* is taken into the formula ϕ at the same position where the variable x_2 is existentially bound. Finally, we move one step up and we compute the "ϕ: U" form of the restrictor and of the scope of the highest quantifier, *every1*.

$1(X') = \forall x_1[\text{gambler}(x_1)]$

$2(X') = \{<x_1, \text{gambler}(x_1)>\}$

$1(S') = \exists x_2[\text{horse}(x_2) \wedge \forall w[\text{win}_w(x_2) \rightarrow \text{will-be-surprised}_w(x_1)]]$

$2(S') = \{ \}$

We now apply the EVERY RULE to *every1* and we get the interpretation of (58).

$\forall x_1[\text{gambler}(x_1) \rightarrow \exists x_2[\text{horse}(x_2) \wedge \forall w[\text{win}_w(x_2) \rightarrow \text{will-be-}$
$\text{surprised}_w(x_1)]]] : \{<x_1, \text{gambler}(x_1)>\} - \{<x_1, \text{gambler}(x_1)>\}$
$\cup \{ \} =$

$\forall x_1[\text{gambler}(x_1) \rightarrow \exists x_2[\text{horse}(x_2) \wedge \forall w[\text{win}_w(x_2) \rightarrow \text{will-be-}$
$\text{surprised}_w(x_1)]]]$

The variable restricted by *one horse* is bound at the desired intermediate position.

3.4 Loose ends for Abusch (1994)

The merits of Abusch's discussion are at least the following two. Firstly, she successfully shows that an intermediate reading of an indefinite is neither the narrowing of a wide scope reading, nor the strengthening of a narrow scope one: it is a logically independent reading. Secondly, she points out why an account à la Heim (1982) fails to capture the correct truth conditions of a sentence containing an intermediate indefinite NP: the restriction of an indefinite is forced to be interpreted *in situ*, regardless of whether the latter's variable is interpreted *in situ* or not. However, I believe that Abusch's proposal to determine the scope position of an indefinite by means of a compositional U-set mechanism has the following shortcomings.

First, she defines a semantic storage mechanism that serves no other purpose than that of determining the scope position of an indefinite NP. Furthermore, Reinhart (1997) points out that Abusch's U-set mechanism bears an uncomfortable resemblance to QUANTIFIER RAISING.

Secondly, her account lacks an explanation for why bare plurals in nongeneric contexts cannot get non-narrow scope readings. There is no device to block the generation of a wide scope reading of a bare plural: its free variable and its descriptive content can be stored just like any other indefinite's free variable and descriptive content. In other words, the U-set mechanism predicts that (60) gets a wide and an intermediate reading. This clearly goes against our intuitions.

(60) Each author in this room despises every publisher who would not publish books.

> WIDE # "There are books b such that each author in this room despises every publisher who would not publish b."

> INTERM # "For each author a in this room there are books b such that a despises every publisher who would not publish b."

Thirdly, the U-set mechanism will generate three readings for sentence (61), namely, a narrow, an intermediate and a maximal one.

(61) Every professor invited each committee member who accepted a proposal.

> NARROW "Every professor invited each committee member who accepted an arbitrary proposal."

> INTERM "For every professor q there is a proposal p such that q invited each committee member who accepted p."

> WIDE "There is a particular proposal p such that every professor invited each committee member who accepted p."

The U-set mechanism does not mirror that for the interpretation of sentence (61) people have clear preferences. They take the narrow scope reading (61 NARROW) to be the default reading. Then, they may get the wide scope reading (61 WIDE). And after some more brainwork they may get the intermediate reading (61 INTERM). If we can find a way to deal with the scope properties of indefinites in which these preferences are mirrored, I believe we should favour this way instead of the U-set mechanism.

Fourthly, Abusch fails to see an important link between the resolution of anaphora and the determination of the scope position of an indefinite NP. Although

> one might try to show that an indefinite can get wide scope by virtue of being contained in a phrase which for some independent reason is presupposed [Abusch (1994): 125]

she rejects this option in the light of the following two examples:

(62)   John knows that a man lied.

(63)   Professor Himmel rewarded every student who read a book he had recommended.

In example (62), an indefinite NP is embedded in the presupposed complement of the factive verb *to know*. The presupposition of this sentence can be either (62a), (62b) or (62c):

(62)   a.   There is a man who lied

        b.   It is a man who lied (not a woman).

        c.   A specific man lied.

Regardless of the fact that the indefinite *a man* is embedded in the presupposition triggered by the factive verb *to know*, the former can be understood in a "narrow" way — as in (62a) —, in a contrastive way — as in (62b) —, or "specifically" — as in (62c). Abusch observes correctly that in this case the scope of the indefinite needs to be computed independently of the projection of the presupposed complement sentence. In the other example, (63), the indefinite NP *a book he had recommended* is part of a relative clause which further restricts the domain of the quantifier *every*. Again, the projection of the presupposed set of students does not help us in finding out the scope position of this indefinite. Still, I believe that Abusch fails to mention one important point. Her examples (62) and (63) illustrate cases in which the indefinite is contained in a presuppositional phrase, that is, in the complement of a factive verb or in the domain of a quantifier. What she does not take into account is the fact that an indefinite NP's scope position is sometimes fixed by virtue of itself containing — and not of being contained in — a phrase which is presuppositional.

(64)   Every professor invited each committee member who accepted a proposal *he* made.

Because the indefinite's descriptive material cannot be located higher than the position at which the pronoun it contains is bound, the indefinite gets either an intermediate or a narrow reading:

(64)   INTERM   "For every professor q there is a proposal p such that q invited each committee member who accepted p."

NARROW   "Every professor q invited each committee member who accepted an arbitrary proposal q made.

Finally, because Abusch cannot account for why an indefinite in a sentence initial scope island lacks an intermediate reading, she is forced to call such an indefinite a "referential" indefinite. (65) illustrates that the indefinite *a student in the syntax class* lacks an intermediate reading.

(65)   If a student in the syntax class cheats on the exam, every professor will be fired.

WIDE   "There is a student s in the syntax class such that if s cheats on the exam, every professor will be fired."

INTERM   # "For every professor p there is a student s in the syntax class such that if s cheats on the exam, p will be fired.

In other words, in addition to the variable interpretation of indefinites, Abusch needs a referential interpretation as well. Moreover, apart from this unsatisfactory result Abusch is silent about the narrow interpretation of *a student in the syntax class* in (65).

(65)   NARROW   "If there is a student in the syntax class who cheats on the exam, every professor will be fired."

As opposed to Abusch, I think it is possible to get an intermediate reading of an indefinite in a topicalized island, if its descriptive content contains a pronoun. In that case, the wide reading is impossible.

(66)   If a student in *his* syntax class cheats on the exam, every professor will be fired.

WIDE   # "There is a student s in his syntax class such that if s cheats on the exam, every professor will be fired."

INTERM   "For every professor p there is a student s in p's syntax class such that if s cheats on the exam, p will be fired."

3.5 Reinhart (1997)

For the sake of completeness, I mention a problem for Abusch's approach that has been recently pointed out in Reinhart (1997). It is related to plural existentials. According to Reinhart, Abusch's U-set mechanism gives rise to a reading of (67) which doesn't exist, namely, a wide distributive reading, and fails to capture a reading which does exist, namely, a wide collective reading. The observation and the example are taken from Ruys (1995).

(67)   If three relatives of mine die, I'll inherit a house.

According to Reinhart, Abusch's account assigns (68) as (67)'s wide interpretation.

(68) $\exists x$ [three(x) $\wedge$ relatives-of-me(x) $\wedge$ [x dies $\rightarrow$ I inherit a house]]

Following Ruys, Reinhart writes that

> the only [wide, VVG] interpretation available is where the existential is taken as a collective set of three individuals all of whom must die for the antecedent of the implication to be true [Reinhart (1997): 380].

(68) does not capture this reading because it makes (67) true if only one of the three relatives dies. As Reinhart points out, in a DRT style approach it is always possible to build in the correct collective reading next to the incorrect distributive reading. These are (69) and (70), respectively. The formulae are copied from Reinhart (1997). Note that (70) and (68) are equivalent.

(69) $\exists X$ [three(X) $\wedge$ relatives-of-me(X) $\wedge$ [[X D λz [z dies]] $\rightarrow$ [I inherit a house]]]

(70) $\exists X$ [three(X) $\wedge$ relatives-of-me(X) $\wedge$ X D λz [z dies $\rightarrow$ I inherit a house]]

However, I consider Reinhart's problem for Abusch only as an apparent problem. The reason is that under the wide collective reading (69), namely the one which Reinhart takes to be correct, Reinhart incorrectly interprets the *if*-clause as the restriction of a hidden universal quantification. There is nothing in (67) which motivates the presence of the material implication, the $\rightarrow$, in its "wide" semantic representation. Here is why.

Suppose, on the one hand, we interpret (67) as a narrow indefinite, then we get the following two readings:

(71)   For every t, X [three(X) $\wedge$ relative-of-mine*(X) $\wedge$ die*(X) at t] there will be t' [t' > t $\wedge$ I inherit a house at t' from X] [17]

(72)   There will be t, t', X [three(X) $\wedge$ relative-of-mine*(X) $\wedge$ die*(X) at t $\wedge$ t' > t $\wedge$ I inherit a house at t']

The readings are distinct in the sense that in (71) for any triple of relatives I survive, I get a house, whereas in (72), if I live longer than one triple of three relatives of mine, I get a house. Note that only in the first one of these readings, we have a conditional that can be captured formally in terms of material implication. The universal quantifier that comes with the conditional — this we can agree on —, is triggered by an iterative interpretation of the event expressed by the verb *to die*. The second reading does not contain a conditional: the *if*-clause simply expresses a temporal

---

[17] I add the PP *from X* to this logical representation so that the universal quantifier binding X makes sense. This method I will repeat in some of the LFs below.

restriction of an indefinite time point in the future. Note that the predicate *die** holds of a group when the last member of the group is dead.

On the other hand, if we interpret the indefinite in (73) as an indefinite with wide scope we can only get one reading.

(73) There is X [three(X) $\wedge$ relative-of-mine*(X) $\wedge$ there will be t, t'
      [die*(X) at t $\wedge$ t' > t $\wedge$ I inherit a house at t']]

So, not only is it impossible to give the indefinite an interpretation in which it has scope over a conditional, as in the distributive case (74) — which is Reinhart's (70) —, there is no way to give it a wide collective interpretation either, as in (75) — which is Reinhart's (69):

(74) There is X [three(X) $\wedge$ relative-of-mine*(X) $\wedge$

      for every t, z of X [die(z) at t]

      there will be t' [t' > t $\wedge$ I inherit a house from z at t']]

(75) There is X [three(X) $\wedge$ relative-of-mine*(X) $\wedge$

      for every t [die*(X) at t]

      there will be t' [t' > t $\wedge$ I inherit a house at t']]

The reason is a very simple one: it is only possible to die once. In other words, when combined with a specific indefinite Subject the verb *to die* in (67) cannot be given an iterative reading. As such, it will not trigger a universal quantifier over times (or situations). Hence, there is no motivation for the presence of a conditional in (67)'s wide semantic representations. Rather, with a specific Subject the *if*-clause in (67) can only describe the time at which I will inherit a house as a time after the time at which all three relevant relatives are dead, which is the reading captured by (73).

It follows that Reinhart's claim that Abusch predicts (68) as the only wide reading simply can't be true since there is no conditional which could be made true if only one of the three relatives died. Reinhart should have come up with an example that contains a verb that when combined with a specific Subject can still have an iterative reading. The following is such an example:

(76) If two relatives of mine show up at my place, I pretend that I am not
      at home.

Suppose we interpret the indefinite *two relatives of mine* as a wide plural indefinite (of course, a non-specific reading is available as well). It is then possible, but of course not necessary, to interpret the *if*-clause as a restriction of a hidden universal quantifier, because these two people can show up at my place any time. However, this does not require that they have to show up together. That is, the wide scope reading of (76) can be either collective, as in (77), or distributive, as in (78), and there is no reason to believe with Reinhart that an account which excludes (78) is superior to an account which doesn't.[18]

(77)   There is X [two(X) ∧ relative-of-mine*(X) ∧

       for every t [show-up-at-my-place*(X) at t]

       [I pretend that I am not at home at t]]

(78)   There is X [two(X) ∧ relative-of-mine*(X) ∧

       for every t, z of X [show-up-at-my-place(z) at t]

       [I pretend that I am not at home at t because of z]]

In sum, the only point this kind of example shows is that Abusch's approach has to be extended in such a way that it can deal with collective readings of plural existentials. This in itself is not a problem since Abusch doesn't interpret (plural) indefinites as quantificational per se, that is, as inherently distributive expressions.

3.6 Summary

In this section, I first discussed Abusch's arguments for why it is not possible that indefinites reach their scope position through QUANTIFIER RAISING. Such an approach would leave unexplained why indefinites, as opposed to genuine quantifiers, can escape syntactic scope islands. Then, I discussed Abusch's proposal in which the scope of indefinites is determined by an interpretive U-set mechanism, together with some (apparent) shortcomings that arise with this proposal.

4 The scope of the English bare plural

I pointed out that neither Diesing (1992) nor Abusch (1994) explain why an existential bare plural does not take non-narrow scope positions. One of the earliest and also most interesting attempts to explain the scope properties and other semantic aspects of the English bare plural is Carlson (1977). Indeed, many of the questions that arose with the examples of West Greenlandic incorporated nouns and their West Germanic counterparts in chapter 2, have been put forward by him. His semantic account for the English bare plural is based on the claim that a bare plural always names a kind. Below, we will see that this nonambiguity hypothesis has been successfully refuted in the literature. But Carlson's approach has also advantages, and it is exactly his lexical treatment of the existential reading

---

[18] An account of indefinites which is supposed to do so is elaborated in Reinhart (1997) and Winter (1997). Both authors make use of choice-functions to capture non-narrow existentials. In this book, I do not discuss this kind of approach to indefinites.

of the English bare plural that I will integrate into a uniform semantic account for the semantic behaviour of incorporated nouns, bare plurals and split topics in nongeneric contexts.

4.1 Carlson (1977)

According to Carlson (1977), the English bare plural always functions as the name of a kind which in his ontology is an individual. The meaning of a bare plural is thus unambiguous regardless of whether it is used in a generic context, or in an existential context. For example, Carlson's semantic representation of the generic statement (79) is (80):

(79)   Dogs bark.

(80) λP $(^\vee P$ (dog)) $^\wedge \lambda x$ (bark (x)) $=$ bark (dog)

This means that sentence (79) is true iff

the individual kind denoted by 'dogs' is in the set of things that 'bark' [Carlson (1977): 109].

Moreover, the semantic representation of the existential statement (81) is (82):

(81)   Dogs ran.

(82) λP $(^\vee P$ (dog)) $^\wedge \lambda x$ $(\exists y$ [R (y,x) & run (y)]) $=$

   $\exists y$ [R(y, dog) & run (y)]

Whereas the generic reading of the bare plural *dogs* in (79) follows from its combination with an individual-level predicate, the existential reading of the same bare plural in (81) results from the fact that it is combined with a predicate that applies to "stages" of individuals, namely, a stage-level predicate. The existential quantifier and the realization relation R that relates the existentially bound variable to a kind are both an inherent part of the lexical semantics of a stage-level verb. Carlson concludes that the generic–existential ambiguity that comes with bare plurals is not an inherent part of the meaning of bare plurals themselves.

Exactly these two claims, the nonambiguity of bare plurals and their lexically introduced existential interpretation, have been rejected by many authors and for different reasons. Despite these rejections, I believe that the major advantage of Carlson's view is his account of the narrow scope effects of the English bare plural. It goes as follows.

The existential use of the bare plural only exhibited narrow scope possibilities relative to other quantifiers. The intuitive account of this phenomenon that we will offer here is that the existential quantifier apparently associated with the bare plural actually arises as being a part of the translation of the predicate itself [Carlson (1977): 138].

In other words, the existential quantifier can only be interpreted locally and it cannot take scope over any operator that is introduced by other constituents in the sentence in which it occurs. In chapter 2, I already mentioned one of his examples illustrating this point:

(83)   John didn't see spots on the floor.   [Carlson (1977): 19]

    i.   "It is not the case that John saw spots on the floor."

    ii. # "There were spots on the floor that John didn't see."

Because the existential quantifier that binds the "stages" of the kind named by *spots* comes with the verb *to see*, it cannot take scope over the negation operator that has this verb in its scope.

4.2 Objections against Carlson (1977)

Carlson's theory has been widely discussed in the literature and quite a few objections have been raised against it.[19] On the one hand, we find objections against his view that bare plurals are not ambiguous between an existential and a generic reading. On the other hand, there are objections against his view that stage-level predicates contain a lexicalized existential quantifier.

4.2.1 Are bare plurals ambiguous?

One of Krifka et al.'s (1995) arguments — attributed to Weir (1986) — against the nonambiguity hypothesis is that one cannot explain the distribution of kind denoting expressions.

(84)   The horse has a long tail.

(85)   Horses have a long tail.

Assuming that the definite NP *the horse* in (84) and the bare plural *horses* in (85) denote the same kind, it remains unexplained why the former cannot be used in an existential construction whereas the latter easily can.

(86)   * There is the horse stampeding through the gate.

(87)   There are horses stampeding through the gate.   [Krifka et al. (1995): 117]

The explanation Krifka et al. offer is to say that the bare plural in (87) has an indefinite reading per se which the definite in (86) has not. This, Krifka et al. add, is not only the best way to explain why (87) is good but also to give it the same explanation as for why (88) with a singular indefinite is good.

(88)   There is a horse stampeding through the gate.

---

[19] See Krifka et al. (1995) for an overview.

Carlson has to adopt two different analyses of *there*-insertion. He needs one semantics for the existential predicate that combines with a bare plural, and another one that combines with a singular indefinite.

This may be a good reason to believe that a bare plural has an existential interpretation alongside its kind interpretation. However, whether having an existential reading implies that a nonkind bare plural can also receive different scope readings is still an open question. This brings us to the second kind of objection against Carlson.

4.2.2 Objections against a lexicalized existential quantifier

In this section, I discuss three counterexamples raised against Carlson's claim that a bare plural takes narrow scope with respect to other operators. These examples are supposed to refute Carlson's lexicalized existential interpretation of a bare plural. Two of them, I already mentioned in chapter 2 during my examination of the narrow scope effects of West Greenlandic incorporated nouns, one from Rooth (1995) and one from Kratzer (1980). The third one is again taken from Krifka et al. (1995).

• Rooth (1995)

Rooth (1995) gives (89) as a counterexample to Carlson's observation that the bare plural takes narrow scope with respect to negation.

(89) The Dean failed to act on petitions submitted to his office.

[Rooth (1995): 282]

He writes that

> an ambiguity with respect to negative elements like *fail* is detectable. In [(89), VVG], especially if pronounced with an intonation break after *act on*, the accusation can be that there were some petitions that the dean did not act on [Rooth (1995): 282].

Obviously, the relative clause modifying *petitions* in (89) plays a major role in getting a wide reading of *petitions*. If we drop this modifier, a wide scope reading is out just like for the bare plural in Carlson's example (83).

(90) The Dean failed to act on petitions.

  i. "It is not the case that the Dean succeeded to act on petitions."

  ii. # "There are petitions such that it is not the case that the Dean succeeded to act on them."

To explain the wide scope reading of the modified bare plural in (89) in syntactic terms, Rooth (p.c.) suggests that the relative clause causes some kind of heavy NP shift by which the modified bare plural escapes the scope of the negative element in *to fail*. The S-structure of (73) is then (91).

(91) [$_S$ [$_S$ the Dean failed to act on e] [$_{NP}$ petitions submitted to his office]]

Phonetically, this shift is made visible by means of an intonation break. This in itself is not incompatible with Carlson's proposal that the existential reading of a bare plural is lexicalized. What needs to be added to his proposal is the semantic contribution of intonation breaks.

Still, I doubt whether one should agree with the position that the bare plural in Rooth's example has a wide reading. On Carlson's view that a bare plural names a kind, the bare plural in (89) is modified in such a way that the result names a very specific kind, namely, the kind of petition that has been submitted to the Dean's office. Since this is a kind that obviously holds of a restricted set of objects, the impression arises that the bare plural has to be interpreted as a specific indefinite. This impression is even fortified by the presence of the past participle *submitted* which introduces an additional existential interpretation of the bare plural. Moreover, on my understanding of (89) it is such that the Dean failed to act on *every* petition submitted to his office. If *petitions submitted to his office* really receives a wide scope reading with respect to the negation in *failed*, it must be possible to utter (89) in a context where the Dean fails to act on some petitions submitted to his office but succeeds to act on other such petitions. This, however, is impossible on my universal interpretation of (89) and this impossibility is illustrated through the fact that (92) is a contradiction.

(92)   # The dean failed to act on petitions submitted to his office and he didn't fail to act on petitions submitted to his office.

• Kratzer (1980)

Kratzer (1980) comes up with a second argument against Carlson's lexicalized existential quantifier. Carlson claims that this quantifier causes a bare plural in a modal context to get a de dicto reading only. One of his examples is (93):

(93)   Miles wants to meet policemen.   [Carlson (1977):16]

   i.   "Miles wants to meet any policemen, no matter which one."

   ii. # "There are policemen that Miles wants to meet."

Kratzer (1980) gives a counterexample that goes as follows:

(94)   Otto wollte   Tollkirschen   in den Obstsalat   tun,   weil
       O.   wanted   belladonna.berries in the fruit.salad put,   because

            er   sie   mit   richtigen Kirschen verwechselte.
            he   them   with   real   cherries changed

       "Otto wanted to put belladonna berries in the fruitsalad because he took them for real cherries."

According to Kratzer, there are two pieces of evidence for the NP *Tollkirschen* ("belladonna berries") to take wide scope with respect to the modal operator *wollte* ("wanted"). First, it is possible to pick up the NP with the pronoun *sie* ("them"). *Tollkirschen* establishes an accessible discourse referent and, therefore, this one cannot be embedded into the attitude context triggered by *wollte*. Secondly, she claims that *Tollkirschen* is to be understood de re since we do not believe that Otto wants to poison the fruitsalad. The *because*-sentence tells us explicitly that Otto is uninformed about the real nature of what he wants to put into the salad. For these two reasons, Kratzer interprets the bare plural *Tollkirschen* in (94) as a wide scope indefinite.

(95) ∃X [belladonna berries(X) ∧ Otto wanted to put X in the fruitsalad
      because Otto took X for real cherries]

In what follows I argue that Kratzer's example is not a counterexample to Carlson's view that the existential interpretation of a bare plural is lexicalized.

My first argument is one against Kratzer's wide scope representation of the bare plural *Tollkirschen*. If it were really possible for a bare plural to receive wide scope, it would remain unexplained why (96) is not well-formed.

(96) * Otto wollte   Kirschen   nicht   in den Obstsalat   tun,

       O.   wanted   cherries   not   in the fruit.salad put

       weil   er   sie   mit   Tollkirschen   verwechselte.

       because   he   them   with belladonna.berries changed

In (96), the bare plural *Kirschen* ("cherries") is posited to the left of the negation marker *nicht* ("not") which indicates that it gets a wide scope reading [see section 2.2]. The unwellformedness of (96) illustrates that such a reading is not available. A bare plural has to be within the scope of negation: in the well-formed sentence (97) the indefinite determiner *keine* ("no") bears the negation marker.

(97) Otto wollte   *keine* Kirschen   in den Obstsalat   tun,   weil

       O.   wanted   no cherries   in the fruit.salad put   because

       er   sie   mit   Tollkirschen   verwechselte.

       he   them   with belladonna.berries changed

      "Otto didn't want to put cherries in the fruitsalad because he took
      them for belladonna berries."

What (97) also shows is that although *Kirschen* is embedded under negation, it seems possible to refer to them by means of the plural pronoun *sie*. This indicates that for the resolution of *sie* in (97) we do not find a straightforward antecedent. We should regard this pronoun — and its counterpart in (94) — as an E-type pronoun rather than as a semantically bound pronoun. Kratzer's requirement that for the interpretation of the pronoun in (94) the bare plural itself is interpreted as a wide scope indefinite vanishes.[20]

The next question that arises is how the pragmatic resolution of the plural pronoun *sie* in (94), that is, the description for which this pronoun stands, works. My answer to this question contains my second argument against Kratzer, that is, against her requirement to interpret *Tollkirschen* in (94) de re with respect to actually present objects. Kratzer claims that a de dicto reading of *Tollkirschen* in (94) can only mean that Otto wants to poison the salad. Because we don't believe this, *Tollkirschen* has to be understood de re. From her de re perspective, Kratzer would paraphrase the description for which the E-type pronoun *sie* in (94) stands as in (98).

(98) Otto wollte Tollkirschen in den Obstsalat tun, weil er *die Tollkirschen, die er in den Obstsalat tun wollte (= the belladonna berries that he wanted to put into the salad)*, mit richtigen Kirschen verwechselte.

What is important about this paraphrase is that it requires that there are particular belladonna berries around which Otto wants to put into the salad. I show that this requirement is too strong: for the interpretation of the pronoun *sie* in (94) we only need those belladonna berries that gave rise to Otto's desire to put belladonna berries into the fruitsalad.

Imagine the following scenario. Otto is visiting his aunt who grows fruit in her garden. Otto plans to make a fruit salad for dessert. Looking at all the possible fruit he could put in such a salad (strawberries, currants, grapes, ...), he decides that he also wants to put belladonna berries in the salad, although he knows from his biology teacher that belladonna berries are poisonous and although he does not want to poison anyone. His decision is based on his belief that the belladonna berries he sees in his aunt's garden are real cherries. Using the theory of de re interpretation developed in Cresswell and von Stechow (1982), where a de re interpretation of an expression in an attitude context is captured by representing the second

---

[20] It is a well-known feature of plural pronouns that they often behave as E-type pronouns rather than as semantically bound pronouns. Even within Kamp and Reyle's (1993) DRT, which is a semantic binding framework par excellence, the authors argue in favour of an E-type sort of resolution of plural pronouns.

(i)   Most children were eating apples. They didn't pick them themselves.

According to Kamp and Reyle the resolution of the definite pronouns *they* and *them* in (i) requires a process of antecedent construction through abstraction because neither a set of apple eating children nor a set of apples eaten by children is straightforwardly available as their respective antecedents.

argument of the attitude verb as a structured proposition, Otto's belief can be represented as follows.

(99) believe (otto, <λx[cherry(x)], the belladonna berries in otto's aunt's garden>)

Otto ascribes the property "cherry" to some belladonna berries he is acquainted with. Given this scenario, we can felicitously utter (94). Obviously, the bare plural *Tollkirschen* in (94) has to be understood de re, but only de re with respect to the natural kind it denotes. In Carlsonian terms, only the kind denoted by the bare plural gets a de re interpretation, not its stages. In line with Cresswell and von Stechow, the first part of (94) is then represented as follows.

(100) want(otto, <λk $\exists$y[R(y,k) $\wedge$ put-in-fruitsalad(otto,y)], belladonna berries>)

As opposed to Kratzer's claim, it is thus possible to get a de re reading of a bare plural without dropping the idea that it gets its existential interpretation from the predicate *to put into the salad*.

With (99) and (100), we have an appropriate clue for the pragmatic resolution of the pronoun *sie* in the second part of (94).

(101) Otto wollte Tollkirschen in den Obstsalat tun, weil er *die Tollkirschen im Garten seiner Tante* (= *the belladonna berries in his aunt's garden, i.e., those that motivated his desire*) mit richtigen Kirschen verwechselte.

Note that the belladonna berries that give rise to Otto's desire are not required to be the same belladonna berries that may end up in the fruitsalad. As opposed to the pragmatic resolution of the pronoun *sie* in (98), which is based on Kratzer's object-oriented de re interpretation of the bare plural *Tollkirschen*, I have shown that no actual objects that Otto may want to put into the salad are relevant for the pragmatic resolution of *sie*.

Summarizing, Carlson intended to illustrate with his example (93) that there is no de re reading for the bare plural *policemen* when this bare plural is understood as a set of objects. I have shown that Kratzer's example (94) shows that he did not consider that the kind denoted by a bare plural can be understood de re. Her example shows nothing else, that is, it does not force us to abandon Carlson's view that the existential interpretation of a bare plural is lexicalized.

• Krifka et al. (1995)

The third objection against a Carlsonian existential interpretation of the bare plural is taken from Krifka et al. (1995). According to these authors, the following example in which there are no scope ambiguities shows that Carlson's idea is wrong.

(102) John saw apples$_i$ on the plate, and Mary saw them$_i$, too.

[Krifka et al. (1995): 119]

Given Carlson's representation of the meaning of (102), it is not possible to capture the fact that *apples* and *them* refer to the same set of objects. The first occurrence of the stage-level predicate *saw* introduces an existentially quantified object that is the realization of the kind denoted by *apples*. Krifka et al. claim that it is the presence of a lexicalized existential quantifier which prevents *them* from referring to *apples*.

But isn't Krifka et al.'s sentence a problem for any semantic approach which assigns a "static" existential interpretation to the NP *apples*, regardless of whether the existential quantifier is introduced by the indefinite itself, or lexically, that is, by the stage-level predicate of which *apples* is an argument? I believe the answer is yes. The pronoun *them* in (102) is a syntactically unbound pronoun and it was exactly for this type of pronouns that "dynamic" theories of semantic binding have been created. In fact, Krifka et al.'s apparent counterexample indicates along which lines we can save that part of Carlson's proposal that says that the existential interpretation of a bare plural is lexicalized: the lexicalized quantifier which is responsible for the existential interpretation needs "dynamic" force. This does not affect Carlson's original claim that the bare plural in nongeneric contexts takes narrow scope with respect to other operators. Another way to resolve the pronoun *them* in (102) is by means of the E-type strategy. We just saw in the discussion of Kratzer's example (94) that this strategy does not affect Carlson's approach either.

4.3 Summary and an open end

Summarizing this section, the objections against a lexicalized existential quantifier are in fact objections against the fact that Carlson's theory ignores the semantic contribution of intonation breaks [see Rooth's objection], that it ignores de re interpretations of kinds [see Kratzer's objection] and that it uses a static logic rather than a dynamic one [see Krifka et al.'s objection]. None of these really refute Carlson's idea that the existential interpretation of a bare plural is lexicalized.

Still, Carlson's theory leaves us with an open question. He points out a set of bare plurals that never refer to a natural kind. His examples are the following.

(103) parts of that machine   [Carlson (1977): 316]

(104) people in the next room

(105) books that John lost yesterday

Even though he regards these bare plurals as nonkind denoting, their scope behaviour patterns with that of other bare plurals. This is shown in another set of Carlson's examples.

(106) Parts of that airplane were everywhere.   [Carlson (1977): 318]

(107) Max discovered pieces of that puzzle for three hours.

(108) Fred repeatedly destroyed books that I lost yesterday.

These examples show that bare plurals may be not kind-denoting but that they nevertheless get a narrow existential reading only.[21] So, if we agree, on the one hand, that inherent narrow scope can at best be explained in terms of a Carlsonian lexicalized existential quantifier, and, on the other hand, that the above bare plurals can impossibly denote a kind, an obvious solution to the problem is to say that bare plurals in existential contexts denote properties of a lexically introduced discourse referent. This is exactly the solution I will suggest in the next section.

5 Predicative and free variable indefinite descriptions

In the three foregoing sections, I have discussed three theories that only give a partial solution to a complex task which reads like this. A theory of indefinite descriptions has to tell us *how* an indefinite reaches a particular position, *how* an indefinite receives a partitive interpretation, and *why* particular indefinite descriptions *neither* reach a non-narrow scope position *nor* get a partitive reading. It has to cover the cases of generic interpretations of indefinites as well.

In the previous sections, I paid most of my attention to the weaknesses of the theories presented without talking too much about their strengths. In this section, I first highlight the positive aspects of the theories discussed. Presumably, these aspects have to be part of the "successful" theory of indefinite descriptions. Then, I sketch my contribution to how this ideal could be realized. I will elaborate on this contribution in chapter 5 and chapter 6.

5.1 Some features of the ideal theory of indefinite descriptions

A positive aspect about Diesing's work is that she recognizes that within the class of indefinite descriptions one needs a semantic distinction. Not all indefinites can be treated uniformly. Although I have rejected Diesing's quantifier–variable distinction, we need to look for a distinction that does not give rise to the problems caused by Diesing's distinction.

Abusch's discussion of the scope properties of indefinite descriptions has the following three positive features. Firstly, she successfully shows that an intermediate reading of an indefinite is neither the narrowing of a wide scope reading nor the strengthening of a narrow scope one: it is a logically independent reading. Secondly, she adheres to the view that *all*

---

[21] In fact, my discussion of Rooth's example (89) shows exactly the same: (92) is a contradiction which it shouldn't be if it were possible to interpret the bare plural *petitions submitted to his office* as a wide existential.

indefinites are nonquantificational expressions. Thirdly, she points out that at the syntactic level of LF indefinite NPs always remain *in situ*. That is, at LF an indefinite leaves us with a free variable. Its binding is the result of an interpretive process.

One of the main merits of Carlson's theory of the English bare plural is his account for the narrow scope effects of the bare plural in nongeneric contexts. In a bare plural configuration, it is the verb that introduces both the variable which is an instance of the kind denoted by the bare plural together with the existential quantifier which binds this variable. From my dicussion of the objections raised against this lexicalized existential quantifier, it follows that there is no obstacle to adopting it as a substantial subpart of a theory of indefinite descriptions. Even though his work is integrated into a Montagovian semantic framework, it is remarkable that Carlson allows his theory to regard at least a subpart of natural language nominal expressions as nonquantificational. In this respect, I believe that Carlson's (1977) treatment of the English bare plural anticipates the Kamp-Heim view that the descriptive content of an indefinite NP and the quantificational source binding such an NP are independent semantic components.

5.2 Converting these features into a theory of indefinites

Like Diesing (1992), my account for the scope and partitivity behaviour of indefinite descriptions is based on a semantic distinction within the class of indefinite descriptions. Unlike Diesing, I do not not interpret one type of indefinites quantificationally. Rather, all indefinites are nonquantificational expressions and a distinction is drawn between predicative indefinites, on the one hand, and free variable indefinites, on the other. Whereas the former denote a property only, the latter translate as a property restricting a free variable. Neither a predicative nor a free variable indefinite is a discourse referent introducer in the Kamp-Heim sense.

I adopt Abusch's (1994) view that at LF indefinites remain *in situ*. I argue that the different readings that an indefinite can get are determined not only by the distinction just drawn, but also by the mechanisms used to process the meaning contribution of an indefinite. Whereas predicative indefinites are said to receive their existential interpretation through semantic incorporation, free variable indefinites get their existential interpretation through accommodation. As opposed to standard DRT, I free an indefinite from the discourse-referent-introducing task.

What does it mean for an indefinite to be semantically incorporated? I pursue the idea that predicative indefinites denote a property only. The latter is absorbed as a restriction on an incorporating verb's internal argument, if this verb is an extensional verb. It is absorbed as the internal argument of the verb if this verb is intensional [Zimmermann (1993)]. For the extensional case, I argue that a narrow indefinite receives its existential interpretation from its verbal head. Both absorption processes I call semantic incorporation. I thus adopt Carlson's (1977) view that the existential interpretation of a verbal argument can be lexicalized. From a discourse semantic perspective this means that semantically incorporating verbs take over the task of introducing the discourse referent of predicative indefinites. Typical semantically incorporating verbs are the existential predicate and the relational predicate *TO HAVE*. Typical instances of predicative indefinites are incorporated nouns in West Greenlandic, bare plurals in West Germanic languages and German split Objects, all of which we encountered in chapter 2. Given that we interpret nouns that are incorporated in verbs as indefinites, the semantic notion of indefinite description cannot be identified anymore with the syntactic notion of indefinite NP.

And what does it mean for an indefinite to be accommodated? A free variable indefinite cannot be semantically incorporated. Rather, it is interpreted through the accommodation of its descriptive content. Although accommodation is a mechanism that has been used solely for the purpose of presupposition projection so far, I argue that also this mechanism takes over the task of introducing discourse referents. To carry out my proposal, I adopt the notion of accommodation used in van der Sandt (1992). This notion meets Abusch's requirement that the descriptive content of an indefinite is located at the level at which its variable is bound. In addition, it allows us to capture the order of reading preferences during the semantic interpretation process.

In the class of partitive indefinites, I distinguish between predicative and free variable indefinites as well. Apart from the semantic incorporation of the former and the accommodation of the latter, the interpretation of partitive indefinites requires an additional, independent step. Given that the descriptive content of a partitive indefinite is presuppositional, that is, anaphoric, it will either find an antecedent through direct anaphoric binding or create its own antecedent through accommodation in case it doesn't find one [Heim (1982), van der Sandt (1992)]. Determining the scope of a partitive expression separately from the resolution of its presuppostional content allows us to keep "partitivity" distinct from "scope".

Where do generic uses of indefinites fit into the picture? Looking at generic readings of English bare plurals only, this book only gives a partial answer to this question. The English bare plural is said to be ambiguous between a kind and a property reading. The former is the one we find in its generic uses.

Finally, I propose that the predicative reading of an indefinite is its default interpretation and that global accommodation is the default accommodation mechanism. In this way, we account for the interpretation preferences mentioned in section 3.4.

6 Chapter summary

In this chapter, I started from the assumption that every theory of indefinite descriptions has to present an answer to the questions of how indefinites get into particular scope positions, why particular indefinites receive a partitive interpretation, and why particular indefinites do not get into particular scope positions and do not get a partitive reading. I examined to what extent the theories of indefinites in Diesing (1992) and Abusch (1994), on the one hand, and the theory of bare plurals in Carlson (1977), on the other, answer these questions. I finally got to my own proposal to deal with meaning differences in the class of indefinite descriptions. I proposed that a successful theory of indefinites is based on a semantic disctinction between predicative and free variable indefinites. I furthermore proposed that the descriptive content of an indefinite can either be semantically incorporated by a verb — accounting for its narrow scope interpretation in the way Carlson (1977) does —, or that it is accommodated — yielding its non-narrow readings. The presentation of this proposal will be the topic of chapter 5 and chapter 6.

4

Setting the Syntactic Scene

0 Introduction

In the introductory chapter, I said that I am pursuing two goals in this book. The first and primary goal is to develop a semantic theory of indefinite descriptions within which we can understand West Greenlandic incorporated nouns and their semantic counterparts in Germanic languages as *predicative* indefinite descriptions. To develop such a theory, I discussed the pros and cons of some theories of indefinites in the previous chapter, and I extracted from them some features an "ideal" theory of indefinites should embody. This chapter is devoted to my second goal, which is to figure out whether and to what extent the semantic characteristics of West Greenlandic incorporated nouns — and of predicative indefinite descriptions in general — are visible in the syntax.

To achieve this second goal, I first discuss the two mainstream approaches to the structure of noun incorporation, the lexicalist [Mithun (1984), Di Sciullo and Williams (1987), Rosen (1989), Anderson (1992)] and the transformational approaches [Baker (1988), Bok-Bennema (1991), Bittner (1994)]. I investigate whether the structural representations suggested by these approaches contain appropriate triggers for the semantic interpretation of noun incorporating configurations. The central claim of the lexicalist theory is that noun incorporating configurations are lexical compounds and, hence, syntactic atoms. Incorporated nouns are not visible in the syntax and for this reason this lexicalist approach cannot deliver semantically transparent syntactic representations. The transformational theory regards noun incorporation as the result of a syntactic transformation, namely, head movement. The most central claim in this theory is that incorporated nouns are syntactically visible because at D-structure they are the nominal head of an NP. Nevertheless, I argue that this "phrasalization" of noun incorporation does not ensure the syntactic transparency of the semantic pecularities associated with incorporated nouns either.

As an alternative to these mainstream approaches, I propose that West Greenlandic noun incorporating constructions have to be regarded as syntactically base generated complex words, a view that has already been suggested in Dowty (1979). West Greenlandic noun incorporation falls in the domain of syntax, more particularly, of *subphrasal* syntax. I argue that in addition to the *strong* and *weak Case* positions in a syntactic V-projection [de Hoop (1992)], we have to distinguish the position of an incorporated noun as yet another substantial, underived slot in a VP. On top of that, we need to distinguish different types of VPs in the syntax, a distinction that West Greenlandic makes visible through the (lack of) Object agreement morphology on the verb. In the construction of semantic representations, it are these morphosyntactic features (case, agreement morphology) that help us to derive the semantic distinction between predicative and free variable indefinite descriptions drawn at the end of the previous chapter.

In section 1 of this chapter, I present one representative of each of the two classical approaches to noun incorporation, that is, the lexicalist qualifier theory and the syntactic transformational approach. The second section is devoted to a syntactically base generated analysis of noun incorporation as an alternative approach. Section 3 is about the syntax of those configurations that I called the semantic counterparts of West Greenlandic incorporated nouns, West Germanic bare plurals and German split topics.

1 Two mainstream approaches

Most of the literature on noun incorporation deals with its morpho-syntactic aspects. This literature concentrates on the question of whether noun incorporation is a lexical or a syntactic phenomenon. That is, it looks for an answer to the question of whether noun incorporation falls in the domain of the lexicon or in the domain of syntax.

In this section, I first discuss a representative of the lexicalist perspective, namely, Di Sciullo and Williams (1987). Next, I discuss Baker (1988) as a representative of the view that noun incorporation is a syntactic phenomenon.

1.1 A lexicalist approach

The view that incorporated nouns are parts of lexicalized complex words has also been defended in Mithun (1984), Rosen (1989) and Anderson (1992). Di Sciullo and Williams, however, devote a large part of their 1987 monograph to the theoretic aspects and consequences of a lexicalist approach and it is for this reason that I primarily focus on their work.

1.1.1 Di Sciullo and Williams (1987): The qualifier theory

On the strong lexicalist view developed in Di Sciullo and Williams (1987), noun incorporating configurations are lexical compounds. The verbal complexes "airplane-make", "wing-have" and "rudder-have" in the West Greenlandic example (1) are constructed in the lexicon.

(1)   a.   Suulut   *timmisartu-liur*-p-u-q.   [Sadock (1980): 311]

　　　　　S.ABS   airplane-make-IND-[-tr]-3SG

　　　　　"Suulut made an airplane."

　　　b.   *Suluusa-qar*-p-u-q   *aquute-qar*-llu-ni-lu.

　　　　　wing-have-IND-[-tr]-3SG   rudder-have-INF-3SG.PROX-and

　　　　　"It has wings and a rudder"

According to Di Sciullo and Williams,

> an incorporated noun is added to the verb as an act of word formation, governed by the principles of morphology ... [Di Sciullo and Williams (1987): 64].

They furthermore claim that

> a morphological operation can affect the syntactic distribution of the resulting word only in two ways: it can affect the features of that word or it can affect the argument structure of that word. ... The 'qualifier' theory falls under the second of these possibilities because the incorporated noun becomes a qualifier on one of the arguments of the verb [Di Sciullo and Williams (1987): 65].

In other words, noun incorporation does not change the thematic argument structure of a transitive verb but links the lexical content of an incorporated noun to the internal argument of a verb. This procedure is illustrated in (2) and (3) for the complex verbs "airplane-make" and "wing-have", respectively.[1]

(2)   timmisartu- + -liur-   →   timmisartu-liur-

　　　airplane + make($\underline{A}$, Th)   →   make($\underline{A}$, Th)

　　　　　　　　　　　　　　　　　　　　　　|

　　　　　　　　　　　　　　　　　　　airplane

(3)   suluusa- + -qar-   →   suluusa-qar-

　　　wing + have($\underline{A}$, Th)   →   have($\underline{A}$, Th)

　　　　　　　　　　　　　　　　　　　|

　　　　　　　　　　　　　　　　wing

The incorporated nouns *timmisartu* ("airplane") and *suluusa* ("wings") are added as a qualifier on the theme argument of the verbal affixes *-liur-* ("to make") and *-qar-* ("to have"), respectively. With this in mind, the following tree represents the simplified S-structure of the noun incorporating configuration in the first sentence under (1) from this lexicalist perspective.

---

[1] "$\underline{A}$" stands for "external agentive argument" and "Th" for "internal theme argument."

(4)

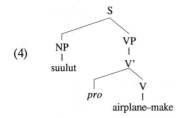

Note that the incorporated noun itself is not "visible" in the syntactic representation of a sentence in which it occurs. This is in accordance with Di Sciullo and Williams' ATOMICITY HYPOTHESIS which says that words — both simple and compound ones — are "atomic" at the level of phrasal syntax and what they call phrasal semantics.[2]

In (4), *pro* fills the syntactic position that realizes the thematic role of the transitive verb *to make*: *pro* is the latter's "real" Object. Although Di Sciullo and Williams are not explicit about this point, following Baker (1995) I regard this representation as a reasonable way of capturing their view that

> the Atomicity Hypothesis further predicts that the syntax of syntactic arguments will be independent of whether or not there is an incorporated noun on the verb [Di Sciullo and Williams (1987): 65].[3]

If we modify the incorporated noun by means of an external modifier, as in (5), it is this modifier which is regarded as the "real" Object of the verb.

(5)   Suulut   qisum-mik   timmisartu-liur-p-u-q.   [fw]

       S.ABS   wood-INST.SG   airplane-make-IND-[-tr]-3SG

       "Suulut made a wooden airplane."

---

[2] I suppose that Di Sciullo and Williams use the term "phrasal semantics" to cover that part of a semantic representation which is made up from phrasal syntax. However, from a truth conditional perspective a distinction between a phrasal and a morphological semantic level is not useful because the construction of the truth conditional meaning of a sentence makes use of phrasal and morphological information simultaneously [e.g. the role of plural morphology in plural semantics and inflectional information in temporal semantics]. This means that from a truth-conditional perspective, we need *one* syntactic representation containing both the relevant phrasal *and* subphrasal information as the input for semantic interpretation.

[3] Yet another way to represent this strong lexicalist analysis of incorporated nouns in the syntax is by saying that the VP does not even contain a *pro*.

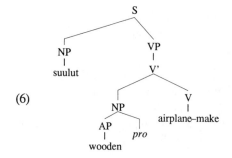

(6)

The claim that incorporated nouns are syntactically invisible is clearly meant as an attempt to save the THETA CRITERION [Chomsky (1981)] which contains the requirement that a thematic role can only be assigned once.

(7)   THETA CRITERION

Every argument must be assigned one and only one Theta role;

Every Theta role must be assigned to one and only one argument.

In (4) and (6), it are the "real" Objects that are assigned a Theta role. From a compositional semantic perspective, the lexicalist view can be understood in such a way that for the interpretation of (4) and (6) the respective incorporated nouns simply denote a predicate of the verb's internal argument's variable. The "real" Objects, *pro* in (4) and the NP with the externally modifying adjective in (6), contribute the existential interpretation of this variable.

1.1.2 Some problems for the qualifier theory

First, Sadock (1991) points out that one of the problems that come with the qualifier theory is that

> on this analysis, an external argument to an incorporating verb represents a more specific entity of the kind selected for by the incorporated noun stem. ... While such a semantic theory might be plausible in the case where the incorporated nominal is quite general and the external argument is necessarily a more specific entity of the same kind, ..., it is much less plausible where the two sets have no necessary relationship to one another [Sadock (1991): 92-93].[4]

A case in point Sadock gives as an illustration is one where an incorporated noun is modified by means of a numeral.

---

[4] Apart from this problem, Sadock (1991) discusses other problems a lexicalist treatment of noun incorporation gives rise to. I will not repeat them here but refer the reader to pp. 82-100 in Sadock's book.

(8)   Suulut   marlun-nik   timmisartu-liur-p-u-q.   [fw]

       S.ABS   two-INST.PL   airplane-make-IND-[-tr]-3SG

       "Suulut made two airplanes."

There is no way in which we could think of the numeral "two" in this example as being a more specific type of airplane. Similarly, when the external modifier is an intensional adjective, as in (9),

> the suggestion that the incorporated modifier simply restricts the range of arguments of the verb fails [Sadock (1991): 95].

(9)   Peqquserluut-nik   aningaasaq-liur-tuq.   [Sadock (1991): 95]

       false-INST.PL   money-make-REL.[-tr].ABS.SG

       "one who makes false money, a counterfeiter."

Rather, the intensional adjective modifies the incorporated noun itself and as such it cannot be the "real" argument of the verb.

Secondly, some incorporating languages allow "doubling" as illustrated in the following Mohawk example.

(10)   Kikv   rabahbot wa-ha-its-a-hnini-'

       this   bullhead FACT-M.SG.SUBJ-fish-buy-PUNCT

             ki   rake-'niha.   [Baker (1995): 9]

             this   my-father

       "My father fish-bought this bullhead."

The complex verb "fish-buy" combines with a full NP "this bullhead." According to the proponents of the lexicalist approach, one cannot accept that the incorporated noun "fish" is syntactically visible since otherwise both this incorporated noun and the full NP would be syntactic arguments of the verb. This would clearly be a violation of the THETA CRITERION. However, I wonder whether this kind of doubling data really supports the lexicalist view that an incorporated noun cannot be a syntactic constituent. It appears to me that we can think about "argument doubling" from a more abstract perspective on how exactly verbal argument structure is linguistically realized and what exactly is semantically contributed by which syntactic argument. This way of thinking is reminiscent of the treatment of other instances of doubling phenomena in natural language. For instance, if we look at the phenomenon of negative concord. An illustration of this are the following two examples from my own South Dutch dialect spoken in the neighbourhood of Antwerp.

(11)   Ik   hemme-k-ik   zoiet   nog *nooit nie* gezien.

       I   have-1SG-1SG   such.a.thing   yet   never   not   seen

       "I haven't seen such a thing ever before."

(12)   Ik   hemme-k-ik   da   *niemand   nie*   wille   zegge.

    I   have-1SG-1SG   that   nobody   not   want   say

    "I didn't want to tell this to anybody."

Although from a logical perspective these examples contain a double negation and should therefore be understood in a positive way, they are understood as if they only contained one negation. Recent studies in the semantics on negation have been devoted to this possibility of realizing sentence negation at different positions in one sentence [Jacobs (1982), Ladusaw (1992), Dowty (1994)]. The basic idea these semantic studies have in common is that several negative elements in a sentence can mark the presence of one abstract negation operator. Notice that the above Antwerp examples illustrate yet another case of doubling. In both sentences it is fully grammatical to repeat the first singular pronoun *ik* ("I") twice as a sort of Subject agreement marker or clitic on the verb.[5] There is no reason to think of one of these first singular markers as being lexicalized. Again, one could think of them as the multiple syntactic realizations of a more abstract notion of agreement.

Interestingly, one case of doubling that is very reminiscent of the above Mohawk example is split topicalization in German. Fanselow (1993) points out that it is possible to realize one verbal argument through two syntactically independent NPs.[6]

(13)   *Raubvögel*   glaube   ich   kennt   Gereon

    birds.of.prey   believe   I   knows   G.

      nur   Bussarde.   [Fanselow (1993): 63]

      only   buzzards

    "As for birds of prey, I believe that Gereon knows only buzzards."

(14)   *Impfungen*   werden   in der Regel   von der Krankenkasse

    vaccinations   are   in the rule   by the health.insurance.fund

      nur die Standardimpfungen   gezahlt.

      only the standard.vaccinations   paid

    "As a rule, only the standard vaccinations are paid by the health insurance fund."

---

[5] I thank Jerry Sadock for drawing my attention to this case of clitic doubling.

[6] In section 3.2, I return to the syntax of split topics, and I discuss Fanselow's proposal that the topicalized constituent and the remnant constituent in a split construction are independently generated in the syntax.

In these German examples, the constituent that names the less specific realization of the theme role of the respective verbs — and in this sense it is the counterpart of the Mohawk incorporated noun in (10) — is a topicalized phrasal constituent. There is no way of treating it as a lexicalized and syntactically invisible element.

In sum, "doubling" phenomena are widespread in natural language and present interesting challenges for a formal grammarian. Trying to get rid of them in the way the qualifier theory tries to get rid of syntactic argument doubling in noun incorporating configurations is, I believe, not the right way to tackle them. In the next chapter, I propose a rather straightforward semantic way to deal with doubling and external modifiers of West Greenlandic incorporated nouns. In this proposal, incorporated nouns as well as their external modifiers are syntactically visible and, except for the intensional modifiers, all of them are semantically interpreted as predicates of the internal argument's variable of an incorporating verb.

1.2 A syntactic approach

If we reject the view that incorporated nouns are parts of lexicalized complex words, as we just did, what could be a proper alternative? The other main approach in the debate on noun incorporation is Baker's (1988) view that noun incorporation is the result of a syntactic transformation and that therefore an incorporated noun is syntactically visible.[7]

1.2.1 Baker (1988): Noun incorporation by head movement

In Baker (1988), the syntactic incorporation of a noun is defined as the following structure dependent operation.[8]

---

[7] Sadock (1991) is another important proponent of the syntactic line in the noun incorporation debate. He developed the theory of autolexical syntax in which the structure of a sentence is represented as a double tree. In Van Geenhoven (1992), I pointed out that it is unclear how these double trees are interpreted semantically. In particular, it is unclear whether the phrase structure tree or the word-structure tree is taken as the input for the semantics, and it is even more unclear how the structural information of both trees could be regarded as the input for the semantics. I do not discuss autolexical syntax in this book.

[8] It was Baker's (1988) primary concern to explain grammatical function [GF] changing phenomena in terms of syntactic head movement [e.g. dative shift, passive, antipassive]. "The heart of all apparent GF changing processes is the movement of a word or (more technically) a lexical category [Baker (1988): 19]." In addition to that, he analyzes noun incorporation in terms of head movement as well. His general concern is to reduce GF changing and noun incorporation to the common denominator called "syntactic incorporation."

(15)   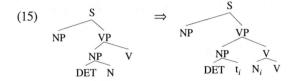

At S-structure, the head noun of a D-structural NP is adjoined to the V-node that governs this NP. Although at the surface an incorporated noun is morphologically dependent on a verb, syntactically it projects independently. In Baker's view, the Onondaga example (16a) and its nonincorporated counterpart (16b) have the same syntactic D-structure.

(16)   a.   Pet wa-ha-hwist-ahtu-t-a.   [Woodbury (1975)]

           P. PAST-3ms/3N-money-lost-CAUS-ASP

           "Pat lost money."

    b.   Pet wa-ha-htu-t-a   ne o-hwist-a.

           P. PAST-3ms/3N-lost-CAUS-ASP the PRE-money-SUF

           "Pat lost the money."

D-structure is the level of representation that satisfies the THETA CRITERION [see (7)]. According to Baker, the independent projection hypothesis of incorporated nouns yields the desired result. His syntactic treatment captures the fact that (16a) and (16b) are in some sense synonymous, that is, they are different surface realizations of the same thematic structure. This is in accordance with the UNIFORMITY OF THETA ASSIGNMENT HYPOTHESIS [UTAH]:

(17)   UNIFORMITY OF THETA ASSIGNMENT HYPOTHESIS   [Baker (1988): 46]

    Identical thematic relationships between items are represented by identical structural relationships between those items at the level of D-structure.

In Baker's transformational approach the THETA CRITERION is as central as in Di Sciullo and Williams' qualifier theory. Also Baker does not allow the double realization of one syntactic relation.

What seems interesting about Baker's approach is that it follows from his theory that in the noun incorporating languages studied so far Subjects are never incorporated.[9] If the head noun of the Subject NP in (15) were

---

[9] From his head movement approach, Baker (1988) also derives an explanation for why a ditransitive verb does not incorporate its goal argument. See Van Geenhoven (1998) for a discussion of noun incorporating di-transitives in West Greenlandic and an alternative view on this point.

adjoined to the V, its trace would be ungoverned and the resulting S-structure would violate the EMPTY CATEGORY PRINCIPLE.

(18)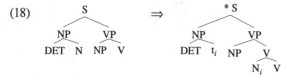

1.2.2 Some problems for the transformational approach

Like the lexicalist's account, Baker's account does not allow the double realization of a verbal argument in the syntax. The price the lexicalist pays to save the THETA CRITERION is the loss of syntactic visibility of incorporated nouns. The price Baker pays is the loss of the independence of a morphological process. A noun incorporating configuration is reduced to a nonincorporating configuration. That is, morphology is reduced to phraseology. I don't think one reaches more adequate grammars of synthetic languages by pretending that they are fundamentally nonsynthetic. Moreover, Baker's approach gives rise to some concrete problems. In the following two examples a numeral is incorporated and therefore they each are a severe problem for the idea that morphological incorporation is the result of head movement.

(19) Kaali   natser-nik   *marlu*-raar-p-u-q.   [fw]

    K.ABS   ringed.seal-INST.PL   two-catch-IND-[-tr]-3SG

    "Kaali caught two ringed seals."

(20) Festi-mi   qallunaar-*passua*-qar-p-u-q.   [fw]

    party-LOC   white-many-have-IND-[-tr]-3SG

    "There were many Danes at the party."

Furthermore, the question which the present study hinges on is whether the stipulation that an incorporated noun has a phrasal base is semantically useful.

First, the transformational approach implies that incorporated nouns are reconstructed for their semantic interpretation. Bittner (1994), however, argues that this cannot be true for the case of West Greenlandic incorporated nouns. In chapter 2, we saw that the latter always receive narrow scope. Bittner suggests that if reconstruction applied, nothing would prevent the construction of an LF with the reconstructed phrase taking wide scope. If, in contrast, the phrase remains unreconstructed, the trace it contains prohibits its raising since raising would give rise to an EMPTY CATEGORY PRINCIPLE violation. In the next chapter, I discuss Bittner's approach in more detail and compare it with my proposal of semantic incorporation.

Secondly, West Greenlandic noun incorporating configurations with an external numeral modifier cannot get a partitive interpretation.

(21) Nuka   marlun-nik   iipili-tur-p-u-q.   [fw]

N.ABS   two-INST.PL   apple-eat-IND-[-tr]-3SG

i.   "Nuka ate two apples."

ii.   # "Nuka ate two of the apples."

Under the assumption that the incorporated noun and the numeral modifier build a phrase, it remains unexplained why this phrase lacks a partitive reading, since NPs with a numeral determiner often receive such a reading.

Thirdly, Baker (1988) takes the discourse transparency of an incorporated noun to be a direct consequence of the view that such a noun is transformationally related to a phrase. In other words, he regards the discourse transparency of the incorporated *qimmi-* ("dog") in (22) as an argument in favour of his approach. In this example, the Subject agreement marker *3SG* that is part of the inflectional ending functions as a pronominal element.

(22) Aani   qimmi-qar-p-u-q.

A.ABS   dog-have-IND-[-tr]-3SG

Miki-mik   ati-qar-p-u-q.   [Bittner (1994): 67]

M.-INST   name-have-IND-[-tr]-3SG

"Aani has a dog. Its name is Miki."

This idea has been adopted in the literature without proof [Baker (1988), Bok-Bennema (1991), Bittner (1994)]. However, the fact that an incorporated noun can act as the antecedent of a definite pronoun has nothing to do with the syntactic stipulation that it is a part of a D-structural phrase. Among the studies about anaphoric relations between pronouns and their antecedents, we find authors who believe that these relations are pragmatic in nature (the E-type strategy) and authors who believe that they are semantic in nature [the semantic binding strategy]. In the question of anaphora resolution neither of these strategies primarily relies on the *phrasal* nature of the antecedent constituent. At the end of chapter 5, I return to the discourse transparency of incorporated nouns, and I discuss to what extent the anaphora resolution strategies proposed by discourse semantic frameworks can deal with it [Kamp (1981), Heim (1982), Kamp and Reyle (1993)].

1.3 Summary

In this first section, I have discussed two approaches to noun incorporation and some of their shortcomings. Whereas the strong lexicalist approach ignores the syntactic visibility of incorporated nouns, the transformational approach ignores the basically morphological nature of a noun incorporating configuration.

The proponents of both approaches think of noun incorporation as if it has to be either a lexical or a syntactic phenomenon. The possibility that within one linguistic theory lexical *and* syntactic noun incorporation could and should live next to each other, is not considered. I believe that the apparent incompatibility of the two is an artifact, that is, it does not follow from the phenomenon of noun incorporation itself. As a matter of fact, Sadock (1991) defends a similar view. He shows that in West Greenlandic a noun incorporating construction often is syntactic but that one simultaneously finds such constructions lexicalized. The example he gives is the following:

(23)   Nuna-mi tassa-ni   nuna-qar-p-u-q.   [Sadock (1991): 100]

       land-LOC that-LOC   land-have-IND-[-tr]-3SG

       "He lives on that land."

Although we can identify the stem *nuna-* ("land") and the verbal affix *-qar-* ("have") as a noun incorporating complex verb, this complex verb now has the lexicalized meaning "to live somewhere." Interestingly, Baker (1995) presents a more moderate view of noun incorporation as well and gives examples from Mohawk illustrating that this language has lexicalized and syntactic cases of noun incorporation. Nevertheless, Baker (1995) still regards the syntactic cases as the result of head movement.

2 The excluded middle: Noun incorporation syntactically base generated

The two analyses of noun incorporation discussed in the previous section were presented as the two "mainstream" approaches in the ongoing discussions of the interplay of morphological and syntactic principles in natural language theories. These two approaches play their arguments off against one another in such a way that both operate on the presupposition that they are the only possible theoretical approaches. However, there are good reasons to believe that this presupposition is wrong. This does not only follow from the fact that we rejected both approaches in the previous section. Despite the fact that it has been hardly considered in the literature, it appears rather straightforward to develop a third approach in which noun incorporation is regarded as a case of syntactically base generated word formation, an approach that is distinct from both the transformational and the lexicalist approach. In fact, Dowty (1979) already suggested such a treatment for noun incorporation in West Greenlandic, and I will outline his suggestion below. The need for regarding subphrasal syntax as a substantial and elementary part of the syntactic component is also pointed out by Sells

(1994) for Korean, by Neeleman (1994) for Dutch and by Mohanan (1995) for Hindi.[10]

An interesting side effect of regarding noun incorporation as a base generated configuration is that morphological incorporation can show up in both the syntax *and* the lexicon. That is, it can be analyzed as a syntactically base generated configuration or as a lexicalized such configuration. In this way, we can account for the fact expressed at the end of the preceding section, namely, that noun incorporation is sometimes syntactic and sometimes lexicalized.

This section is organized in the following way. I first present Dowty's concept of syntactic noun incorporation. Then, I show that the position of an incorporated noun is a substantial and underived part of a syntactic V-projection. In particular, I show how the idea of base generated noun incorporation can be integrated into the syntactic V-projection theory developed in de Hoop (1992). Finally, I point out the advantages of syntactically base generated noun incorporation with respect to its semantic interpretation.

2.1 Dowty's (1979) proposal

Dowty (1979) develops a clear picture of grammar that allows syntactic and lexical word formation within one linguistic framework. Dowty's picture lies in the tradition of Montague grammar [Montague (1974)] and is based on a useful distinction between linguistic operations, on the one hand, and grammar rules, on the other. The latter are made up by (combinations of) the former. As an illustration, I give Montague's syntactic rule for English that combines an intransitive verb like *sleep* with *Jim* as its Subject and forms the sentence *Jim sleeps*.

(24) If δ is an intransitive verb and α a name or a pronoun, then $F_1(\alpha, \delta)$ is a sentence and $F_1(\alpha, \delta)$ is $\alpha\delta'$, where δ' is the result of replacing the main verb in δ by its third person singular present form.

Following the lexicalist tendencies in generative grammar [Chomsky (1972), Bresnan (1978)], Dowty extends the Montagovian framework in that he defines syntactic rules and lexical rules. Like the former, the latter are made up by phrase-level and word-level operations. Given this cross-classification, one is not forced to think of word formation as being either a

---

[10] Mohanan (1995) defends the view that noun incorporation in Hindi is a matter of syntactically base generated word formation. To contrast her approach with Baker's syntactic transformational approach, Mohanan calls it a *lexicalist* approach. I believe that this is only a terminological matter, and as far as I can see Mohanan defends the view that Hindi noun incorporation belongs to that part of syntax that takes care of *subphrasal* syntax. Note in this respect that, as opposed to West Greenlandic, Hindi noun incorporation does not involve a morphological process.

syntactic or a lexical phenomenon. Like all other subphrasal operations, word-level operations can show up both in syntactic and in lexical rules. The following diagram taken from Dowty (1979) summarizes the main points of his framework.

(25)

kind of rule	SYNTACTIC RULES	LEXICAL RULES
kind of operation		
SYNTACTIC OPERATIONS	traditional syntactic rules (phrase structure and transformational).	rules forming lexical units of more than one word (English V-Prt combinations and factitives).
MORPHOLOGICAL OPERATIONS	1. rules introducing inflectional morphology; 2. rules introducing derivational morphology when unrestricted and semantically regular (polysynthetic languages).	rules introducing derivational morphology, zero-derivation, compounding where partially productive and less than predictable semantically.

Dowty points out that

> the upper left and lower right boxes are the traditional classes, the upper right and lower left are more novel. ... Morphological operations which are used by syntactic rules will correspond to those traditionally classed under inflectional morphology. However, even morphological operations usually classed as derivational should in my view be classed with syntactic rather than lexical rules if these morphological operations are used in a completely productive way and in a completely regular way semantically. The best candidates for this class probably come from polysynthetic languages like Eskimo [Dowty (1979): 302-303].

In other words, whereas much of the compounding and derivation in English is captured by means of lexical rules, West Greenlandic noun incorporating complexes are regarded as the result of syntactic word formation.[11] [12]

---

[11] Sadock (1991) points out that in some languages noun incorporation is derivational whereas in others it is compounding. "Word formation" is a cover term for both cases.

[12] The diagram under (25) shows that Dowty (1979) regards English verb–particle combinations [see (i)] and resultatives [see (ii)] as lexical constructs.

(i)   I will call you up.
(ii)   I painted the door red.

I am not so much interested in the fact that Dowty spells out his ideas within Montague grammar, but rather in how his basic idea that the syntax of natural language contains both word- *and* phrase-level combinatorial and derivational principles could be integrated into other linguistic approaches. Dowty's attempt of bringing phrasal syntax and word-level syntax together into one syntactic component is, I believe, more adequate with respect to natural language than the classical distinction between a morphological and a syntactic component adopted in most generative frameworks. To make Dowty's view compatible with these frameworks, one has to dispense with the "idée fixe" that syntax is *phrasal* syntax and that the analysis of subphrasal phenomenona belongs into a lexical or a morphological component. Fortunately, some authors working within the tradition of generative grammar have abandoned this idée fixe [Sells (1994), Neeleman (1994), Mohanan (1995)] and for purely syntactic reasons they have arrived at the conclusion that subphrasal syntax *is* syntax. I think that only with this amount of flexibility it is possible to gain more insight into the contribution of morphology to semantics, in particular, to the construction of semantic representations of morphologically complex configurations such as noun incorporation in West Greenlandic.

How can we translate the insight that the West Greenlandic noun incorporating configuration under (26) is the result of syntactic word formation?

(26)   Suulut   timmisartu-liur-p-u-q.   [Sadock (1980): 311]

       S.ABS   airplane-make-IND-[-tr]-3SG

       "Suulut made an airplane."

I propose that we regard such a configuration as a syntactically base generated construction. With respect to example (26), this view is represented in the following way:

See Neeleman (1994) for a recent discussion of Dutch and English verb-particle combinations and resultatives.

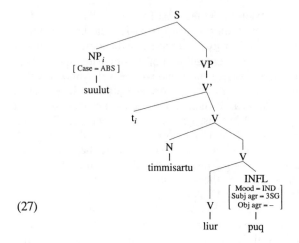

(27)

This picture illustrates what syntactically base generated noun incorporation has in common with transformational noun incorporation: it regards noun incorporation as an instance of word formation which takes place in the syntax. Hence, incorporated nouns are visible for the semantic interpretation. The merit of this transformation-free syntactic word formation is that we do not need to stipulate the existence of a phrasal base for morphological complexes: syntactic visibility is not necessarily identical with phrasal visibility. (27) also shows that, like in a lexicalist account, noun incorporation is a base generated configuration, with the important difference that it is a syntactic configuration. Note that I adopt Bittner's (1994) view that the Subject is base generated in the VP and moves to the ABSOLUTIVE case position to receive Case. Moreover, since Pollock (1989) proposed the split of INFL there has been a trend in generative linguistics to represent all syntactically relevant morphological information as projections of functional categories. I do not follow this trend. Rather, I regard the INFL-node as collection of the information contributed by the inflection morpheme. In the next chapter, I show how these features trigger the presence of the relevant operators at LF.

In sum, (27) illustrates that one syntactic representation can embody different categories and combinatorial principles. If two people get married, it does not necessarily follow that one becomes dependent on the other.

2.2 The syntactic position of incorporated nouns

The tree structure under (27) is only a first approximation of representing the idea that a West Greenlandic incorporated noun is a basic part of a syntactic V-projection. As a next step, I want to integrate the syntactic reality of an incorporated noun into a broader perspective. The perspective I have in mind is a novel and useful concept of the V-projection defended in de Hoop (1992), who distinguishes between a strong and a weak Case NP position in the VP. I argue that in addition to de Hoop's distinction we need a Case-less syntactic position as a slot for syntactically base generated incorporated nouns. Furthermore, I suggest that in the syntax we need to distinguish weak from strong V-projections.

2.2.1 De Hoop (1992): Weak and strong Case

De Hoop (1992) studies the relationship between case and the interpretation of NPs. On independent syntactic grounds, she distinguishes two types of structural Case, namely, weak Case and strong Case. This abstract Case distinction is meant to capture the observation made in many languages that there are two objective cases. Whereas Belletti (1988) revisits the observation that Finnish has two possible cases for an Object NP — that is, ACCUSATIVE and PARTITIVE — , it has been observed for West Greenlandic that the Direct Object argument of a verb can occur in the ABSOLUTIVE or in the INSTRUMENTAL case [see chapter 2, Bittner (1988)]. Similarly, in Turkish the Object of a verbal predicate may either bear an ACCUSATIVE case marker or lack it [Enç (1991)]. According to Butt (1993), the same holds for Hindi/Urdu. The following examples illustrate the case distinctions in these typologically different languages.

(28) a. Ostin   *leipää*.   [Finnish, Belletti (1988)]

        buy.1SG   bread.PART

        "I buy bread."

    b. Ostin   *leivän*.

        buy.1SG   bread.ACC

        "I buy the bread."

(29) a. Jaaku *arna-mik* tuqut-si-v-u-q.   [West Gr., Bittner (1988)]

        J.ABS   woman-INST   kill-AP-IND-[-tr]-3SG

        "Jacob killed a woman."

    b. Jaaku-p *arnaq*   tuqut-p-a-a.

        J.-ERG   woman.ABS   kill-IND-[+tr]-3SG.3SG

        "Jacob killed the/a particular woman."

(30) a. Ali bir *piyano* kivalamak istiyor.   [Turkish, Enç (1991)]

         A. one piano to.rent   wants

         "Ali wants to rent one piano."

      b. Ali bir *piyano-yu* kivalamak istiyor.

         A. one piano-ACC to.rent   wants

         "Ali wants to rent a certain piano."

(31) a. Adnaan-ne *rotii*   paka-yii.   [Urdu, Butt (1993)]

         A.MAS-ERG bread.FEM-NOM cook-PERF.FEM.SG

         "Adnaan made (a/the) bread."

      b. Adnaan-ne *rotii-ko*   paka-yaa.

         A.MAS-ERG bread.FEM-ACC cook-PERF.MAS.SG

         "Adnaan made a particular/the bread."

The respective distinctions in objective case correlate with a distinction in semantic interpretation and it is de Hoop's primary goal to figure out the exact nature of this correlation [see section 2.3 below]. Whereas the Objects in the respective a-examples tend to get a "nonspecific" reading, the Objects in the b-examples tend to get a "specific" interpretation. Without repeating her discussion in full detail, the syntactic picture we get is the following.

> Weak Case [PARTITIVE in Finnish, INSTRUMENTAL in West Greenlandic, ZERO CASE in Turkish and Hindi/Urdu, VVG] can be licensed on an NP in a certain configuration at D-structure. This type of Case is a weak Case in the sense that it can no longer be licensed as soon as the NP moves out of the original position. That means that if an NP moves out of its original weak Case position, strong Case must be licensed at S-structure to avoid a violation of the Case Filter. In certain cases, at S-structure this will show up as an adjacency requirement for NPs bearing weak Case and their licenser [de Hoop (1992): 80].[13]

As a matter of fact, the adjacency requirement shows up in those cases where weak Case is not overtly realized as illustrated in the Turkish and Hindi/Urdu a-examples above. Interestingly, such weak "zero" Case configurations have often been called instances of noun incorporation in the literature [Szabolsci (1986), Mohanan (1995)], an issue to which I return below.

---

[13] The CASE FILTER, a basic principle of generative grammar, is defined in the following way [see Rouveret and Vergnaud (1980)]:

> Every phonetically realized NP must be assigned (abstract) Case.

The following tree structure skeletons visualize de Hoop's weak–strong Case distinction.

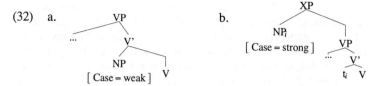

(32) a.   b.

The West Greenlandic examples (29a) and (29b) illustrate that it is not only the structural Case distinction which supports the view that in the syntax we have different Direct Object positions. The Case distinction corresponds with a distinction in the agreement morphology that is realized in the inflectional ending on a verb. If the Object of a verb is realized as a weak Case NP — as the INSTRUMENTAL in (29a) —, no overt Object agreement marker appears on the verb. If it is realized as a strong Case NP — as the ABSOLUTIVE in (29b) —, we do find Object agreement on the verb. I suggest that we add this agreement information to (32a) and (32b) as feature information on the verbal node. (33a) and (33b) are the VP skeletons for West Greenlandic.

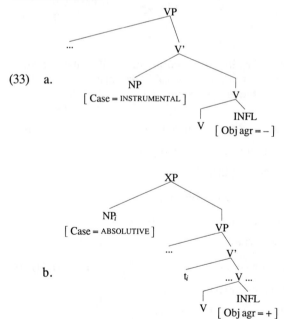

(33) a.

b.

2.2.2 Incorporated nouns as constituents in a V-projection

At this stage, we have two Object positions available in the syntactic representation of a West Greenlandic VP. In section 2.1, I presented the option of regarding noun incorporation in West Greenlandic as a syntactically base generated configuration. From this it follows rather straightforwardly that we want to distinguish a third syntactic Object position, namely, the position of a syntactically base generated incorporated noun. This means that in addition to (33a) and (33b), I distinguish (33c) as a well-formed V-projection in West Greenlandic. Note that the verb bears no Object agreement.

(33) c.

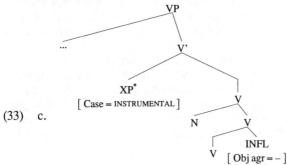

Apart from the Case-less N position, this incorporating VP contains a weak Case NP position. This is the slot for the possible INSTRUMENTAL modifiers of incorporated nouns as in the above examples (5), (8) and (9), repeated here.

(34) Suulut *qisum-mik*   timmisartu-liur-p-u-q.   [fw]

     S.ABS   wood-INST.SG airplane-make-IND-[-tr]-3SG

     "Suulut made a wooden airplane."

(35) Suulut *marlun-nik* timmisartu-liur-p-u-q.   [fw]

     S.ABS   two-INST.PL airplane-make-IND-[-tr]-3SG

     "Suulut made two airplanes."

(36) *Peqquserluut-nik* aningaasaq-liur-tuq.   [Sadock (1991): 95]

     false-INST.PL   money-make-REL.[-tr].ABS.SG

     "one who makes false money, a counterfeiter."

The category X in XP stands for adjective, numeral, *wh*-word or relative clause [see chapter 2, section 1]. The * on XP indicates that any number of INSTRUMENTAL constituents can show up.

2.3 Semantic interpretation and the base generated approach

De Hoop (1992) is primarily interested in the correlation between the structural Case and the semantic interpretation of Object NPs. Her weak–strong Case distinction is part of the preliminaries needed to establish this correlation. Given that I regard the position of an incorporated noun as yet another independent constituent in a V-projection, the proposed noun incorporating VP configuration under (33c) becomes a part of these preliminaries as well. That is, in addition to the correlation between the Case and the interpretation of Object constituents, I am interested in the correlation between noun incorporation and the interpretation of Object constituents.

In this section, I first revisit the main aspects of how de Hoop links the weak–strong Case distinction to possible NP interpretations. For reasons that will become clear below, I do not follow her in the actual elaboration of the Case–interpretation correlation. I present an alternative view of the semantic contribution of Case and noun incorporation. Whereas weak Case NPs and incorporated nouns are uniformly interpreted as predicative indefinites, strong Case NPs are either free variable indefinites, definites or quantifiers.

2.3.1 De Hoop's semantic picture

De Hoop (1992) distinguishes three possible semantic types for the interpretation of Object NPs: the type of a quantifier ($<<e,t>,t>$), the type of an individual object (e) and the type of a predicate modifier ($<<e,t>,<e,t>>$). Assuming that an NP bears the type of a quantifier if it has a quantificational, a specific, a partitive or a generic, that is, a "strong" interpretation in the sense of Milsark (1977), de Hoop interprets an Object as a generalized quantifier if it bears strong Case [see (32b)]. This means that the Object constituents in the above b-examples in (28) through (31) are interpreted as quantificational expressions. In contrast, an Object NP that bears weak Case is always interpreted as a "part-of-the-predicate." De Hoop's understanding of the notion "part-of-the-predicate" is that a weak Case Object is either interpreted as a term of type e, that is, as an individual, or as a predicate modifier of type $<<e,t>,<e,t>>$. In the latter case, the syntactic Object is not regarded as a semantic argument of a transitive verb but rather as a modifier of an intransitive verb. Depending on whether the verbs in the a-examples under (28) through (31) are lexically characterized as telic or atelic, the weak Objects in these examples are interpreted either as individuals or as predicate modifiers. In the former case, the weak NP gets a weak, existential interpretation. De Hoop illustrates that NPs with a definite determiner (= strong) can denote a weak semantic type as well. This is needed to understand the difference in interpretation between the Dutch examples (37a) and (37b): depending on its position with respect to the verbal complex *gaat doen* ("go do"), the definite NP *de was* ("the laundry") gets a "part-of-the-predicate" and a strong, referential reading respectively.

(37) a. Omdat   Paul zondag *de was*   gaat doen. [de Hoop (1992): 112]

         because   P.   Sunday the wash   goes do

         "Because Paul (always) does the laundry on Sunday."

      b. Omdat   Paul *de was*   zondag gaat doen.

         because   P.   the wash   Sunday goes do

         "Because Paul (will) do the laundry on Sunday."

With this kind of example, de Hoop suggests that weak Case on a strong NP gives rise to a weak interpretation.

2.3.2 Some problems for de Hoop

Bittner (1994) gives the following pair of West Greenlandic examples illustrating that the interpretation of the partitive Object NP with respect to the modal operator *-sariaqar-* ("must") depends on the Case assigned to this NP.

(38) a. *Atuartu-t*   *ila-an-nik*

         student-ERG.PL   part-3PL.SG-INST.PL

         ikiu-i-sariaqar-p-u-nga.   [Bittner (1994): 138]

         help-AP-must-IND-[-tr]-1SG

         "I must help one of the students (lit. students one part of them), any will do."

      b. *Atuartu-t*   *ila-a-t*

         student-ERG.PL   part-3PL.SG-ABS.PL

         ikiur-tariaqar-p-a-ra.   [Bittner (1994): 138]

         help-must-IND-[+tr]-1SG.3SG

         "There is one of the students that I must help."

Overt partitive NPs bearing weak Case do not fit into de Hoop's semantic picture.[14] The INSTRUMENTAL (= weak Case) constituent *ilaannik* as well as the ABSOLUTIVE (= strong Case) *ilaat* are the head of an overt partitive and

---

[14] If weak Case is assigned in the VP — and de Hoop (1992) provides us with independent evidence that this really is the case — Diesing (1992) has a problem with the fact that in West Greenlandic partitive NPs can bear weak Case as well. The problem arises because Diesing requires that partitive NPs necessarily move out of VP. This means that we have an additional problem for Diesing's approach [see chapter 3, section 2.3].

regardless of which Case they bear, they require a partitive interpretation, which is in de Hoop's picture a strong and therefore quantificational interpretation. Obviously, this requirement is not compatible with the requirement that weak Case constituents always receive a "part-of-the-predicate" interpretation. The weak–strong Case distinction in the examples under (38) shows that de Hoop's interpretation of weak Case does not cover all the cases.

Moreover, in the previous chapter I discussed Abusch (1994), who succesfully shows that genuine quantifiers and indefinites have different scope properties. She shows that the different scope readings of indefinites cannot be the quantificational readings because indefinites but not quantifiers can escape scope islands. Abusch's view suggests, and I follow this suggestion, that de Hoop's proposal that all strong Case Object NPs are quantifiers is wrong. Apart from denoting a quantifier, a strong Case object NP can also translate as a free variable indefinite that in some way or other reaches an intermediate or a wide scope position.

A final aspect of de Hoop's semantic picture that I want to discuss here is directly related to our main topic, namely, noun incorporation. She writes that

> if object NPs on their weak reading have to be interpreted as part of a one-place predicate, then the phenomenon of object incorporation can be conceived as the ultimate morphological realization of this interpretation [de Hoop (1992): 113].

In chapter 2, we indeed characterized West Greenlandic incorporated nouns as narrow indefinite descriptions. The question that arises is whether this narrowness can be appropriately captured in terms of de Hoop's part-of-the-predicate interpretation, that is, by assigning incorporated nouns the semantic types e or $<<e,t>,<e,t>>$. I argue that to cover the meaning aspects of West Greenlandic incorporated nouns and other narrow indefinites we must define in a more fine-grained way what "part-of-the-predicate" means. Those constituents that are understood as "part-of-the-predicate" will be interpreted as properties (type $<s,<e,t>>$).

2.3.3 Weak Case NPs and incorporated nouns denote properties

At the end of the previous chapter, I concluded that for an appropriate understanding of indefinite descriptions we need to draw a distinction between predicative and free variable indefinites. Whereas the former cover the set of narrow indefinites, the latter cover the indefinites that receive wide and intermediate interpretations. With this distinction in mind, I propose that in West Greenlandic weak Case NPs as well as incorporated nouns are predicative indefinites and that strong Case NPs are either free variable indefinites, definites or quantifiers. The details of this proposal are elaborated in the next two chapters and here I only give a foretaste.

Given the weak V-projections (33a) and (33c), the idea is that a verb absorbs the meaning of a weak Case Object, or of an incorporated noun together with its external weak Case modifiers as the predicate of its internal argument's variable. This absorption process, called "semantic incorporation", can capture what "part-of-the-predicate" means. In fact, weak Case NPs and incorporated nouns can be regarded as being "part-of-a-predicate" because they restrict the internal argument's variable of that predicate even though this variable has been bound already. They neither modify the predicate itself, as in the case of de Hoop's $<<e,t>,<e,t>>$ weak reading, nor do they introduce an object variable, as in the case of de Hoop's e weak reading.[15]

I mentioned before that in West Greenlandic the weak–strong Case distinction is not the only morphological trigger for the proper semantic interpretation of West Greenlandic Object constituents. The West Greenlandic examples given so far show that this Case distinction correlates with the absence vs. presence of Object agreement on the verb. Intuitively, the morphological realization of agreement on the verb functions as a marker for keeping track of the arguments of this verb. In West Greenlandic, this is only necessary if this argument bears strong Case, that is, if it is not in the VP. On the one hand, I suggest that the lack of Object agreement on a West Greenlandic verb indicates that its Object constituent — an incorporated noun with its weak Case modifiers or a weak Case Object — is locally bound, or, as people sometimes say it in more syntactic terms, is existentially closed in the VP. In chapter 5, I argue that this local binding is always the result of semantic incorporation. On the other hand, the presence of Object agreement on a verb indicates that its Object constituent is not locally bound. It is either a quantificational expression, a definite or a free variable indefinite.

A side effect of interpreting the noun incorporating V-projection under (33c) in the way proposed is that from a semantic perspective there is no need to create a derivational link between the incorporated noun and its external modifiers as proposed in Baker (1988). The reason that we can dispense with this syntactic link is that (33c) contains enough information to semantically identify an incorporated noun and its external modifiers as the predicates of a variable that is introduced by the verb. Once the VP of a West Greenlandic sentence is recognized as the syntactic structure under (33c), this provides sufficient information for the semantic construction component to regard each nominal or adjectival node in this configuration as a predicative expression. In the next chapter, I present a detailed overview of

---

[15] Also Bittner (1994) proposes to regard a West Greenlandic incorporated noun as a predicate modifier. In the next chapter, I compare Bittner's proposal with my proposal. See also Van Geenhoven (1995).

the semantic interpretation of various base generated noun incorporating constructions.[16]

Still, sceptical transformational minds may wonder how the base generation approach accounts for the fact that Subjects never incorporate. In section 1.2.1, I showed how Baker (1988) accounts for this fact by means of a syntactic principle, the ECP. In my approach to noun incorporation, this fact is not syntactically but semantically accounted for. I suggest that the reason for why Subjects never incorporate follows from the fact that external arguments are not true arguments of the verb [Marantz (1984), Kratzer (1994)]. Hence, a verb cannot absorb a predicate of this argument in the way it absorbs a predicate of its internal argument.[17]

Finally, the present base generated approach to noun incorporation in West Greenlandic and the proposed semantics indirectly account for the discourse semantic pecularities of incorporated nouns. Again, I only present the basic ideas here. First, assuming with Heim (1982) that a definite description translates as a variable that looks for an antecedent we can explain the fact that an incorporated noun lacks a definite interpretation as a direct consequence of the fact that the variable of which this noun is a predicate has to meet the NOVELTY CONDITION [see chapter 3, section 1.2]. Secondly, the discourse transparency of a West Greenlandic incorporated noun is in no way a valid argument for the transformational account of Baker (1988). Rather, the idea that an incorporating verb introduces the existential quantifier binding its internal argument means that from a discourse semantic perspective such a verb introduces the discourse referent occupying its internal argument's position. The discourse transparency of this referent can then be captured in terms of semantic binding. Thirdly, the fact that a noun incorporating configuration lacks a partitive interpretation follows from the fact that the incorporated nominal material is not an overt partitive. This holds for English predicative indefinites as well: a narrow indefinite is only semantically interpreted as a partitive NP if it is an overt partitive. Imagine the following situation. You know that there were five ice cream bars in the fridge and at some point you want to eat one of them.

---

[16] In Van Geenhoven (1997) I elaborate a Case-indexing device to deal with more complex data, namely data in which more than one INSTRUMENTAL occurs and in which these INSTRUMENTAL constituents are predicates of different variables. (i) is a case in point.

(i)   Nuka   puisi-mik   qasertu-mik   ami-ir-i-v-u-q.   [fw]
       N.ABS   seal-INST   grey-INST   skin-remove-AP-IND-[-tr]-3SG
       "Nuka removed a seal's grey skin."

I do not discuss such data in this book.

[17] Of course, this raises the related question of how we account for predicative indefinites in Subject position. I return to this question in chapter 5. — Because it is not relevant for my argumentation in the remainder of this book, I represent the external argument as an argument of the verb. The reader should keep in mind that this is a representational matter only.

Opening the fridge you ascertain the fact that they are all gone. You may ask the first person entering the kitchen the following question:

(39)   Did you eat the ice cream bars?

This person, fully innocent, can give two negative answers. Either she uses an overt partitive or she uses a normal indefinite NP as the Object constituent.

(40)   a.   I didn't eat one of your ice cream bars.

        b.   I didn't eat one ice cream bar.

On their narrow reading, the main difference between the two answers under (40) is that in the b-answer the Object NP is not interpreted as a partitive. (40b) means that the person asked did not eat any ice cream bar at all. That this really is the case can be illustrated by adding *but I ate one I bought myself* to (40). Whereas (40a) does not give rise to a contradiction, it does give rise to a contradiction if added to (40b).

(41)   a.   I didn't eat one of your ice cream bars but I ate one I bought myself.

        b.   # I didn't eat one ice cream bar but I ate one I bought myself.

My explanation of why *one ice cream bar* in (40b) lacks a partitive interpretation is that this NP lacks an overt partitive marker and, moreover, bears weak Case. Therefore, it is automatically interpreted as a predicate that is semantically incorporated by the verb *to eat*. Note that this does not prevent us from having overt partitives bearing weak Case, as in the above West Greenlandic example (38a) and in the English example (40a). Weak Case is compatible with semantic partitivity if it is assigned to an overt partitive construction.

2.4 Summary

In this section, I presented an analysis of noun incorporation which is an alternative to both the lexicalist and the transformational approach. In my analysis, West Greenlandic noun incorporating configurations are regarded as syntactically base generated constructs. I sketched how such an analysis correlates with the semantic features of these configurations. For more semantic details, the reader has to wait until the next chapter.

3 The syntactic position of predicative indefinites in German

In chapter 2, I presented German bare plurals and split topics as semantic counterparts of West Greenlandic incorporated nouns. This view gives rise to the question of whether they are syntactic counterparts as well. In a sense, they are. For instance, what German bare plurals in Object position have in common with West Greenlandic incorporated nouns is adjacency to their verbal head. Furthermore, I provide supporting evidence that the structure underlying German split topics is very similar to the West Greenlandic noun incorporating V-projection (33c).

3.1 Adjacency and the German bare plural in Object position

In my presentation of de Hoop's (1992) structural Case distinction, I briefly mentioned that in some languages weak Case Objects must be adjacent to their verbal head. De Hoop borrows a pair of Turkish examples from Kornfilt (1990) to illustrate this adjacency requirement.

(42) a. Ben dün aksam çok güzel *bir biftek* yedim.

       I yesterday evening very nice a steak ate

       "Yesterday evening, I ate a very nice steak."

    b. * Ben çok güzel *bir biftek* dün aksam yedim.

De Hoop explains this requirement as being the consequence of the syntactic fact that weak Case is only licensed in Object position at D-structure. If we scrambled the Object, the latter would lose its weak Case. From a semantic perspective, the syntactic adjacency requirement functions as a trigger to interpret the Object as a "part-of-the-predicate." We just saw that unlike de Hoop, my understanding of "part-of-the-predicate" is that the Object is interpreted as a predicate of the internal argument of an incorporating verb. From this perspective, it is understandable that some authors used the term noun incorporation for those configurations in which the Object is strictly adjacent to its verbal head even though no morphological noun incorporation has taken place [Szabolsci (1986) for Hungarian, Mohanan (1995) for Hindi].

In German — and similarly in Dutch —, bare plural Object NPs prefer to be adjacent to the verbal component as well. If such an Object does not meet this requirement, the sentence tends to be ungrammatical.[18]

(43) a. Daß Jan gestern *Kartoffeln* geschält hat, scheint

       that J. yesterday potatoes peeled has, seems

       niemanden zu beeindrucken.

       nobody to impress

       "The fact that Jan peeled potatoes yesterday seems to impress nobody."

    b. * Daß Jan *Kartoffeln* gestern geschält hat, scheint niemanden zu beeindrucken.

---

[18] Note that the b-sentences become better if we focus the adverbial modifiers *gestern* ("yesterday") and *tagelang* ("for several days").

(44) a   Obwohl Julia tagelang *Eimer* herangeschleppt hatte,

          although J.   days.long buckets along.dragged   had,

          wirkte sie   nicht müde.

          looked she   not   tired

          "Although Julia had been dragging along buckets for days, she didn't look tired."

     b. * Obwohl Julia *Eimer* tagelang herangeschleppt hatte, wirkte sie nicht müde.

These examples show that in German the bare plural can only be realized as a weak Case NP. This correlates with the semantic fact that in existential contexts a German bare plural — like a West Greenlandic incorporated noun — only receives a predicative interpretation.

Moreover, I suggest that in German phrasal adjacency triggers semantic incorporation is not restricted to bare plurals. In general, German indefinite Object NPs which are adjacent to the verb are likely to receive a predicative interpretation. The following examples illustrate how the presence versus absence of adjacency mirrors a semantic distinction in the interpretation of a singular indefinite.

(45) a. daß   Jan   mit viel Lärm   *einen Schrank* verschoben hat.

         that   J.   with a.lot.of noise   a wardrobe   pushed   has

         i.   "... that John pushed a wardrobe with a lot of noise."

         ii.   # "... that John pushed a prtc./one of the wardrobe(s) with a lot of noise."

     b. daß   Jan   *einen Schrank* mit viel Lärm   verschoben hat.

         that   J.   a wardrobe   with a.lot.of noise pushed   has

         i.   # "... that John pushed a wardrobe with a lot of noise."

         ii.   "... that John pushed a prtc./one of the wardrobe(s) with a lot of noise."

(46) a. daß   Julia   gestern   *ein Pferd* gestriegelt hat.

         that   J.   yesterday   a horse   curried   has

         i.   "... that Julia curried a horse yesterday."

         ii.   # "... that Julia curried a particular/one of the horse(s) yesterday."

b. daß Julia *ein Pferd* gestern gestriegelt hat.

   that J. a horse yesterday curried has

i.   # "... that Julia curried a horse yesterday."

ii.   "... that Julia curried a particular/one of the horse(s) yesterday."

3.2 Split topics in German

This section is devoted to one of the never-ending stories in the literature on German syntax, namely, to the syntactic representation of split topicalization. The syntax of German split topics has been discussed by many authors and represented in many ways. We can distinguish two main approaches in these discussions. In the first approach, split topicalization is analyzed as if the topicalized constituent and the "Mittelfeld" remnant were one D-structural NP [van Riemsdijk (1987), Diesing (1992)]. The other, and less popular, approach does not stipulate the existence of a derivational link between the topicalized constituent and the "remnant" [Fanselow (1988), (1993)]. Both approaches have been presented under different guises and I will not recapitulate all of them here. Rather, I first present van Riemsdijk's (1987) proposal together with the semantic predictions of his proposal as defended in Diesing (1992). In their view, split topicalization is NP split. Then, I present a novel analysis of split topicalization in which two nominal constituents are base generated independently in the VP, and in which the topicalization of the innermost of these constituents is explained as raising for the purpose of Case checking. In my view, split topicalization is V split.

3.2.1 Split topics as NP split

Van Riemsdijk (1987) proposes that split topicalization literally results from cutting a "Mittelfeld" NP in two pieces. The structure of (47) is (48).

(47) *Katzen* hat jedes Kind *fünf* gesehen.

   cats has every child five seen

   NARROW "As for cats, every child saw five such animals."

   WIDE   # "There are five cats such that every child saw them."

(48) $[_{NP} Katzen]_i$ hat jedes Kind $[_{NP} fünf\ t_i\ ]$ gesehen

In the previous chapter, I showed how Diesing (1992) takes van Riemsdijk's NP split proposal as the basis for her explanation for why German split topics lack strong readings. According to Diesing, an NP can only get a strong reading when it leaves the VP, either at S-structure or at LF. Her explanation for why (47) lacks the wide reading goes as follows. A strong

reading of the discontinuous NP *Katzen ... fünf* ("cats ... five") requires that
before the topicalization of *Katzen* takes place its D-structural source *fünf
Katzen* ("five cats") is scrambled out of the VP.

(49)   jedes Kind hat [NP fünf Katzen]k [VP tk gesehen]

Being in this scrambled position means that the NP is in an ungoverned
position. Topicalizing the head *Katzen* would give rise to a violation of
Huang's (1982) CONSTRAINT ON EXTRACTION DOMAIN which prohibits
extraction from an ungoverned position. The result would be the
unwellformed S-structure in (50).

(50)   * [NP Katzen]i hat jedes Kind [NP fünf ti]k [VP tk gesehen]

What Diesing adds to van Riemsdijk's proposal is that a split topic is the
result of splitting an NP that is in the VP. This is illustrated in (51).

(51)   [NP Katzen]i hat jedes Kind [VP [NP fünf ti]   gesehen]

Diesing wraps up her explanation of the narrow scope effect of split topics
into the following syntactic generalization [see chapter 3, section 2.2].

(52)   REVISED EXTRACTION CONSTRAINT   [Diesing (1992): 128]

>   Extraction cannot take place out of an NP that must raise out of VP
>   before tree splitting.

3.2.2 Problems for NP split

Fanselow (1988) brings empirical supporting evidence for why a
transformational account of split topics à la van Riemsdijk cannot be on the
right track. I repeat some of his arguments here.

First, it is not always possible to regard the remnant as a determiner of
a D-structural NP for the simple reason that it never belongs to this
category. In other words, (53b) is illformed because *welche* is a full-fledged
NP and it can never serve as a determiner. Hence, it cannot serve as the D-
structure of (53a).

(53)   a.   Katzen   hat   jedes Kind   welche   gesehen.

>   Cats   has   every child   some   seen

>   "As for cats every child saw some."

>   b.   * Jedes Kind hat [NP *welche Katzen*] gesehen.

Secondly, (54) and (55) illustrate further cases taken from Fanselow (1993)
where both the topicalized constituents and the "remnants" are full NPs.

(54) *Einen neuen Wagen* kann ich   mir   leider

a.ACC new car   can   I.NOM I.DAT unfortunately

    keinen leisten.

    no.ACC afford

"As for a new car, I unfortunately cannot afford one."

(55) *Raubvögel*   glaube ich kennt Gereon nur   *Bussarde.*

birds.of.prey think   I   knows Gereon only bussards.

"As for birds of prey, I think Gereon knows only bussards."

Apart from these empirical problems for van Riemsdijk's approach, I believe that there are also empirical problems for Diesing's REVISED EXTRACTION CONSTRAINT which is based on this approach. We do find sentences containing a "strong" NP from which a part has been extracted.

(56) Von den Hunden$_i$ hat Johann einen t$_i$ [$_{VP}$ nicht gesehen]

of the dogs   has J.   one.ACC   not seen

"Of the dogs, there is one that John didn't see."

(57) Von den Äpfeln$_i$ hat Karl   die kleinsten t$_i$ [$_{VP}$ den Pferden gegeben]

of the apples   has K.   the.ACC smallest   the.DAT horses given

"Of the apples, Karl gave the horses the smallest ones."

These sentences are fully well-formed although they clearly violate the above REVISED EXTRACTION CONSTRAINT. Obviously, this constraint cannot be the final explanation for why split topics have a "weak" interpretation only.

3.2.3 Split topics as V split

Fanselow (1988) proposes (58) as the syntactic representation of (47).

(58) [$_{NP}$ Katzen]$_i$ hat jedes Kind [$_{NP}$ fünf *pro*$_i$] [$_V$ [$_{NP}$ t$_i$] gesehen]

The idea behind his analysis is that the topicalized constituent is nonreferential and therefore it is not a "real" Object argument of the verb *to see*. It is syntactically licensed through the fact that it is coindexed with a property denoting *pro* that is the head of the verb's "real" Object argument. Obviously, Fanselow builds this coindexation trick into the representation of split topics to save the THETA CRITERION [see (7)]. With Fanselow, I argue that split topics are the result of splitting a V. A crucial part in which my proposal departs from Fanselow's is that the topic NP is generated in the "Mittelfeld" independently from other "Mittelfeld" material. I take (59) as the underlying VP structure of a German split Object. Note that this is very similar to the West Greenlandic noun incorporating V-projection in (33c) presented in section 2.2.2 and repeated here for the sake of comparison.

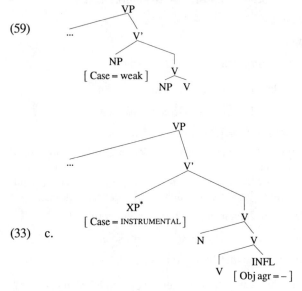

(59)

(33) c.

Whereas (33c) is the noun incorporating skeleton capturing the basic structure of West Greenlandic noun incorporating configurations, (59) is the NP incorporating skeleton that captures the basic structure of German split Objects. A direct consequence of my proposal is that split objects are not split NPs but rather split Vs. The S-structure of our example (47) now looks as follows:

(60)   [NP Katzen]ᵢ hat jedes Kind [V' [NP fünf] [V [NP tᵢ] gesehen]]

Sceptical minds may raise the question of why (60) cannot be realized at S-structure, that is, they may ask why the ungrammatical structure under (53b) could not be assigned the following well-formed S-structure?

(61)   jedes Kind hat [V' [NP welche] [V [NP Katzen] [V gesehen]]]

Here is my answer. Unlike nouns in West Greenlandic, the NP that is adjacent to the verb in (59) cannot remain in this Case-less position because the CASE FILTER [see fn. 13] requires that every NP has to be assigned Case. According to (59), weak Case is assigned to the constituent *welche*. To receive Case, the incorporated NP *Katzen* necessarily moves at S-structure into the topic position yielding the grammatical sentence (53a). Note that my proposal to analyze split topics as the split of a complex verb also covers the case of VP topicalization. A case is point is (62).

(62) Katzen gesehen hat   jedes Kind   welche.

      cats   seen   has   every child some

From the tree skeleton under (59) it follows that the topicalized *Katzen gesehen* ("cats seen") builds a verbal constituent at D-structure, a prediction which is clearly absent in the NP split proposal of van Riemsdijk (1987).

(63) [$_V$ Katzen gesehen]$_i$ hat jedes Kind [$_{V'}$ [$_{NP}$ welche] [$_V$ t$_i$]]

What does the analysis of split topicalization as V split predict with respect to the semantic peculiarities of split topics? We know that these configurations lack wide and partitive readings. Again, our example (47) will serve as a case in point.

(47) Katzen hat   jedes Kind   fünf gesehen.

      cats   has   every child five seen

      NARROW "As for cats, every child saw five such animals."

      WIDE   # "There are five cats such that every child saw them."

      PART   # "Of the cats, every child saw five."

The narrow reading is the result of semantic incorporation. Like the incorporated noun and its modifiers in (33c) the nominal material in V' in (59) gets a predicative interpretation. Hence, (47) does not have a wide reading. (47) lacks a partitive reading because the split material is not an overt partitive construction. Hence, there is no trigger for creating the membership relation.

Finally, from our perspective that split topicalization applies to verbs we can give a very straightforward answer to the question of why strong Case NPs never split: the head of a German NP is simply never topicalized.

(64) a. Lisa hat   im   Keller   einige   schwarze   Spinnen

          L.   has   in.the cellar   some   black   spiders

          nicht gesehen.

          not   seen

      "There are some black spiders that Lisa didn't see in the cellar."

      b. * Schwarze Spinnen hat Lisa im Keller einige nicht gesehen.

Aren't the examples (56) and (57) that were called problematic for Diesing's REVISED EXTRACTION CONSTRAINT problematic for my approach as well? No, they aren't. Unlike Diesing, I do not define the constraint on split topicalization as a constraint on extraction. From the perspective that the topicalized PPs are adjoined to the head NP of the respective partitive phrases [Hoeksema (1983b)], they can be topicalized like any other full-fledged phrase can. This perspective is illustrated in the following more detailed bracketings of these examples.

(65)   Von den Hunden$_i$ hat J. [$_{NP}$ [$_{NP}$ einen e][$_{PP}$ t$_i$]] [$_{VP}$ nicht gesehen]

(66)   Von den Äpfeln$_i$ hat K. [$_{NP}$ [$_{NP}$ die kleinsten e][$_{PP}$ t$_i$]] [$_{VP}$ den Pferden gegeben]

3.3 Summary

In this third and final section, I have considered some syntactic aspects of those configurations that I called the semantic counterparts of West Greenlandic noun incorporating configurations. Given that the German bare plural in Object position meets the adjacency requirement, we can conclude that this bare plural — like other adjacent phrases in German — bears weak Case. Moreover, the split topic construction in German is assigned nearly the same underlying VP structure as the noun incorporating configuration in West Greenlandic. The main difference is that in German not nouns, but NPs fill the Case-less position. To meet the CASE FILTER, these NPs have to move at S-structure.

4 Chapter summary

In this chapter, I first discussed the lexicalist and the transformational approach to noun incorporation and the (semantic) problems raised by these approaches. I then proposed to analyze the structure of West Greenlandic noun incorporating configurations as syntactically base generated constructions. In this vein, I argued that in addition to weak and strong Case Object constituents, the grammar of West Greenlandic distinguishes incorporated nouns as independent syntactic Object constituents. It follows that in the interpretation of Object constituents we have to consider not only weak and strong Case but Case-less incorporated nouns as well. Finally, I argued that split topicalization in German is a matter of V split rather than of NP split.

In the next chapter, I give a detailed analysis of the semantics of West Greenlandic incorporated nouns and West Germanic weak Case constituents, which is based on the syntactic insights gained in this chapter. It will become clear why I stressed the need for the syntactic visibility of incorporated nouns.

5

Semantic Incorporation

0 Introduction

This chapter investigates how the meaning aspects of a West Greenlandic incorporated noun and its semantic counterparts can be dealt with in a theory of indefinite descriptions. As such, it presents my answer to the question of why some indefinites do not reach a non-narrow scope reading. Narrow indefinites usually introduce a predicate only. This predicate is absorbed or *semantically incorporated* by a verb as the restriction of the verb's internal argument. Semantic incorporation embodies Carlson's (1977) idea that verbal predicates are responsible for the existential interpretation of the English bare plural. In other words, a West Greenlandic incorporated noun and its semantic counterparts receive their existential interpretation from a verbal incorporator.

Chapter 5 contains seven sections. In the first section, I present semantic incorporation as a way of dealing with narrow scope indefinites. I compare my proposal with Carlson's theory of the English bare plural. In section 2, I elaborate a compositional semantic analysis of West Greenlandic incorporated nouns. I furthermore discuss how semantic incorporation deals with modifiers of these incorporated indefinites, and which role is played by the view that noun incorporating configurations in West Greenlandic are syntactically base generated [see chapter 4]. In the third section, I present the West Greenlandic noun incorporating affix *-qar-* ("to have", "there is/are") as a typical semantically incorporating verb. From this section onwards, I relate the discussion of the West Greenlandic data to that of its semantic counterparts in West Germanic languages. Section 4 is about the narrow scope effects arising with a predicative indefinite. In section 5, I discuss how intensional verbs fit into the semantic incorporation picture. In section 6, I contrast my proposal with another account of the semantics of West Greenlandic incorporated nouns, namely Bittner's (1994) predicate modifier view. Finally, section 7 is about the discourse transparency of predicative indefinites. It concludes with an answer to the question of which words are anaphoric islands.

1 The semantic incorporation of predicative indefinites

1.1 The proposal

My proposal contains two basic claims. First, a narrow indefinite denotes a *predicate* only. Secondly, this predicate is absorbed by a verb as the predicate of that verb's internal argument's variable. This absorption is what I call "semantic incorporation."[1] Using an extensional language like Gallin's (1975) Ty2, the lexical meaning of an incorporating verb can be represented as in (1). For the sake of transparency, I add the semantic types as indices on the respective λ-abstracted variables.

(1) $\lambda P_{<s,<e,t>>} \lambda w_s \lambda x_e \exists y [\text{Verb}_w(x,y) \wedge P_w(y)]$

Note that the number of the internal argument is not determined: the value of the variable y can be an atomic object or a nonatomic one. Below, we will see that the absorption of additional predicates that are marked for number, determines this value.

One important aspect about (1) is that the existential interpretation of a predicative indefinite is contributed by the verb.[2] From this it follows that the narrow scope effects of a predicative indefinite are explained in the way in which Carlson (1977) explained the narrow scope effects of the English bare plural [see section 4 below]. Moreover, (1) can be contrasted with a nonincorporating extensional verb whose lexical semantics is that of an ordinary n-place predicate [see (2)], or with an intensional verb that, following Zimmermann (1993), I regard as a relation between an individual and a property [see (3)].

(2) $\lambda w_s \lambda y_e \lambda x_e [\text{Verb}_w (x, y)]$

(3) $\lambda P_{<s,<e,t>>} \lambda w_s \lambda x_e [\text{Verb}_w (x, \lambda w' P_{w'})]$

Another important aspect about (1) is that semantically incorporated indefinites are interpreted as nominal expressions that do not have quantificational force of their own. Although this idea is clearly reminiscent of the Kamp-Heim treatment of indefinites as nonquantificational expressions, the main difference between a Kamp-Heim indefinite and an

---

[1] Independently, McNally (1995) presents an analysis for the Spanish bare plural that is similar to my proposal. My proposal is more radical than McNally's in that I regard every narrow indefinite as a property denoting expression and, moreover, that I regard the predicative meaning as the default interpretation of an indefinite [see chapter 6].

[2] Dowty (1981) uses the mechanism of lexicalized existential interpretation to account for the inherent narrow scope of a missing Object, as in (i).

(i)   John didn't eat.
    i.   "It is not the case that John ate something."
    ii. # "There is something that John didn't eat."

Unlike my proposal, Dowty does not regard lexicalized existential interpretation as *the* mechanism to treat narrow indefinite Objects.

incorporated indefinite is that the latter does not introduce a novel variable but only a predicate. The variable of which this predicate holds comes with the verb that absorbs the predicate. The novel idea behind semantic incorporation is that a verb is regarded as a quantificational source of an indefinite description. In DRT terms: the verb introduces the "novel" discourse referent occupying its internal argument position.

In the present proposal, the verb clearly plays a crucial role. Most transitive verbal concepts can combine with semantically distinct Object NPs. Consider the verb *to eat*.

(4)   a.   Tim ate apples.

       b.   Tim ate every apple.

If it combines with a bare plural, as in (4a), — or with some other predicative indefinite — it receives the interpretation of a semantically incorporating verb [see (1)]. If it combines with a quantificational NP, as in (4b), it is interpreted as a two-place relation [see (2)]. From a technical perspective, this means that depending on the semantic type of its complement a verbal concept receives different lexical meaning representations. Following Dowty (1981), one could say that the incorporating version of a verb and its nonincorporating counterpart are linked by means of a lexical redundancy rule.[3] A good argument for the view that the link between the semantically incorporating version of a verb and its nonincorporating counterpart is located in the lexicon is that some verbs are strictly semantically incorporating and other verbs are strictly nonincorporating. A typical example of the latter case are individual-level predicates. (5) and (6) illustrate that they never take a property denoting expression as its argument.

(5)   ?? Parts to this machine are quite common.   [Carlson (1977): 318]

(6)   ?? Dogs that are sitting here are rare.

---

[3] As I said in the previous footnote, Dowty (1981) discusses the inherent narrowness of missing Objects. For Dowty, intransitivized *to eat* in (i) is linked to transitive *to eat* in (ii) by means of a lexical rule. Such a rule explains "how the meaning of a verb in one "subcategorization frame" is related to its meaning as it appears in a different frame [Dowty (1981): 80]."

(i)   John didn't eat.
(ii)   John didn't eat an/the/every apple.

In Dowty's approach, a semantically intransitivized verb is only used when no Object is present, as in (i). In all other cases, the semantically nonintransitivized version of a verb is used regardless of whether it is combined with an indefinite, a definite or a quantifier, as in (ii). In my approach, the semantically incorporating or intransitivized version of a verb becomes active whenever the Object is missing and, most importantly, when the Object denotes a property. When the latter denotes a quantifier or a free variable expression, its nonincorporating version is activated.

Typical examples of the former case are those that can only take a property as their argument. The existential predicate is an example par excellence [McNally (1992)], and others will be discussed at length in this chapter. Still, as we proceed, we will see that there are also reasons to believe that not all links between the semantically incorporating and nonincorporating versions of a verb can be lexicalized.

1.2 Semantic incorporation vs. Carlson (1977)

Apart from the idea that the existential interpretation of a predicative indefinite is lexicalized as a part of the lexical semantics of its verbal head, my proposal differs from Carlson's theory of the English bare plural in two important respects. For one, I do not adopt Carlson's view that in a nongeneric context the English bare plural denotes a kind individual. Rather, the bare plural — like any other semantically incorporated expression — denotes a property. For another, the idea that the existential interpretation of a predicative indefinite is contributed by a verb must be integrated into a "dynamic" semantic theory of indefinites.

1.2.1 Properties vs. kinds

Semantic incorporation is not intended to be a theory of the English bare plural only. Rather, it encompasses a uniform treatment of the class of narrow indefinite descriptions, to which West Germanic bare plurals as well as West Greenlandic incorporated nouns belong. Carlson's view that a bare plural names a kind and that the existential interpretation of a kind-naming expression comes from the stage-level predicate of which it is an argument, cannot be generalized towards a theory of narrow scope indefinites. For instance, many examples given in chapter 2 showed that it is possible to modify West Greenlandic incorporated nouns and German topicalized bare plurals.

(7)   Juuna   Kaali-mit   marlun-nik   allagar-si-nngi-l-a-q. [Bittner (1994): 72]

        J.ABS   K.-ABL   two-INST.PL   letter-get-NEG-IND-[-tr]-3SG

        "It is not the case that Juuna got two letters from Kaali."

(8)   Briefe   hat   Julius   nicht   mal   zwei   gekriegt.

        letters   has   J.   not   even   two   got

        "As for letters, Julius didn't get even two."

To capture the narrowness of the discontinuous numeral–noun constituents in (7) and in (8) in a Carlsonian approach, we would have to allow for individuals in our model that are of the kind "two letters." Undoubtedly, such a requirement sounds rather counterintuitive.

An important aspect in which my proposal differs from Carlson's is that I take an existential bare plural — like any other narrowest indefinite —

to denote a property rather than a kind individual. In my theory of semantic incorporation, there is room for the discontinuous indefinites in (7) and (8). The intuitive idea behind semantic incorporation is that it is possible to predicate something of a bound variable, that is, of the internal argument of an incorporating verb [see (1)]. The presence of the external modifiers in (7) and (8) shows that it is possible to predicate more than one thing of this bound variable.

Also our discussion of some data from Krifka et al. (1995) in chapter 3 illustrated that the English bare plural can not always name a kind. We saw that if one sticks to Carlson's view that the bare plural always names a kind, it remains unexplained why (9) is out and (10) is good.

(9)   * There is the horse stampeding through the gate.

(10)   There are horses stampeding through the gate.

Krifka et al. also point out that it is preferable to have *one* explanation for why (10) and (11) are good rather than two explanations, as in Carlson (1977).

(11)   There is a horse stampeding through the gate.

In section 3 below, I present the existential construction as a typical case of semantic incorporation: the existential predicate can only combine with property denoting expressions [McNally (1992)]. What the bare plural in (10) and the singular indefinite in (11) have in common is the fact that they are predicative indefinites absorbed by the existential predicate.

My proposal should not be understood in such a way that a bare plural and other narrowest existentials have the same semantic features in every respect. As observed by Carlson, only the bare plural can be used as the internal argument of an achievement verb combined with a *for*-adverbial.

(12)   Max killed rabbits for three hours.   [Carlson (177): 29]

(13)   * Max killed a rabbit for three hours.

(14)   * Max killed several rabbits for three hours.

My proposal only says that the bare plurals and other narrowest existentials receive their existential interpretation from the same semantic source, which is the verb. The *for*-adverbial comes with the additional requirement that the number of the internal argument of the verb in the adverbial's scope remains unspecified. In English, only bare plurals (and mass nouns) can meet this requirement and, therefore, (13) and (14) are ungrammatical. According to Krifka (1992), this requirement is a consequence of the more general requirement that the predicate which the *for*-adverbial applies to is atelic/cumulative.[4]

---

[4] See Zucchi and White (1996) for a discussion of some problems with Krifka's approach.

Finally, I return to the bare plurals of the parts-of-that-machine kind shortly discussed at the end of chapter 3. Carlson (1977) pointed out that these bare plurals do not fit into his nonambiguity hypothesis because they never denote a kind. I repeat his examples.

(15)   parts of that machine   [Carlson (1977): 316]

(16)   people in the next room

(17)   books that John lost yesterday

In existential contexts, the scope behaviour of nonkind bare plurals patterns with that of other bare plurals, as illustrated in another set of Carlson's examples.

(18)   Parts of that airplane were everywhere.   [Carlson (1977): 318]

(19)   Max discovered pieces of that puzzle for three hours.

(20)   Fred repeatedly destroyed books that I lost yesterday.

If we agree that inherent narrow scope can at best be explained in terms of a Carlsonian lexicalized existential quantifier, an obvious solution to the problem is to say that all bare plural existentials denote properties rather than kinds. Thus, non-kind denoting bare plurals do not present an obstacle for the semantic incorporation approach.

1.2.2 Dynamic vs. static

According to Krifka et al. (1995), the lexicalization of the existential interpretation of the English bare plural blocks an adequate representation of a sentence in which this bare plural antecedes a definite pronoun [see chapter 3, section 4.2.2]. I rejected this objection, saying that it is not the lexicalization of the existential quantifier binding the stages of a kind named by a bare plural which blocks an adequate representation of the discourse transparency of that bare plural, but rather the fact that Carlson's lexicalized quantifier is a *static* existential quantifier. If we give this quantifier a *dynamic* interpretation, Krifka et al.'s problem could be solved.[5] This "dynamization" of a lexicalized existential quantifier is another novelty contained in the present proposal. It follows that the verb takes over the task of introducing a discourse referent. In other words, a semantically incorporating verb underlies Heim's (1982) NOVELTY CONDITION [see chapter 3, section 1.2].

The idea that the existential interpretation of an indefinite description introduced by an incorporating verb is "dynamic" can be realized within two

---

[5] Krifka et al.'s problem could be solved for those cases in which the bare plural is not in the scope of some operator. For those cases in which the bare plural is embedded, we need the sort of anaphora resolution proposed by Kamp and Reyle (1993), i.e., the abstraction method which is reminiscent of the E-type strategy in the resolution of syntactically unbound anaphora.

different approaches to discourse semantics. One is dynamic semantics in the line of dynamic Montague grammar [Groenendijk and Stokhof (1990)]. Taking this route would keep us close to the compositional framework of Montague grammar within which Carlson (1977) presented his theory of the English bare plural. What is also interesting is that with the integration of semantic incorporation into this framework, we can abandon the view that indefinites are always existential quantifiers. This means that even in a strictly compositional framework, it becomes possible to represent indefinites as expressions that receive their existential interpretation from an external source.

The other kind of discourse semantic framework into which we can integrate semantic incorporation is a representational one such as DRT-93 [Kamp and Reyle (1993)]. I believe that taking this route is justified for the following reasons. First, I mentioned in chapter 3 that DRT-93 does not have an account for why particular indefinites receive narrow interpretations only. Building semantic incorporation into DRT means that we build a narrow scope account into this kind of framework. Secondly, I show in chapter 6 that for the proper treatment of free variable indefinites as well as for the projection of presuppositions, we need a representational framework.

1.2.3 Generic readings of bare plurals

Semantic incorporation covers the existential interpretations of bare plurals. Unlike Carlson's theory, semantic incorporation does not present a uniform theory of the English bare plural. To make the picture of bare plurals more complete, I adopt Carlson's view that in a generic context a bare plural denotes a kind. The most straightforward case is the one in which a bare plural is the Subject of an individual-level predicate, as illustrated in (21).

(21)   Cats are intelligent.

To be intelligent is a predicate that holds of an individual, in our case of an individual kind. This is represented as follows:

(22)   intelligent(cat)

An apparently less straightforward case is (23), an example taken from McNally and Van Geenhoven (1997), with a bare plural as the Subject of a conditional's antecedent.

(23)   If rivers are wide, they are likely to be deep.

In chapter 3, I briefly mentioned Heim's suggestion that if we treat an indefinite as a variable introducer, this variable can be unselectively bound by a silent generic operator. The meaning of (24) with a singular indefinite is then represented as under (25). It says that if something is a river and it is also wide it is likely to be deep.

(24)   If a river is wide, it is likely to be deep.

(25) GEN_x [river(x) $\wedge$ wide(x)] [likely-to-be-deep(x)]

It has been argued that the bare plurals in (21) and (23) behave like indefinites in that they also introduce a free variable which is bound by a generic operator [Krifka et al. (1995)]. However, (23) means that if it is a general characteristic of rivers that they are wide, then it is a general characteristic of rivers that they are deep. Hence, (25) is not an appropriate representation of (23)'s meaning. In other words, like *cats* in (21) *rivers* in (23) denotes a kind.

Also in the following example borrowed from Van Geenhoven and McNally (1997) the bare plural denotes a kind and does not introduce a variable.

(26)   Well-trained dogs always sit quietly.

(26) entails that if some relevant numer of well-trained dogs sit, they sit quietly. It is this entailment which give rise to the impression that we are quantifying over objects. We suggest that *always* quantifies over situations: all sittings with well-trained dogs are quiet sittings.[6]

(27) ALWAYS_s [sit(s,well-trained dog)] [quietly(s)]

In sum, I do not adopt Heim's view when it comes to generic readings of bare plurals. Even though what I have presented here is not a complete picture of indefinites in generic contexts, this book does not attempt to further elaborate this issue and focuses on existential readings of indefinites.

1.3 Logical Form and its interpretation

Although the dynamization of semantic incorporation improves our understanding of the discourse semantic properties of West Greenlandic incorporated nouns and of other predicative indefinites, this issue will remain in the background until section 7. Before I discuss the discourse-level properties, I first want to convince the reader that semantic incorporation explains the sentence-level semantic pecularities of West Greenlandic incorporated nouns and their semantic counterparts. To reach this goal, I assume that Logical Form [LF] is the syntactic level that delivers the input relevant for the semantic interpretation. The S-structure of a sentence delivers its default LF.

Each LF node bears its semantic translation. This translation is an ordered pair $<\varepsilon,\sigma>$ consisting of an expression ε of an interpreted formal language and a possibly empty store of variables σ.[7] Following Bittner

---

[6] Note that I have represented the bare plural *well-trained dogs* in (27) as a kind even though it clearly does not name a natural kind. I assume that there is a partial map from the domain of properties to the domain of kinds and that the latter domain contains both natural and context-dependent kinds.

(1994), the semantic type of a syntactic trace is locally determined. In this chapter, I only deal with traces occurring in a syntactic argument position. Their interpretation is captured in the following rule:

TRACE RULE

Let $[e]_i$ be an empty node indexed i, let α be a node translated as $<\varepsilon,\sigma>$ and τ and ρ be types, and let: $[e]_i$ is in an arg-position and sister to α, and type(ε) = $<\tau,\rho>$ hold,

then $[e]_i$ is translated as $<v_{i,\tau}, \{v_{i,\tau}\}>$.

This rule says that a trace is translated as a variable, which can serve as the argument of the trace's sister. The translation rule for the lexical items, the translation of those nodes that have one daughter only, and functional application are defined in the following three rules.

LEXICAL ITEM RULE

If α is a lexical item of category κ and α translates as α',

then $[_\kappa \alpha]$ translates as α'.

TRANSFER RULE

Let α be the only daughter of β with some translation, and let α translate as α',

then β translates as α'.

FUNCTION APPLICATION RULE

Let α and β be daughters of γ, α translates as α', β translates as β', and $<\alpha',\beta'> \in \text{Dom}(f)$,

then γ translates as $f(\alpha',\beta')$.

The TRANSFER RULE takes care of the semantic type transfer from a single daugther to its mother node. The function f referred to in the FUNCTIONAL APPLICATION RULE is defined in the following way.

f, the default operation, is a function such that

(i) $\text{Dom}(f) = \{<<\varepsilon,\sigma>,<\varepsilon',\sigma'>>: \text{ME} \cap \{\varepsilon'(\varepsilon), \varepsilon(\varepsilon'), \varepsilon'(\lambda w\ \varepsilon_w), \varepsilon(\lambda w\ \varepsilon'_w)\} \neq \varnothing\}$

(ii) for any $<<\varepsilon,\sigma>,<\varepsilon',\sigma'>> \in \text{Dom}(f)$, $f(<\varepsilon,\sigma>,<\varepsilon',\sigma'>) = <\varepsilon'', \sigma \cup \sigma'>$, where $\varepsilon'' \in \text{ME} \cap \{\varepsilon'(\varepsilon), \varepsilon(\varepsilon'), \varepsilon'(\lambda w\ \varepsilon_w), \varepsilon(\lambda w\ \varepsilon'_w)\}$

where ME is the set of meaningful expressions.

---

[7] I adopt this mode of representation from Bittner (1994). In Bittner's system, the formal language is ILP, an intensional logic with plurals [Montague (1974), Link (1983)].

If function application cannot apply, a type-adjusting rule can derive a secondary translation of some expression.

TYPE-ADJUSTING RULE

Let α be a sister of β, α translates as α', β translates as β', $<\alpha',\beta'>$ $\notin$ Dom(f), and let ω be a type-lifting operator such that $<\alpha', \omega>$ $\in$ Dom(f),

then α translates as $f(\alpha', \omega)$.

I assume that the following type-lifting operators apply.

TL-1

from $P_{<s,<e,t>>}$ to $\lambda M_{<<s,<e,t>>,<s,<e,t>>>}$ [M(P)]

TL-2

from $M_{<<s,<e,t>>,<s,<e,t>>>}$

to $\lambda F_{<<s,<e,t>>,<s,<e,t>>>}$ $\lambda P_{<s,<e,t>>}$ [M](F(P))

and

from $M_{<<s,<e,<e,t>>>,<s,<e,t>>>}$

to $\lambda F_{<<s,<e,t>>,<s,<e,<e,t>>>>}$ $\lambda P_{<s,<e,t>>}$ [M](F(P))

TL-3

from $P_{<s,<e,t>>}$ to $\lambda Q_{<s,<e,t>>}\lambda w_s \lambda x_e$ [$P_w(x) \wedge Q_w(x)$]

TL-4

from $P_{<s,<e,t>>}$ to $\lambda Q_{<s,<e,t>>}\lambda w_s$ [$P_w(x) \wedge Q_w(x)$]

TL-5

from $R_{<s,<e,<e,t>>>}$

to $\lambda Q_{<s,<e,t>>} \lambda w_s \lambda x_e$ [$R_w(x) \wedge Q_w(x)$]

TL-1 is an instance of Montague raising and TL-2 is known as the Geach rule. TL-3 is in charge of modifier creation. The predicates it applies to become restrictions of a "novel" variable. TL-4 applies to predicates that become appositive, i.e., they become predicates of a free variable [e.g. proper names]. TL-5 is like TL-3, the difference being that it applies to relational predicates. Note that I restrict the type-driven system in such a way that I assume that those expressions that are functors remain functors, and that those that are arguments remain arguments. The relevance of this restriction will become clear below.

I assume with Bittner (1994) that in addition to type-adjusting by means of a type-lifting operator, the system also allows type-adjusting by means of λ-binding. The following rule then applies to those expressions whose LF translation <ε,σ> contains a stored variable.

TYPE-ADJUSTING RULE "BITTNER"

Let α be translated as <ε,σ>, let α or a sister of α have the index i, and let u_i be a stored variable,

then α is translated as <λu_i[ε], σ - {u_i}>.

Finally, Bittner's STORE FILTER makes sure that the stored variables are bound at some point in LF.

STORE FILTER

The root node has a translation <ε,σ>, where σ = ∅.

In sum, to show the reader what semantic incorporation is about, I adopt a classical approach, that is, a type-driven system based on the ideas of the work of Montague (1974), Partee and Rooth (1983) and Klein and Sag (1985), and enriched with two new perspectives of Bittner (1994).

2 West Greenlandic incorporated nouns are semantically incorporated

In light of the West Greenlandic noun incorporating configurations discussed in chapter 2, I first relate my proposal of semantic incorporation to the simplest among these configurations, namely the one in which no external constituent modifies the incorporated noun. Then I show how my approach extends to cases with an incorporated *wh*-word and to those with external INSTRUMENTAL modifiers.

2.1 The simple case

Let us start with a simple example.

(28)   Arnajaraq *iipili*-tur-p-u-q.   [fw]

A.ABS   apple-ate-IND-[-tr]-3SG

"Arnajaraq ate an apple/apples."

Given what we said in chapter 4 about the syntax of noun incorporation, I take (29) to be the syntactic analysis of this sentence.

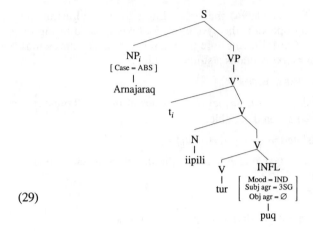

(29)

I represent the inflectional morphology as feature information on an INFL-node, and thereby regard inflectional information as syntactic information. Below, I largely ignore the contribution of inflectional information to the construction of (28)'s LF. Following Bittner (1994), the Subject leaves the VP to receive Case. What is more important in the present context, is that I regard a West Greenlandic noun incorporating construction as a syntactically base generated configuration, that is, the incorporated noun is visible in the syntactic tree.

(30) is the LF of (28) in which each node bears its semantic translation <ε,σ>. In this LF and the ones that follow, I do not consider the trace of the Subject NP.

(30)

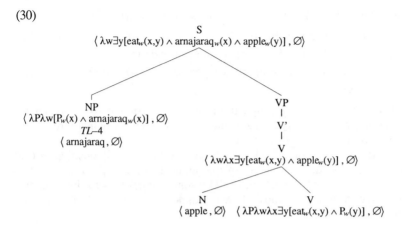

The semantic translation of the verbal node shows that the verb is the semantic head, that is, the functor of a noun incorporating configuration. Regardless of the fact that its internal argument's variable is existentially bound, the verb leaves a slot for a predication over this variable. Note that the number of the internal argument's variable y remains unspecified. This captures the fact that the incorporated noun in (28) can either mean "an apple" or "apples." Later we will see when this variable y can be restricted as atomic or nonatomic. Finally, I treat names as the predicate of a free variable at LF, and I adopt van der Sandt's (1992) view that these variables find their binder either through direct anaphoric linking to their antecedent, or through accommodation [see chapter 6]. Accommodation transforms LFs like (30) into interpretable semantic representations.

2.2 An incorporated *wh*-word

The following example presents the interesting case in which the *wh*-affix *su-* ("what") is incorporated.

(31) Nuka *su*-tur-p-a?   [fw]

   N.ABS   what-drink/eat-INTER-[-tr]-3SG

   "What did Nuka drink/eat?"

The person asking the question in (31) wants to know a property of the object Nuka consumed. That is, he wants to figure out the predicate that holds of the internal argument's variable introduced by the incorporating verb *-tur-* ("to consume"). Following Karttunen's (1977) view that the meaning of a question is the set of its true answers, the meaning of (31) is represented in the following way.

(32) $\lambda p \; \exists P \; [\; p(@) \wedge p = \lambda w \; \exists y \; (\; eat_w(x,y) \; \& \; nuka_w(x) \wedge P_w(y) \;) \;]$

where p is a variable ranging over propositions (type $<s,t>$), w is a variable ranging over possible worlds (type s), P is a variable ranging over properties (type $<s,<e,t>>$) and @ is the actual world.

(32) denotes the set of propositions which are of the form "Nuka ate something with property P" for some property P, and which are true in the actual world.

The next question is how the LF representing the composition of (32) is derived from the S-structure of the noun incorporating construction of (31)? To answer this question, I follow some suggestions for interrogative LFs sketched in von Stechow (1993). Suppose we have the following base generated S-structure of (31).

(33)

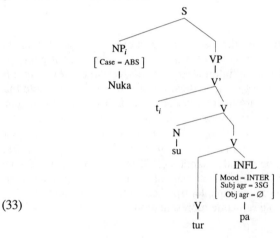

I assume that the interrogative morphology in the INFL-node indicates that we adjoin an abstract question operator to S at LF.[8] Moreover, to obtain the LF representing (32) as the meaning of (31), we have to raise the incorporated *wh*-morpheme. Our decision to regard an incorporated nominal as an independent *syntactic* constituent becomes highly relevant. Being a syntactic constituent, nothing prevents us from raising this noun at LF.[9]

---

[8] It is also possible to think of an INTER-node at S-structure which licenses the interrogative morphology on the verb, like it is possible to think of an abstract NEG-node licensing negative elements.

Note that in the LF below, the trace of the incorporated *su*- ("what") is interpreted as a property variable [see TRACE RULE].

(34)

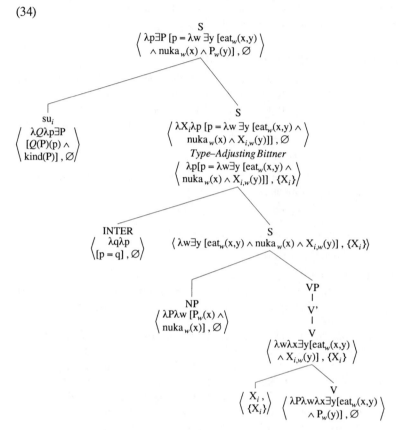

The semantic analysis I present for the West Greenlandic morpheme *su*- is essentially the same analysis presented for English *what* in Heim (1987).[10]

---

[9] N-RAISING at LF is also needed for other purposes. For instance, von Stechow (1993) argues that we need it for the interpretation of nonconstituent coordination.

Furthermore, I adopt the following suggestion of Beck (p.c.) who attributes it to Heim. The *wh*-element *su-* ("what") applies to an expression of type $<<s,<e,t>>,<<s,t>,t>>$. This guarantees that at the root node the propositional variable p is properly bound.

2.3 When incorporated nouns are modified

In chapter 2, I gave many examples illustrating the possibility of modifying West Greenlandic incorporated nouns by means of an adjective, a numeral, a *wh*-modifier or a relative clause. Here, I show how these modified incorporated nouns can be regarded as semantically incorporated predicates.[11]

2.3.1 Adjectives

I start with an example illustrating the possibility of modifying an incorporated noun by means of an adjective.

(35) Esta   *nutaa-mik*   *aalisagar*-si-v-u-q.   [fw]

  E.ABS   fresh-INST.SG   fish-buy-IND-[-tr]-3SG

  "Ester bought fresh fish."

The adjectival modifier *nutaamik* ("fresh, new") of the incorporated noun *aalisagar* ("fish") bears the INSTRUMENTAL case and it is exactly this Case information that will serve as an important clue in the construction of (35)'s LF.

The apparent problem that arises in the construction of a semantic representation of a "discontinuous" nominal expression such as *nutaamik ... aalisigar-* ("fresh fish") is to figure out whether, and at which point, its parts have to be brought together. Since they are both predicates of one and the same variable, that is, of the internal argument's variable of the incorporating affixal verb *-si-* ("to buy, to get"), it seems as if we must regard them as a unit at some syntactic level. In chapter 4, we saw that Baker (1988) argues that a modifier of an incorporated noun and the incorporated noun constitute a syntactic unit at D-structure and that the incorporation of the noun into the verb is the result of a Head-Movement transformation. However, I showed that this phrasal mirror is too weak to

---

[10] Heim furthermore argues that *what* is the interrogative counterpart of *such*. I do not agree with her on this point because the meaning of *what* lacks a presuppositional component (i.e., the contextual presence of a kind or property) which is an essential part of the meaning of *such*. In section 2.3.4 below, I suggest that the interrogative counterpart of *such* is the kind-partitive interpretation of *which*.

[11] In chapter 2, I related these discontinuous nominal configurations in West Greenlandic to another discontinuous configuration, namely, Object split in German arguing that there are good semantic reasons to believe that this correlation makes sense. In section 4.4 below, I return to this German configuration.

capture the semantic fact that an INSTRUMENTAL modifier of an incorporated noun and the incorporated noun are predicates of one and the same variable. The syntactic phrasalization of an incorporated noun alone cannot account for the semantic peculiarities that are inherently related to a noun incorporating configuration. I then suggested that a syntactic distinction between incorporated, weak Case and strong Case Object constituents helps us to determine which of these can receive which interpretation. It was said that in West Greenlandic incorporated nouns and weak Case Objects are uniformly interpreted as predicative indefinites. In other words, if we exploit the fact that a West Greenlandic noun incorporating configuration is a word-level syntactic construct together with the fact that external modifiers in such a configuration appear in the INSTRUMENTAL (= weak) case, there is no semantic need to regard an incorporated noun and the INSTRUMENTAL modifier(s) as one syntactic unit. Let me illustrate how I proceed.

I assume that the syntactic representation of (35) is (36):

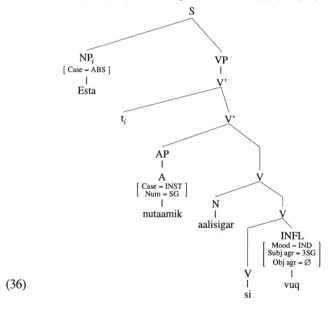

(36)

Ignoring the inflection information, we start building up the LF of this structure. First, the noun "fish" is semantically incorporated by the verb "to buy."

(37)

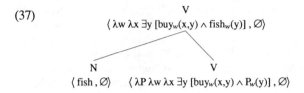

$$V$$
$$\langle \lambda w\, \lambda x\, \exists y\ [\mathrm{buy}_w(x,y) \wedge \mathrm{fish}_w(y)]\ ,\ \varnothing \rangle$$

$$N \qquad\qquad V$$
$$\langle\, \mathrm{fish}\, ,\, \varnothing \rangle \qquad \langle\, \lambda P\, \lambda w\, \lambda x\, \exists y\ [\mathrm{buy}_w(x,y) \wedge P_w(y)]\ ,\ \varnothing \rangle$$

Next, we arrive at the external modifier "fresh." In the previous chapter, I said that an INSTRUMENTAL adjectival constituent in a noun incorporating configuration like the one under (36) can be unambiguously identified as a predicate of the verb's internal argument. However, the question mark below the V'-node in (38) indicates that there is no way to combine the complex verb "fish-buy" with the property denoted by "fresh." Note that the fact that the external modifier *nutaamik* ("fresh") in (36) bears a singular number feature triggers the presence of the predicate *at* for "atomic."

(38)

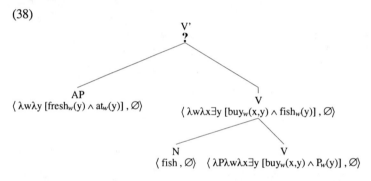

$$V'$$
$$?$$

$$AP$$
$$\langle\, \lambda w \lambda y\ [\mathrm{fresh}_w(y) \wedge \mathrm{at}_w(y)]\ ,\ \varnothing \rangle$$

$$V$$
$$\langle\, \lambda w \lambda x \exists y\ [\mathrm{buy}_w(x,y) \wedge \mathrm{fish}_w(y)]\ ,\ \varnothing \rangle$$

$$N \qquad\qquad V$$
$$\langle\, \mathrm{fish}\, ,\, \varnothing \rangle \qquad \langle\, \lambda P \lambda w \lambda x \exists y\ [\mathrm{buy}_w(x,y) \wedge P_w(y)]\ ,\ \varnothing \rangle$$

In Van Geenhoven (1995), I proposed a re-compose strategy to deal with this problem. This strategy amounts to the following. Because the complex verb "fish-buy" lacks a slot to absorb the property "fresh" as yet another predicate of its internal argument, I suggest that we de-compose the complex verb and re-compose it. That is, we go back one step in the LF construction and before the noun "fish" is semantically incorporated, we adjust the latter's type by changing its predicative meaning into the meaning of a restrictive modifier [see TL-3]. Also, we apply the Geach rule [see TL-2] to the incorporating verb so that it is able to absorb the "enriched" meaning of "fish." The result of this recomposition approach is illustrated in the following LF.

(39)

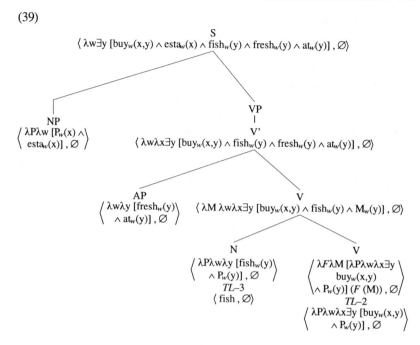

The recomposition strategy is triggered by the presence of an external INSTRUMENTAL modifier. In case more than one such modifier is present, each of them will trigger the recomposition of the complex verb that should absorb it. What is crucial is that despite the type-adjusting processes the verb remains the functor, and the incorporated noun and its modifiers remain its arguments. This prohibits the generation of impossible interpretations.

For some readers, my semantic treatment of externally modified noun incorporating configurations may taste like a bad λ-soup. However, the idea behind the type-lifting strategy is a very straightforward one. It ensures that every INSTRUMENTAL constituent as well as the incorporated noun are predicates of one and the same variable, namely the existentially bound internal argument of the incorporating verb.

2.3.2 Intensional adjectives

The adjectival modifier discussed in the previous subsection belongs to the class of intersective modifiers. The following example illustrates the case in which the external modifier is an intensional adjective.

(40)   Kaali   *peqquserluuti-nik aningaasaq*-liur-p-u-q.   [fw]

    K.ABS   false-INST.PL   money-make-IND-[-tr]-3SG

"Kaali made false money."

Whereas the intersective adjective *nutaamik* ("fresh") was simply regarded as yet another predicate of the verb's internal argument's variable, the intensional adjective *peqquserluutinik* ("false") modifies the predicate introduced by the incorporated noun *aningaasaq* ("money"). This means that we cannot simply apply the recomposition strategy illustrated before. Rather, instead of adding an intersective modifier slot to the incorporated noun, we add an intensional modifier slot to it.

I proceed in the following way. The tree under (41) is the syntactic structure of (40).

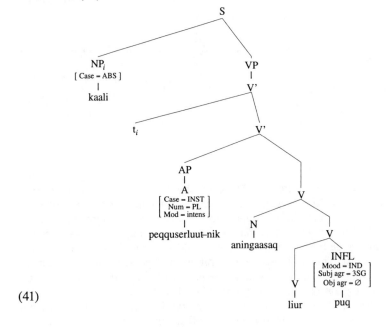

(41)

I suggest that it is the lexical feature *Mod = intens* on the adjective which informs us about the fact that we are dealing with an intensional modifier. This information triggers the creation of an intensional modifier slot on the incorporated noun rather than an intersective one. Again, the syntactic transparency of the incorporated noun is highly relevant for the semantic composition because if it weren't syntactically visible, how could we semantically designate it as the property to which the intensional modifier applies? The "enriched" meaning of the incorporated noun is absorbed by the verb after Geach's rule has been applied to the latter. The interpretation of (40) is exemplified in the LF in (42).

(42)

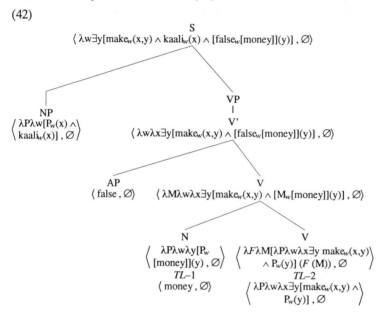

2.3.3 Numerals

In chapter 2, we saw that a numeral in the INSTRUMENTAL case makes the number of an incorporating verb's internal argument explicit. This is what *marlunnik* ("two") does in (43) and in (44):

(43) *Marlun-nik   ammassat-*tur-p-u-nga.   [Sadock (1991): 94]

two-INST.PL   sardine-eat-IND-[-tr]-1SG

"I ate two sardines."

(44) Juuna Kaali-mit *marlun-nik allagar-*si-v-u-q.   [Bittner (1994): 72]

J.ABS   K.-ABL   two-INST.PL   letter-get-IND-[-tr]-3SG

"Juuna got two letters from Kaali."

I propose to interpret the numerals in these examples as cardinality predicates [Klein (1980), Hoeksema (1983a)].[12] This gives us the possibility of representing the LF of (44) in the following way:

(45)

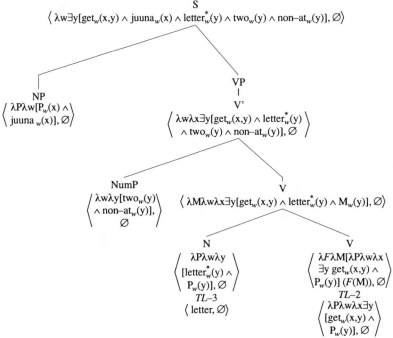

This LF informs us about yet another aspect of the incorporated noun. The modifier *two* makes explicit that the internal argument of the verb denotes a nonatomic object. I adopt Link's (1983) *-operator, which transforms a predicate of individual objects into one of plural objects.

I already spent some time discussing the issue of partitivity, in particular, on the fact that West Greenlandic numeral–noun incorporating configurations lack a partitive reading.

---

[12] Note in passing that on this view cases with incorporated numerals do not pose a problem. See chapter 4, section 1.2.2.

(43)   Marlun-nik   ammassat-tur-p-u-nga.

two-INST.PL   sardine-eat-IND-[-tr]-1SG

"I ate two of the sardines."

(44)   Juuna   Kaali-mit   marlun-nik   allagar-si-v-u-q.

J.ABS   K.-ABL   two-INST.PL   letter-get-IND-[-tr]-3SG

"Juuna got two of the letters from Kaali."

To account for the fact that numeral–noun incorporating configurations never get a partitive interpretation, I argue in chapter 6 that an indefinite that is not overtly partitive gets a partitive interpretation only if it introduces a variable by itself. This variable is then interpreted as an element of a familiar set. Since the nominal material in a numeral–noun incorporating configuration is purely predicative, there is no trigger to create the required membership relation.

2.3.4 *Wh*-modifiers

Apart from the possibility of incorporating a *wh*-word [see section 2.2], a *wh*-word can also fill the position of an INSTRUMENTAL modifier in a noun incorporating configuration. I present two *wh*-modifiers, the West Greenlandic correspondents of English *how many* and *what kind of.*

• *How many?*

The following examples illustrate the possibility of asking for the number of the internal argument of the incorporating verbs *-qar-* ("to have") and *-tur-* ("to consume"), respectively. More specifically, *qassinik* ("how many") asks for the cardinality of the variable bound by these verbs, and restricted by the respective incorporated nouns.

(46)   *Qassi-nik*   *qimmi*-qar-p-i-t?   [fw]

how.many-INST.PL   dog-have-INTER-[-tr]-2SG

"How many dogs do you have?"

(47)   Nuka   *qassi-nik*   *aalisaga*-tur-p-a?   [fw]

N.ABS   how.many-INST.PL   fish-eat-INTER-[-tr]-3SG

"How many fish did Nuka eat?"

Following mostly the semantics of English *how many*-questions presented in Rullmann (1995), we can paraphrase the meaning of the question in (47) in the following way.

(48)   "What is the number n such that n is the cardinality of the set of fish that Nuka ate."

The LF under (49) represents how this question's meaning is composed.[13]

(49)

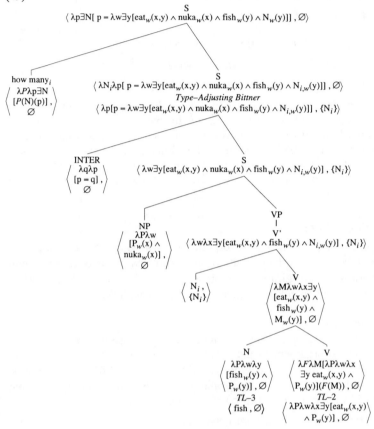

• *What kind of?*

The following example illustrates the case in which an external *wh*-modifier asks for a kind. In particular, *qanoqittumik* ("what kind of") asks for a subkind of the kind denoted by the incorporated noun *aalisaga-* ("fish").

---

[13] Rullmann (1995) builds a maximality requirement into the truth conditions of questions. This requirement makes sure that a *how many* question selects the maximal number of a particular set of objects whose number is being asked for. I ignore Rullmann's maximality requirement in the present context.

(50) Ole *qanoq-it-tu-mik* *aalisaga*-tur-p-a? [fw]

O.ABS how-be-REL.[-tr]-INST fish-eat-INTER.[-tr]-3SG

"What kind of fish did Ole eat?"

Possible anwers to this question are: Ole ate cod-fish, salmon, raw fish, ... Interestingly, this West Greenlandic question is reminiscent of the German *was für* ("what for") and the corresponding Dutch *wat voor* questions that are often realized as discontinuous constituents as well. (51) and (52) are the German and the Dutch equivalents of (50), respectively.

(51) *Was* hat Ole *für einen Fisch* gegessen?

(52) *Wat* heeft Ole *voor een vis* gegeten?

I suggest that these sentences can be semantically analyzed as in (53), which can be formalized as in (54).[14]

(53) For which P, P is a property: Ole ate a fish with P.

(54) $\lambda p \exists P [p = \lambda w \exists y [eat_w(x,y) \wedge ole_w(x) \wedge P_w[fish](y)]]$

I adopt this analysis for the West Greenlandic "what kind of" question in (50). (55) is the LF of the West Greenlandic question (50). Note that the incorporated "fish" and the *wh*-constituent are generated and interpreted independently.

---

[14] Beck (1996) proposes that (51) is analyzed as in (i) and formalized as in (ii).

(i) For which property P: there is a fish that has P and Ole ate this fish.

(ii) $\lambda p \exists P [p = \lambda w \exists y [ate_w(ole,y) \wedge fish_w(y) \wedge P_w(y)]]$

My proposal differs from Beck's in that I regard the *what kind of* predicate as an intensional modifier rather than an intersective one. This captures that *what kind of* does not necessarily ask for a subproperty of the property denoted by the incorporated noun. The answers to the following questions show that it is possible to interpret *what kind of* in an intensional way.

(iii) Was für Zähne hat Olafs Großmutter?
"What kind of teeth does Olaf's grandmother have?"
Falsche Zähne.
"False teeth."

(iv) Was für Soldaten möchte der deutsche Verteidigungsminister an der Grenze zwischen Serbien und Bosnien einsetzen?
"What kind of soldiers does the German minister of defense want to employ at the boarder between Serbia and Bosnia?"
Ehemalige Bundeswehroffiziere. [Der Spiegel 37/1995: 19]
"Former officers of the Bundeswehr."

(55)

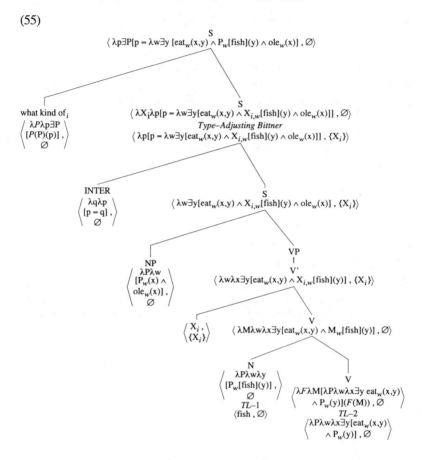

West Greenlandic has yet another *wh*-word that asks for a kind, namely, *sorleq*. In my presentation of the data in chapter 2, I mentioned that *sorleq* is the translation of English *which*. As Heim (1987) points out, English *which* can only be understood in a partitive way. That is, question (56) can only be uttered against a background in which either a set of houses, or different kinds of houses (for instance in a brochure of a building-contractor) are available.

(56)   Which house did you buy?

     i.   "Which of the houses available did you buy?"

     ii.   "What kind of house of the kinds available did you buy?"

These two meanings of the English example each have their own West Greenlandic translation. As one expects, the object-partitive question (56i) is realized as the transitive configuration under (57), and the kind-partitive (56ii) as the intransitive incorporating configuration under (58).

(57) Illu   *sorleq*   pisiari-v-iuk?   [fw]

 house.ABS   which.ABS   buy-INTER-[+tr].2SG.3SG

 i.   "Which of the houses available did you buy?"

 ii. # "What kind of house of the kinds available did you buy?"

(58) *Sorlem-mik*   illu-si-p-i-t?   [fw]

 which-INST   house-buy-INTER-[-tr]-2SG

 i.   # "Which of the houses available did you buy?"

 ii. "What kind of house of the kinds available did you buy?"

The meaning difference between *qanoqittumik* ("what kind of") in (50), and *sorlemmik* ("what kind of") in (58) is that only the latter has to be interpreted against a background in which a familiar set of kinds — in this case, kinds of houses — is available. Like English *which*, West Greenlandic *sorleq* has a presuppositional meaning component which *qanoqittumik*, like English *what*, lacks. Note in this respect that *which* on its the kind-partitive interpretation [see (56ii)] is the interrogative counterpart of the interpretation of English *such*, rather than the *wh*-word *what* as proposed in Heim (1987) [see fn. 10]. Like *which*, *such* has a presuppositional aspect which *what* clearly lacks.

2.3.5 Relative clauses

The last type of modifier in a West Greenlandic noun incorporating construction discussed in chapter 2 is the relative clause. I repeat the examples.

(59) Juuna kalaalli-sut   oqalus-sinnaa-su-mik

 J.ABS   Greenlander-EQU speak-can-REL.[-tr]-INST.SG

 ilinniartitsisu-siur-p-u-q.   [Bittner (1994): 70]

 teacher-seek-IND-[-tr]-3SG

 "Juuna is looking for a teacher who can speak West Greenlandic."

(60) Arne   qatanngute-qar-p-u-q   *Canada-mi*

 A.ABS   sister-have-IND-[-tr]-3SG   C.-LOC

najuga-lim-mik. [fw]

dwelling.place-have.REL.[-tr]-INST.SG

"Arne has a sister who lives in Canada."

I assume that a relative clause — let it be restrictive or appositive — denotes a predicate only. The predicate denoted by a restrictive relative clause is a predicate of the variable introduced by an incorporating verb, that is, a "novel" variable in the sense of Heim (1982). The predicate introduced by an appositive relative clause is a predicate of a "familiar" variable.[15]

The present theory of semantic incorporation predicts that a relative clause in a semantically incorporating configuration is always restrictive. This follows from the fact that the internal argument of an incorporating verb is always novel. At first sight, this prediction does not seem to be compatible with the rather widespread view that an indefinite modified by a relative clause tends to get a specific, namely, a wide scope reading [Fodor and Sag (1982)]. On this view, it should be possible to get a wide scope reading of a West Greenlandic incorporated noun if the latter is modified by a relative clause. In example (61), it seems to be the case that the relative clause modifying the incorporated noun forces us to regard the discourse referent of which this noun's descriptive content holds as a specific individual. In other words, we appear to be talking about a particular dog.

(61) Ullumi qimme-rniar-p-u-gut ippassa-mat

today   dog-sell-IND-[-tr]-1PL yesterday-CAUS

meeqqa-mik kii-si-sima-su-mik. [fw]

child-INST bite-AP-PERF-REL.[-tr]-INST

"Today, we sold a dog that has bitten a child yesterday."

However, once we introduce negation into the noun incorporating configuration it becomes clear that this "specific" reading is only an apparent reading. (62) gives rise to laughter: it can only be interpreted in such a way that there exist dogs with the property of having bitten a child yesterday.

(62) Ullumi qimme-rniar-nng-l-a-gut ippassa-mat

today   dog-sell-NEG-IND-[-tr]-1PL yesterday-CAUS

meeqqa-mik kii-si-sima-su-mik. [fw]

child-INST bite-AP-PERF-REL.[-tr]-INST

---

[15] My view is compatible with Doron's (1993) view that for the interpretation of an apposition we need an antecedent. Moreover, Doron presents a set of facts showing that an apposition should indeed be interpreted as a predicate.

i. :-) "It is not the case that today we sold a dog that has bitten a child yesterday."

ii. # "There is a dog that has bitten a child yesterday and it is not the case that we sold it today."

This indicates that the relative clauses in (61) and in (62) are restrictive: they only make a property more specific. A restrictive clause sometimes makes a property so specific that the resulting property can only hold of one object. This then leads to the impression that in (61) we are talking about a specific dog. Despite this impression, the only correct semantic interpretation of this incorporated noun is that of a predicative indefinite.

2.4 Summary

This section presented the treatment of West Greenlandic incorporated nouns as semantically incorporated, predicative indefinites. I illustrated how various types of external modifiers of incorporated nouns can be straightforwardly embedded into this treatment.

3 The West Greenlandic affix *-qar-*

This section is about one particular incorporating affix, namely, about the verbal affix *-qar-*. This affix denotes both the relational predicate *TO HAVE*, and the existential predicate *THERE IS*. The interesting point about this West Greenlandic affix is that it tells us quite a bit about the semantic constraints on these two predicates. It is a well-known fact about the existential predicate that it manifests the definiteness restriction [Milsark (1977)]. In chapter 2, I illustrated that relational *TO HAVE* underlies a similar constraint.

In the first part of this section, I discuss the relational meaning of *-qar-* and I show that West Greenlandic *-qar-* only covers a part of the meanings English *to have* bears. The second part is devoted to the existential construction.

3.1 The relational meaning of *-qar-*

One basic interpretation of West Greenlandic *-qar-* is that of relational *TO HAVE*. Under this interpretation, the incorporated noun is a relational predicate.

3.1.1 Relational *TO HAVE*

The following examples illustrate the relational meaning of the affix *-qar-*.

(63) Nuka   qimmi-*qar*-p-u-q.   [fw]

       N.ABS   dog-have-IND-[-tr]-3SG

       "Nuka has a dog."

(64) Arne   qatanngute-*qar*-p-u-q   Canada-mi

       A.ABS   sister-have-IND-[-tr]-3SG C.-LOC

           najuga-lim-mik.   [fw]

           dwelling.place-have.REL.[-tr]-INST.SG

       "Arne has a sister who lives in Canada."

(65) Angut   taanna   atur-sinnaa-nngit-su-nik

       man.ABS   that.ABS   be.used-can-NEG-REL.[-tr]-INST.PL

           qimmi-*qar*-p-u-q.   [Fortescue (1984): 117]

           dog-have-IND-[-tr]-3SG

       "That man has useless dogs."

I consider the fact that in West Greenlandic the relational predicate *TO HAVE* is realized as a morphologically incorporating affix as a structural mirror of the fact that this predicate is semantically incorporating and, hence, of the semantic constraints that are related to it. These constraints can at best be illustrated if we look at a more familiar language like English: the relational meaning of the verb *to have* can combine with "narrow" indefinites only.

(66) Jim doesn't have one sister.

       i.   "It is not the case that Jim has a sister, not even one."

       ii. # "There is one sister that Jim doesn't have."

(67) * Jim has every sister.

(68) * Jim has the sister.

First of all, the NP *one sister* in (66) can only take narrow scope with respect to the negation in this sentence. Secondly, (67) and (68) illustrate that relational *TO HAVE* can neither combine with a genuine quantifier nor with a definite description.[16]

---

[16] My observations about relational *TO HAVE* are the same as those made in Heim (1987) about the preposition *with*: "possessional *with* (under certain conditions at least) selects for a weak NP [Heim (1987): 26]." Her example:

Under the view that relational *TO HAVE* has an incorporating interpretation only, the lack of a wide reading of its Object argument, as well as the impossibility of combining this predicate with a quantificational expression is predicted. The meaning of relational *TO HAVE* is captured in such a way that it can only absorb relational predicates. Any other combination leads to a type clash.

(69) $\lambda R_{<s,<e,<e,t>>>} \lambda w_s \lambda x_e \exists y [R_w(x,y)]$

(68) is ungrammatical even though a definite description can be relational. However, it can only predicate something of a familiar variable. The internal argument's variable introduced by an incorporating verb is novel and, therefore, whatever is predicated of this variable has to be restrictive.

Note with respect to (63) that Greenlanders can think of *dog* as a relational noun. In more formal terms, this means that the one-place predicate *DOG* is reinterpreted as the restriction of the internal argument's variable of a relational predicate.[17]

(70) $\lambda w \lambda y [dog_w(y)] \implies \lambda w \lambda y \lambda x [dog_w(y) \wedge \text{rel-have}_w(x,y)]$

It is the relational requirement on the noun which explains the ungrammaticality of (71a): Greenlanders cannot think of a reindeer as a domestic animal, as an animal one bears a relation to. If a noun is not or cannot be understood as a relational noun, it is combined with the morpheme *-ute-* before it combines with the verbal affix *-qar-*.

(71) a. * Tuttu-qar-p-u-q.   [Sadock (p.c.)]

       reindeer-have-IND-[-tr]-3SG

    b. Tuttu-*ute*-qar-p-u-q.   [Sadock (p.c.)]

       reindeer-PSV-have-IND-[-tr]-3SG

       "He/she has a reindeer (to eat)."

The relational requirement also accounts for the meaning difference between *-illu-* ("house") in (72a) and (72b).

(72) a. Illu-qar-p-u-q.   [fw]

       house-have-IND-[-tr]-3SG

       "He/she has a house in which he/she lives him/herself."

(i)   a house with many/no/27/* all the/* most windows

[17] I thank Ede Zimmermann for pointing this out to me.

b. Illu-*ute*-qar-p-u-q. [fw]

house-PSV-have-IND-[-tr]-3SG

"He/she owns a house."

The meaning of the West Greenlandic morpheme -*ute*- is that of a possessive relation.

(73) $\lambda P_{<s,<e,t>>} \lambda w_s \lambda y_e \lambda x_e$ [poss-have$_w$(x,y) $\wedge$ P$_w$(y)]

That is, if -*qar*- incorporates -*ute*-, the resulting noun incorporating affix -*uteqar*- will give us the incorporating version of possessive *TO HAVE*. From the present semantic perspective, we apply the Geach rule TL-2 to the meaning of -*qar*- in (69) first. The resulting "enriched" meaning of -*qar*- is shown in (74).

(74) $\lambda F_{<<s,<e,t>>,<s,<e,<e,t>>>>} \lambda M_{<s,<e,t>>}$ [$\lambda R_{<s,<e,<e,t>>>} \lambda w_s$ $\lambda x_e \exists y [R_w(x,y)]$] ($F$ (M))

We now apply (74) to (73), the meaning of -*ute*-. The result is the meaning of incorporating possessive *TO HAVE* that has a slot for a nonrelational predicate.

(75) $\lambda M_{<s,<e,t>>} \lambda w_s \lambda x_e \exists y$ [poss-have$_w$(x,y) $\wedge$ M$_w$(y)]

3.1.2 Relational vs. possessive *TO HAVE*

(75) does not only capture the lexical meaning of West Greenlandic -*uteqar*- but accounts for another set of data as well. I pointed out in chapter 2 that in West Greenlandic possessive *TO HAVE* is realized as the verb *pigi*-.

(76) Juuna illu-nik   marlun-nik *pigi*-v-u-q.   [fw]

J.ABS house-INST.PL two-INST.PL have-IND-[-tr]-3SG

"Juuna owns two houses."

(77) Juuna-p illu-t   marluk   *pigi*-v-a-i.   [fw]

J.-ERG house-ABS.PL two.ABS have-IND-[+tr]-3SG.3PL

"Juuna owns the two/two particular houses."

Pigi- is a verbal stem whose Object argument can either bear the weak INSTRUMENTAL case, or the strong ABSOLUTIVE case. The former configuration is known as the antipassive construction in West Greenlandic [Bittner (1988)]. The verb lacks Object agreement and the Object is interpreted as an unspecific indefinite.[18] Hence, the meaning of *pigi*- in (76) is exactly the

---

[18] Bittner (1994) shows that under particular circumstances it can receive a specific or a definite interpretation, but since these are mostly readings enforced by the context I ignore them here.

one represented under (75). In the latter construction, namely (77), the verb bears Object agreement and the Object is interpreted as a specific indefinite or as a definite . Hence, the meaning of *-pigi-* in (77) is represented as the semantically nonincorporating two-place predicate under (78).

(78)   λw λy λx [poss-have$_w$(x,y)]

(78) represents the meaning of English *to have* that we find in the following sentences.

(79)   Paul has every shop in this part of town.

(80)   Patricia has the key.

(79) illustrates that, unlike the above example (67) in which relational *TO HAVE* is combined with a quantificational argument, the combination of nonincorporating possessive *TO HAVE* with a quantifier is grammatical. (80) shows that it is also possible to combine nonincorporating possessive *TO HAVE* with a definite NP.

Our discussion of possessive *TO HAVE* shows that I treat the antipassive as an instance of semantic incorporation. This brings us back to the question of how we link the semantically incorporating version of a verb to its nonincorporating counterpart. In section 1, I suggested with Dowty (1981) that this link is possibly a matter of lexical redundancy. The West Greenlandic antipassive data, however, indicate that this may be only a partial truth. First of all, the antipassive is a fully productive construction in this language. Secondly, as opposed to the above example with possessive *TO HAVE* many antipassives come with an overt antipassive morpheme. The following examples taken from Bittner (1988) are some cases in point.

(81)   Jaaku   arna-mik   tuqut-*si*-v-u-q.   [Bittner (1988): 5]

         J.ABS   woman-INST   kill-AP-IND-[-tr]-3SG

         "Jacob killed a woman."

(82)   Jaaku   puu-mik   aa-*llir*-p-u-q.   [Bittner (1988): 5]

         J.ABS   bag-INST   fetch-AP-IND-[-tr]-3SG

         "Jacob fetched a bag."

In Van Geenhoven (1997), I suggest that it is exactly the semantic contribution of these morphemes to turn a nonincorporating verbal stem into a semantically incorporating one. The link between them can therefore not simply be regarded as a matter of lexical redundancy. In section 4, we will discuss yet another case of semantic incorporation which probably cannot be dealt with in terms of lexical redundancy either, namely, the case of predicative Subjects.

3.1.3 *TO HAVE* vs. *TO HAVE AS*

At first sight, one may not agree with my claim that relational *TO HAVE* cannot combine with a definite NP, as illustrated in (68). This disagreement may be caused by examples such as the following:

(83)   The German soccer team has Vogts as *its trainer*.

(84)   Jimmy has Mr. Jones as *his math teacher*.

The meaning of the predicate *TO HAVE AS* is distinct from the relational predicate *TO HAVE* in that the former is not semantically incorporating in the sense discussed so far. Again, West Greenlandic can help us in figuring out the exact denotation of this predicate. In this language, the noun incorporating affix *-gi-* that comes with transitive agreement inflection denotes *TO HAVE AS*. (85) illustrates a case in point.

(85)   Nuka-p   Esta   anaana-*g*-a-a.   [fw]

      N.-ERG   E.ABS   mother-have.as-IND.[+tr]-3SG.3SG

      "Ester is Nuka's mother (lit. Nuka has Ester as his mother)."

I suggest that the meaning contribution of *TO HAVE AS* is as follows.

(86) $\lambda R\ \lambda w\ \lambda y\ \lambda x\ [\ R_w(x,y)\ ]$

Like relational *TO HAVE*, *TO HAVE AS* absorbs a two-place predicate. It is distinct from relational *TO HAVE* and the other incorporating verbs discussed so far in that it does not deliver the existential binding of the internal argument. If we combine (86) with the relational noun *mother*, we get the complex verb *to have y as mother* in (87).

(87) $\lambda w\ \lambda y\ \lambda x[\ mother_w(y) \wedge rel\text{-}have_w(x,y)\ ]$

3.2 The existential meaning of *-qar-*

I now turn to the other meaning of West Greenlandic *-qar-*, namely, that of the existential predicate.

(88)   Nillataartarfim-mi   tallima-nik   manne-*qar*-p-u-q.   [fw]

      fridge-LOC   five-INST.PL   egg-have-IND-[-tr]-3SG

      "There are five eggs in the fridge."

(89)   Festi-mi   qallunaar-passua-*qar*-p-u-q.   [fw]

      party-LOC   dane-many-have-IND-[-tr]-3SG

      "There were many Danes at the party."

West Greenlandic is surely not the only language that uses one verbal stem to express relational *TO HAVE* as well as the existential predicate. As I pointed out in chapter 2, in some South German dialects the verb *haben* is not only used to denote relational [see (90a)] and possessive *TO HAVE* [see (90b)], but can receive an existential interpretation as well [see (90c)].

(90)   a.   Karl *hat*   einen Bruder.

            K.   has   a brother

            "Karl has a brother."

     b.   Karl *hat*   die meisten Wohnungen   in diesem Haus.

            K.   has   the most appartments   in this house

            "Karl owns most of the appartments in this house."

     c.   Heute *hat*   es   wieder   frische Milch.

            today   has   it   again   fresh milk

            "Today, there is fresh milk again."

In English, the verb *to have* can receive an existential interpretation as well: (91a) and (91b) are synonymous.[19]

(91)   a.   The car has scratches on it.

     b.   There are scratches on the car.

In parallel to my treatment of the relational meaning of the affix *-qar-*, I regard the fact that in West Greenlandic the existential predicate is realized as a morphologically incorporating affix as a structural mirror of the meaning of this predicate and the semantic constraints related to it. Since Milsark (1977), these constraints are derived from the definiteness restriction, which has been widely discussed and analyzed by many authors [Heim (1987), Keenan (1987), McNally (1992)]. This restriction can be briefly captured in the following way. On the one hand, it is not possible to combine the English existential predicate with a genuine quantifier. On the other hand, it is not possible to combine it with a definite description.

(92)   * There is every cow in the meadow.

(93)   * There is the cow in the meadow.

I explain the ungrammaticality of both sentences in exactly the same way in which I explained the ungrammaticality of (67) and (68). That is, adopting (94) as the lexical semantics of the existential predicate makes clear that this predicate cannot combine with an expression that does not denote a property of a novel variable.

---

[19] Jack Hoeksema (p.c.) pointed out that in Dutch *hebben* ("to have") can receive an existential interpretation as well. His example:

(i)   Op dit eiland   heb   je   maar drie huizen.
     on this island   have   you   only three houses
     "On this island, there are only three houses."

(94) $\lambda P \, \lambda LOC \, \lambda w \, \exists y \, [\, P_w(y) \wedge LOC_w(y) \,]$

Assuming that a genuine quantifier denotes type $<<e,t>,t>$, it follows that it cannot be absorbed as the predicate of the argument of the existential predicate. Therefore, (92) is ungrammatical. Details aside, we find essentially the same explanation for why the existential predicate in English cannot have a quantificational argument in McNally (1992). According to McNally, the argument of the existential predicate is interpreted as a nominalized function and only nonquantificational expressions — including the definite descriptions — are interpretable as nominalized functions.[20] According to McNally, definite descriptions are not excluded from the existential construction because they denote the wrong type, but rather because definites are associated with the condition that their referent is familiar. As such, they do not meet the requirement that the discourse referent corresponding to the instantiation of the nominalized function argument of the existential predicate is novel. Therefore, (93) is ungrammatical.

McNally's explanation for why definite descriptions cannot be the argument of the existential predicate is stated as a NOVELTY CONDITION on the argument of the existential predicate [see chapter 3, section 1.2]. Similarly, Kamp and Reyle (1993) assume

> that the semantic function of there-insertion sentences is to assert that an individual, or set of individuals, with certain specified properties exists ... the remainder of the sentence must provide a discourse referent to represent the individual or set whose existence is being asserted; and for this it is crucial that this discourse referent is not bound already, or anaphorically linked to some discourse referent outside the representation itself [Kamp and Reyle (1993): 456].

From a discourse semantic perspective, the existential predicate in my approach introduces the discourse referent standing for its internal argument and guarantees that this referent is novel [see section 7]. The NOVELTY CONDITION is thus a condition on the lexical semantics of a semantically incorporating verb rather than on its argument.

Finally, the present perspective makes it possible to give a uniform analysis of the existential predicate combining with apparently semantically different arguments. Here are some examples.

---

[20] McNally elaborates the idea that the argument of the existential predicate denotes a property in the framework of property theory [Chierchia (1984)]. For the sake of completeness, I should mention her account of the following kind of example.

(i)   There was every kind of beer at the party.

According to McNally, *every kind of beer* quantifies over properties rather than over individuals. If we raise this quantifier, the remaining trace can serve as the argument of the existential predicate since its type is that of a property. This explains why (i), unlike (92), is grammatical.

(95)   There are *eggs* in the fridge.

(96)   There is *an egg* in the fridge.

(97)   There are *five eggs* in the fridge.

Under Carlson's (1977) proposal that the English bare plural is unambiguously interpreted as a kind denoting expression [see chapter 3, section 4.1], we need two different lexical semantic analyses for the existential predicate: one to combine with a kind denoting expression as in (95), and the other one to combine with a quantifier thereby capturing the meaning of (96) and (97). Krifka et al. (1995) point out that any proposal which can give a uniform semantic analysis for the existential predicate is to be preferred to Carlson's proposal [see chapter 3, section 4.2]. I suggest that what the bare plural in (95), the singular indefinite in (96), and the numeral indefinite in (97) have in common is that they all denote properties which are predicates of the argument's variable of the existential predicate.[21]

As a final illustration, I give the LF of (88), the West Greenlandic counterpart of (97). To save space, I ignore the world index in this LF and I silently assume the presence of the *-operator.[22]

---

[21] McNally (to appear) shows how this claim remains unproblematic for cases in which the argument of the existential predicate contains the numeral *zero*, the determiner *no* and downward entailing quantifiers.

[22] Like the other presuppositions, I represent definite descriptions as free variables at LF.

(98)

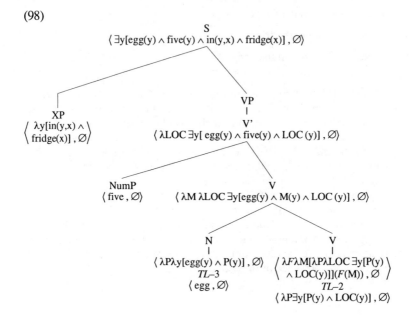

3.3 Summary

In sum, the noun incorporating West Greenlandic affix *-qar-* is the morphological realization of two semantically incorporating predicates, viz., relational *TO HAVE* and existential *THERE IS*. A semantic constraint on the internal argument of these predicates, Milsark's definiteness restriction, is explained as the direct consequence of semantic incorporation. That is, incorporating predicates only absorb property-denoting expressions that can serve as the predicate of their novel internal argument. Moreover, given that my approach regards the NOVELTY CONDITION as a condition on the lexical semantics of semantically incorporating predicates, only restrictive predicates can be absorbed.[23]

---

[23] An apparent counterexample is the following taken from Doron (1993)

(i)   There is a doctor in Manchester, Welsh I think.

At first sight, the apposition *Welsh I think* seems to be yet another predicate that holds of the novel referent introduced by the existential predicate. However, this predicate is not simply absorbed by the predicate in the way *a doctor* is. Rather, as Doron points out an apposition is a predicate that triggers a process of anaphora resolution. This view is supported by the fact that (i) is synonymous with (ii).

(ii)   There is a doctor in Manchester. She is Welsh I think.

4 "Scope" effects and other predicative indefinites

In the previous section, I argued that the semantic constraints on the internal argument of the relational predicate *TO HAVE*, as well as the constraints on the argument of the existential predicate are directly related to their semantic interpretation as semantically incorporating predicates. In the same spirit, the narrow scope effects that show up with West Greenlandic incorporated nouns are directly related to the semantic analysis of the affixes that incorporate these nouns. That is, it is a direct consequence of the idea that the existential interpretation of an incorporated noun is part of the lexical semantics of the incorporating affix.

In this section, I revisit some of the scope phenomena related to West Greenlandic incorporated nouns presented in chapter 2 and discuss them within the present semantic incorporation approach. My discussion of scope goes beyond the West Greenlandic data, and in this sense this section is about the scope of their West Germanic semantic counterparts as well. As such, it contains my answer to the question of why particular indefinites never reach non-narrow scope positions.

4.1 Negation

Once sentence negation is involved, an incorporated noun can only take narrow scope with respect to it. To my knowledge, this observation was first made by Bittner (1994).

(99) Arnajaraq aalisaga-si-*nngi*-l-a-q. [fw]

    A.ABS   fish-buy-NEG-IND-[-tr]-3SG

    i.   "It is not the case that Arnajaraq bought (a) fish."

    ii. # "There is/are (a) fish that Arnajaraq didn't buy."

(100) Juuna Kaali-mit marlun-nik allagar-si-*nngi*-l-a-q. [Bittner (1994): 118]

    J.ABS K.-ABL two-INST.PL letter-get-NEG-IND-[-tr]-3SG

    i.   "It is not the case that Juuna got two letters from Kaali."

    ii. # "There are a two letters that Juuna didn't get from Kaali."

Obviously, the view that the verbal affixes in these examples are semantically incorporating, in the sense that they themselves introduce the existential quantification of their internal argument's variable, predicts the narrow scope of these internal arguments. That is, any operator taking scope over the verb automatically takes scope over the semantic components of this verb's meaning. Stating it more precisely, we should not say that

---

By the time that *Welsh I think* in (i) is processed the novel referent introduced by the existential predicate has turned into a salient referent.

the incorporated noun takes narrow scope with respect to negation but rather, that it can be the predicate of a lexically bound variable only.

To illustrate the narrow scope effect, I give the LF of example (99). Following the treatment of negation at LF sketched in von Stechow (1993), I regard the suffixal negation morpheme *-nngi(t)-* as a negative element that is realized on the verb and that indicates the presence of an abstract NEG-node at LF.

(101)

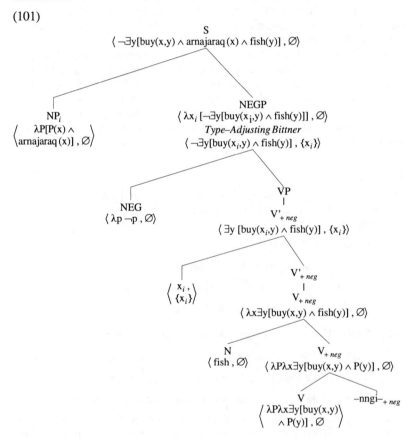

My explanation for the narrow scope effect of West Greenlandic incorporated nouns is essentially the same as Carlson's (1977) narrow scope explanation for the English bare plural. However, the lexicalized existential interpretation of a West Greenlandic incorporated noun and of a Germanic bare plural does not only deliver the answer to why these expressions do not reach non-narrow scope positions. I take it to be the general answer as to how the narrowest scope reading of most indefinites is processed. In this sense, it goes beyond Carlson (1977). Carlson (1977) gave the pair of examples (102) and (103) to illustrate that the bare plural always takes narrowest scope whereas a singular indefinite has two scope options.

(102) John didn't see spots on the floor. [Carlson (1977): 19]

    i.   "It was not the case that John saw spots on the floor."

    ii. # "There were spots on the floor and John didn't see them."

(103) John didn't see a spot on the floor.

    i.   "It was not the case that John saw any spot on the floor."

    ii. "There was a spot on the floor and John didn't see it."

In the spirit of Montague (1974), Carlson interprets singular indefinites as existential quantifiers which can scope out of the negation or which can remain in the scope of the negation. In the latter case, we get the narrow scope reading of (103). I explain the ambiguity of (103) not as a scope ambiguity. Rather, the indefinite *a spot* can be either interpreted as a predicate or as a free variable indefinite. In the former case, the indefinite undergoes the same interpretive process as the bare plural in (102), that is, semantic incorporation. From this, the narrow scope reading is a simple consequence. In the latter case, it indergoes a process of global accommodation from which the wide scope reading results [see chapter 6].

4.2 Predicative indefinites and distribution

The following West Greenlandic sentence is ambiguous. It can either be understood in a collective or in a distributive way.

(104) Pinartu-t   tamarmik tuttu-raar-p-u-t.   [fw]

     hunter-ABS.PL all   caribou-catch-IND-[-tr]-3PL

    i.   "All the hunters caught a caribou/caribous together."

    ii. "All the hunters caught a caribou/caribous by themselves."

I take the collective reading (104i) to be the default reading of this example and represent it as in the LF under (105). Note that *tamarmik* ("all") does not have the semantic contribution of a quantifier. It simply focuses on the fact that when something is predicated of a plural definite description, this predication holds of every member of the set denoted by this description.

(105)

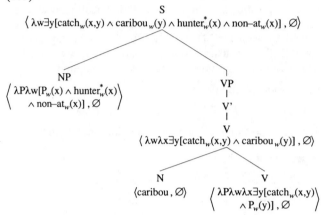

For the representation of the distributive reading (104ii), we add a (silent) distributive operator to the representation of the Subject NP.

(106)

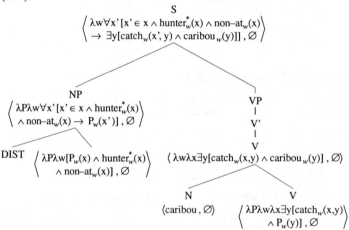

My LF representations (105) and (106) show that I do not regard the ambiguity of (104) as a matter of scope [Kamp and Reyle (1993)]. In both LFs, the incorporated noun is interpreted as an absorbed property. In chapter 2, the following pair of examples was given as an illustration that it is possible to disambiguate (104) if one inserts the adverbs *ataatsimut* ("together") and *immikut* ("by.self"), respectively:

(107) Pinartu-t   tamarmik ataatsimut tuttu-raar-p-u-t.   [fw]

     hunter-ABS.PL   all   together   caribou-catch-IND-[-tr]-3PL

     "All the hunters caught a caribou/caribous together."

(108) Pinartu-t   tamarmik immikut tuttu-raar-p-u-t.   [fw]

     hunter-ABS.PL   all   by.self   caribou-catch-IND-[-tr]-3PL

     "All the hunters caught a caribou/caribous by themselves."

A related point of interest is the following contrastive pair of examples taken from Carlson (1977).

(109) Everyone read books on giraffes.

     i.   "Every person was reading (different) books on giraffes."

     ii.   # "There were books on giraffes that everyone was reading."

(110) Everyone read a book on giraffes.

     i.   "Every person was reading a book on giraffes."

     ii.   "There was a book on giraffes that everyone was reading."

According to Carlson, these examples illustrate that, unlike the English singular indefinite, the English bare plural cannot receive a "wide" reading with respect to a universal quantifier. His explanation goes as follows. On the one hand, the bare plural in (109) receives its existential interpretation from the verb *to read* and therefore necessarily receives a narrow scope reading. On the other hand, the indefinite in (110) is an existential quantifier that can take either narrow or wide scope with respect to the universally quantified subject. In contrast, I defend the view that the narrow reading of the bare plural in (109) as well as that of the indefinite in (110) is the consequence of semantic incorporation. In each case, the direct Object NP denotes a predicate which is absorbed by the verb *to read*. That the former only receives a narrow interpretation is because the English bare plural can only be understood as a predicate and therefore neccesarily incorporates. That the latter receives also a wide reading follows because the singular indefinite in (110) can be interpreted as a free variable indefinite. In chapter 6, I argue that this "wide" reading is not the result of QUANTIFIER RAISING [Abusch (1994)]. Rather, a free variable indefinite receives its existential interpretation through the global accommodation of its descriptive content.

4.3 Split topicalization in German

By now, it should not come as a surprise that I explain the narrow scope effect of German split topicalization as a direct result of semantic incorporation as well. In fact, I already pointed towards a semantic incorporation analysis of this German phenomenon in my discussion of the German *was für* split [see section 2.3.4].

In chapter 3, a lengthy discussion of Diesing's (1992) approach was provided with her syntactic CED explanation of the fact that only "weak" quantifiers can split.

(111) Schwarze Spinnen hat Lisa im Keller keine gesehen.

  black spiders has L. in.the cellar no seen

  "As for spiders, it is not the case that Lisa saw any black ones in the cellar."

(112) * Schwarze Spinnen hat Lisa im Keller einige nicht gesehen.

  black spiders has L. in.the cellar some not seen

Whereas Diesing's approach is based on the view that Object split is the result of NP split, I defended the view that Object Split is the result of V split [chapter 4, section 3.2.3]. The ungrammaticality of (112) follows because heads of German NPs cannot be topicalized. In particular, I related the syntactic representation of German Split to that of modification in West Greenlandic noun incorporating configurations. According to my view, the syntactic representation of the split configuration in (111) is (113).

(113)

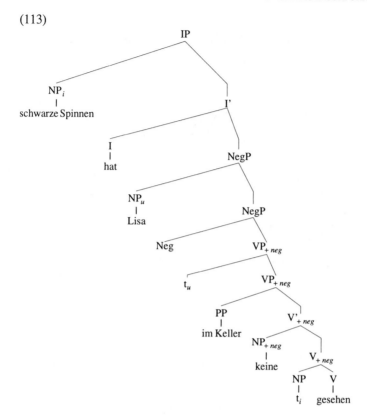

I regard the syntactic similarity between German V Split and West Greenlandic noun incorporation, that is, the fact that both configurations have an incorporated Object position as a structural mirror of the proposal that these configurations are semantic counterparts. In semantic terms, this means that the topicalized material and the Mittelfeld NP are both predicates of one and the same argument, namely of the internal argument of a semantically incorporating verb.

The semantic interpretation of (113) is the LF under (114). I have represented the negative determiner *keine* ("no") as the predicate *SM*.[24]

---

[24] For reasons of space, I have left out the semantic contribution of the auxiliary *hat* in V2 position and that of the PP *im Keller* ("in the basement"). For the same reason, I have left out the world variables.

(114)

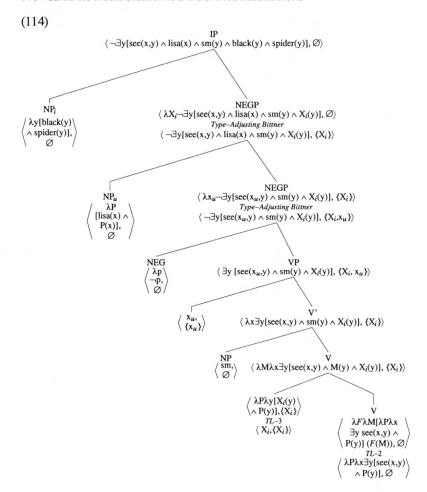

4.4 Predicative Subjects

Up to now, the discussion of semantic incorporation only related to indefinite Objects. How does it extend to Subjects? The following examples taken from Carlson (1977) show that bare plurals also get an existential interpretation in Subject position.

(115) Dogs entered the room.

(116) Books fell on the floor after John had pushed them.

In the previous chapter, I discussed the impossibility of morphologically incorporating Subjects. I explained this fact by adopting Marantz's (1984) and Kratzer's (1994) view that the external argument is not a true argument of the verb. From this it follows that the semantic incorporation of the above predicative Subjects *dogs* and *books* cannot be an inherent lexical property of the verb. Does this mean that semantic incorporation cannot be a uniform explanation of the semantic behaviour of all existential bare plurals? I believe it can and I briefly explain how this can be achieved.

First, also predicative Subjects can only get narrow interpretations. This is supported by the following examples.

(117) Dogs didn't enter the room.

　　i.　"It was not the case that sm dogs entered the room."

　　ii.　# "There were some dogs and they didn't enter the room."

(118) ? Books didn't fall on the floor after John had pushed them.

　　# "Books$_i$ didn't fall on the floor after John had pushed them$_i$."

Dogs in (117) cannot receive a wide interpretation. *Books* in (118) cannot either and therefore the whole sentence sounds odd because there is no accessible antecedent for the pronoun *them*.

Secondly, the Dutch counterparts of (115) and (116) cannot occur in sentence initial position. They have to be embedded into some sort of existential context using the expletive *er* ("there").[25]

(119) a.　?* Honden　kwamen　de kamer　　binnen.

　　　　　　dogs　　came　　　the room　　in

　　　b.　Er　　kwamen　honden　de kamer　　binnen.

　　　　　there　came　　　dogs　　the room　　in

　　　　　"Dogs entered the room."

(120) a.　?* Boeken　vielen　op de grond　nadat　Jan　ze

　　　　　　books　　fell　　on the floor　after　J.　them

　　　　　weggeschoven　had.

　　　　　away.pushed　　had

---

[25] Sentences like the a-examples are possible if used in a kind-contrastive, listing context as in the following description of a chaotic household.

(i)　　Honden liepen het huis in en uit. Katten sprongen over de meubels. Kippen scharrelden in de keuken.
　　　"Dogs were running in and out of the house. Cats were jumping around on the furniture. Chicken were scratching in the kitchen."

b. Er   vielen   boeken op de grond   nadat Jan æ

    there fell   books   on the floor   after J.   them

    weggeschoven had.

    away.pushed   had

    "Books fell on the floor after John had pushed them."

Rullmann (1989) argues that Dutch Subjects can stay in or raise out of the VP and that this syntactic distinction correlates with the well-known semantic weak–strong distinction. Whereas the "weak" VP-internal Subjects receive their existential interpretation through Heimian EXISTENTIAL CLOSURE at the VP, VP-external Subjects are "strong", that is, either quantifiers or referential NPs. Given their inherent weakness, bare plurals have to remain in their VP-internal position and that is why the above a-examples are ungrammatical. Dutch seems to give us a clue as to how predicative Subjects can be integrated into the present proposal. I suggest that the presence of existential *er* in the Dutch examples, allows us to assume the presence of existential *there* in the LFs of the above English examples. Details aside, the semantic contribution of this (implicit) existential is to make the VP semantically incorporating with respect to its Subject. Its semantic role is thus similar to that of West Greenlandic antipassive morphemes as discussed in section 3.1.2. Again, we have a case of semantic incorporation which is not simply a matter of lexical redundancy. Rather, it can be triggered by a syntactic element other than the verb.

4.5 Summary

In this section, I explained the narrow scope effects of West Greenlandic incorporated nouns in particular, and of indefinite descriptions in general, as the direct consequence of the idea that the existential interpretation of these expressions is contributed by semantically incorporating verbal predicates. Getting narrowest scope is the consequence of being semantically incorporated.

5 Intensional verbs

The incorporating predicates discussed so far are extensional predicates: they all introduce the existential interpretation of their internal argument. In the following West Greenlandic examples, the incorporating affix has an intensional meaning. Interestingly, the paraphrases below these examples illustrate that the incorporated nouns only have a *de dicto* reading.

(121) Vittu   cykili-ssar-*siur*-p-u-q.   [fw]

    V.ABS bike-FUT-seek-IND-[-tr]-3SG

   i. "Vittus is looking for an arbitrary bike / bikes."

   ii. # "There is a specific bike such that Vittus is looking for it."

(122) Juuna kalaalli-sut   oqalus-sinnaa-su-mik

       J.ABS Greenlander-EQU speak-can-REL.[-tr]-INST.SG

       ilinniartitsisu-siur-p-u-q.   [Bittner (1994): 70]

       teacher-seek-IND-[-tr]-3SG

       "Juuna is looking for a teacher who can speak West Greenlandic."

The meaning difference between the incorporating affixes dicussed so far and the intensional affix *-siur-* ("to seek") is that the latter does not absorb the incorporated noun as the predicate of its internal argument's variable. Rather, the property introduced by this noun *is* the argument of this verb.

(123) $\lambda P \, \lambda w \, \lambda x \, [\, \text{seek}_w(x, \lambda w' \, P_{w'}) \,]$

In my terminology, an intensional verb is semantically incorporating par excellence: it absorbs a property as its argument. The main advantage of my approach is that regardless of whether a noun is incorporated by an extensional or an intensional affix, it gets the same interpretation, namely that of a property. (123) represents exactly Zimmermann's (1993) interpretation of the intensional verb *TO SEEK* as a relation between an individual and a property. However, although the de dicto reading of indefinites is captured in the way as on Zimmermann's analysis, my approach differs from his with respect to the treatment of the de re reading of *TO SEEK*.

    First, Zimmermann suggests that the intensional predicate *TO SEEK* is interpreted as in (123), and that its extensional counterpart is derived from it by interpreting its second argument as a property of being a particular object. This extensional reading is captured in (124).

(124) $\lambda w \, \lambda y \, \lambda x \, [\, \text{seek}_w(x, \lambda w' \, \lambda z \, z = y) \,]$

Furthermore, he assumes that nonreferential NPs are interpreted as intensional quantifiers. It follows that the latter cannot be the argument of intensional *TO SEEK* but that they can combine with extensional *TO SEEK* only. Hence, Zimmermann accounts for why (125) lacks a de dicto reading.

(125) Theo is seeking each unicorn.

However, because in his account intensional verbs are the input for their extensional counterparts, Zimmermann predicts that every NP which gets a de dicto reading gets a de re reading as well. The following sentence shows that this prediction is wrong.[26]

---

[26] In chapter 3, section 4.2.2, I showed that the bare plural cannot be interpreted de re with respect to objects. — Note that Montague's (1974) analysis, in which the complement of an intensional verb is the intension of a quantifier (type $<s,<<e,t>,t>>$), gives rise to the same

(126) Ede is seeking policemen.

   i. "Ede is looking for arbitrary policemen."

   ii. # "There are some policemen p such that Ede is looking for p."

In my account, semantically incorporating verbs are lexically distinguished from nonincorporating verbs. With respect to (123), this means that its nonincorporating counterpart, which is simultaneously its extensional counterpart, is not derived from it. The latter is simply interpreted as (127), a relation between individuals. It can have a quantificational, an anaphoric expression or a free variable indefinite as its Object argument.

(127) $\lambda w \, \lambda y \, \lambda x \, [\, seek_w(x,y) \,]$

My claim that in existential contexts a bare plural only receives a predicative interpretation correctly predicts that a bare plural can only combine with a semantically incorporating verb. That is, if it combines with *TO SEEK*, it will only combine with intensional *TO SEEK*. The same way of reasoning accounts for why the West Greenlandic examples only get a de dicto reading. An incorporated noun always denotes a predicate, and this can only combine with an incorporating verb.

   Finally, my account covers the case illustrated in (122) where an intensional verb's argument is modified by an external modifier. We proceed as follows. Before it is incorporated, we add a modifier slot to the incorporated noun "teacher." Then, we apply Geach's rule to the intensional verb "to seek" so that the latter can apply to an intersective modifier. These two steps allow us to assign the noun incorporating configuration "teacher-seek" the following interpretation.

(128) $\lambda M \, \lambda w \, \lambda x \, [\, seek_w \, (x, \lambda w' \, \lambda y \, (teacher_{w'}(y) \wedge M_{w'}(y)) \,) \,]$

(128) has a slot to absorb the predicate denoted by the restrictive relative clause "who can speak West Greenlandic."

6 Semantic incorporation vs. Bittner (1994)

In my discussion of the syntax of noun incorporating configurations, I rejected, on the one hand, the Bakerian, transformational approach to noun incorporation [see chapter 4, section 1.2.2] and, on the other, the view that incorporated nouns are predicate modifiers [see chapter 4, section 2.3.1]. Now that my proposal has been outlined in some more detail, I contrast it with Bittner's analysis of noun incorporation in West Greenlandic. Her analysis embodies a transformational *and* a predicate modifier approach.

---

wrong prediction. A recent proposal to analyze intensional verbs in a Montagovian way is Moltmann (1997). See Van Geenhoven and McNally (1997) for a discussion and rejection of Moltmann's (1997) arguments.

6.1 Bittner (1994)

Following Baker (1988), Bittner (1994) assumes that noun incorporation is the result of syntactic head movement whereby an incorporated noun leaves a trace in its D-structural NP position. The S-structure of (100), repeated here as (129), then looks like the tree under (130).

(129) Juuna   Kaali-mit   marlun-nik   allagar-si-*nngi*-l-a-q. [Bittner (1994): 118]

     J.ABS   K.-ABL   two-INST.PL letter-get-NEG-IND-[-tr]-3SG

    i.   "It is not the case that Juuna got two letters from Kaali."

    ii. # "There are a two letters that Juuna didn't get from Kaali."

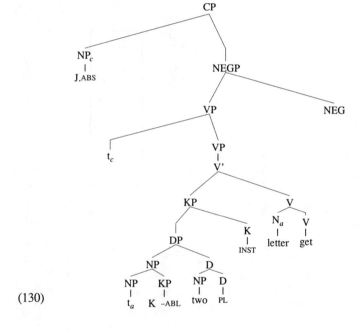

(130)

Bittner takes this S-structure as the input for the acceptable narrow interpretation of (129). Due to space limits, (131) only contains the LF of what is under the NEGP-node in the above tree. The picture of (130)'s interpretation becomes complete when we apply the meaning of the ABSOLUTIVE Subject *Juuna*, namely $\langle \lambda P[P(juuna)] , \varnothing \rangle$, to (131).

(131)

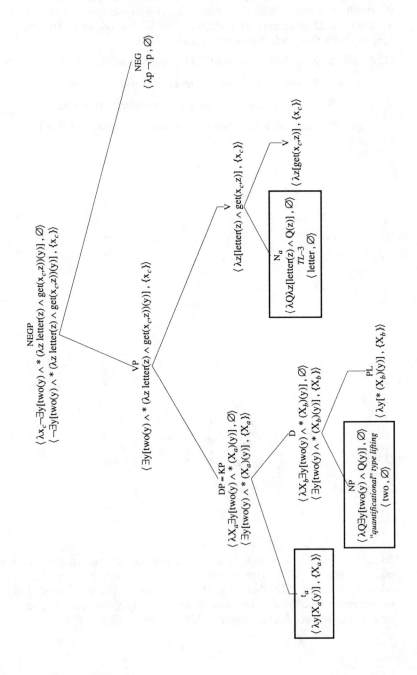

I have boxed three crucial nodes in (131).[27] First, the incorporated noun "letter" is interpreted as a predicate modifier (type $<<e,t>,<e,t>>$). It applies to the two-place predicate "to get" without changing the latter's argument structure. Next, the trace of the incorporated noun is interpreted as a placeholder for the complex V formed by the head movement transformation. That is, it is interpreted as a property (type $<e,t>$). This is based on the general principle stated by Bittner that the trace in a head position is always interpreted as a variable of the same type as the sister of its maximal projection [see TRACE RULE in section 1.3]. Thirdly, through a type-lifting operation called "quantificational type-lifting", the "stranded" numeral modifier "two" becomes the lefthand argument of an existential quantifier. In this way, Bittner smuggles the existential interpretation of the incorporated noun into the truth conditions of a noun incorporating configuration. Note in this respect that there is no (silent) linguistic element which triggers the introduction of this extra semantic information. In Bittner's system, type-lifting creates meaning.

What explains that (129) lacks a "wide scope" reading? To get a wide interpretation for this example, Bittner argues that one has to derive a secondary LF from the S-structure under (130), that is, an LF in which the DP containing the trace of the incorporated noun is raised. However, this derivation cannot take place because the trace would be moved into an ungoverned position and the resulting LF would violate the EMPTY CATEGORY PRINCIPLE [ECP]. Bittner gives a purely syntactic explanation for the excluded reading of (129). This is very reminiscent of Diesing's syntactic account of the narrow scope effect of German split Objects [see chapter 3, section 2.2].

6.2 Some loose ends in Bittner's approach

The questions I address are the following. Is noun incorporation by head movement semantically useful [see chapter 4, section 1.2.2]? Can the predicate modifier view deliver a uniform explanation of the semantic pecularities of West Greenlandic incorporated nouns and their semantic counterparts in West Germanic languages?[28]

---

[27] The reader is invited to study Bittner's syntactic principles, her cross-linguistic semantics and the details of both systems in Bittner (1994). — For reasons of space, I ignore the interpretation of the Subject trace and of the ABLATIVE constituent *Kaalimit*.

[28] The way in which Bittner integrates the predicate modifier view differs from the way in which de Hoop (1992) integrates it. De Hoop interprets the predicate modified by an incorporated noun as an intransitive verb. (131) shows that Bittner interprets the predicate modified by an incorporated noun as a transitive verb.

6.2.1 The head movement part of the proposal

First, Bittner gives one and the same syntactic explanation for the narrow scope effect of West Greenlandic incorporated nouns and for their lack of a definite reading illustrated in (132).

(132) Juuna allagar-si-v-u-q.   [Bittner (1994): 119]

      J.ABS letter-get-IND-[-tr]-3SG

      # "Juuna got the letter."

She assumes that a definite description obligatorily raises at LF to reach its appropriate interpretation position, and argues that ECP violation accounts for the lack of a definite reading of an incorporated noun. Under the widespread view that a definite is an anaphoric expression [Heim (1982)], I fail to see how the syntactic raising of a definite contributes to its appropriate interpretation, that is, to its resolution. However, from a Heimian perspective semantic incorporation simply predicts that (132) lacks of a definite reading: the internal argument's variable of an incorporating verb is always novel and as such it can never be set equal to an antecedent.

Secondly, Bittner's approach accepts narrow readings of incorporated nouns. However, we saw in chapter 2 that a West Greenlandic noun incorporating configuration lacks a partitive interpretation. Similarly, Bittner's example (129) does not get a (narrow) partitive reading either. It cannot mean "Juuna didn't get two of the letters from Kaali." Note that this cannot be explained by the requirement that an NP with a partitive interpretation necessarily raises at LF, because such a requirement would wrongly predict that an NP with a partitive interpretation necessarily takes wide scope. It would be impossible to represent narrow scope readings of partitive NPs. At this point, I see no straightforward way to account for the lack of (narrow) partitive readings of incorporated expressions within Bittner's syntax-driven semantics. In the next chapter, I present an analysis of partitivity in which the partitive relation is interpreted as the membership relation. The prerequisite for a nominal expression to receive a partitive interpretation is that it must translate as a variable that stands in the membership relation to some presupposed set. A numeral–noun incorporating configuration in West Greenlandic lacks a partitive reading because it lacks the variable as the trigger of this membership relation.

The last semantic loose end of Bittner's head movement driven approach, and probably the most important one in the present context, is the nonuniversal nature of this syntactic approach. Because the existential interpretation of an incorporated noun is introduced as a meaning part of its remnant NP, the interpretation of a noun incorporating configuration fully relies upon the existence of a D-structural phrase headed by the incorporated noun. In other words, it lives on the belief that noun incorporation is the result of head movement. However, the data presented in chapter 2 call for a uniform explanation of the (discourse) semantic properties of West

Greenlandic incorporated nouns *and* West Germanic bare plurals. Extending Bittner's syntactic treatment of West Greenlandic noun incorporation to the West Germanic data would require that in the syntactic representation of a bare plural the latter needs to be transformationally related to an empty node in some D-structural phrase. Obviously, the syntactic reality of such a transformation lacks independent evidence. Bittner's ECP account cannot capture the common *semantic* denominator of West Greenlandic incorporated nouns and West Germanic bare plural Objects. In other words, it cannot be a natural consequence of Bittner's theory that an incorporated noun and a narrow indefinite NP are treated in the same way. This chapter has provided enough evidence — I believe — that semantic incorporation is a language independent means of capturing the semantic similarities of nominal constituents in structurally distinct and typologically unrelated languages.

6.2.2 The predicate modifier part of the proposal

The main problem that arises with the predicate modifier view in Bittner's proposal is that the number of INSTRUMENTAL modifiers is not limited to one. Apart from numerals, incorporated nouns can be simultaneously modified by adjectives and relative clauses. The question arises as to which of these contains the designated NP that is type-lifted to the meaning of an existential quantifier in order to introduce the existential interpretation of the incorporated noun [see (131)]. The only principled way to have such a designated NP in Bittner's system is to stipulate that the numeral modifier is this designated NP and, moreover, that if no numeral is among the linguistically realized modifiers, an ARBITRARY numeral has to be present at LF. The non-numeral modifiers are then interpreted as predicate modifiers of the designated numeral modifier before the latter type-lifts. I believe that any approach to West Greenlandic noun incorporation in which no modifier has to be regarded as a designated one is to be preferred to an approach that needs a designated modifier.

The main difference between a predicate modifier approach and mine is that in the former the incorporated noun is the semantically active part in a noun incorporating configuration and in the latter the verb is the semantically active component. In my approach, the distinction between the extensional and the intensional interpretation of an incorporating configuration is located in the semantics of the incorporating verbal predicates involved. The meaning of an incorporated noun is the same regardless of whether it is incorporated by an extensional or an intensional affix. That is, extensional as well as intensional incorporating predicates absorb a property, but only the former lexicalizes the existential reading of its internal argument [see section 5]. In Bittner's approach, the distinction between the extensional and the intensional interpretation of incorporating configurations does not only give rise to an interpretation distinction between the incorporating affixes, but between the incorporated nouns involved as well. If she adopted a Montagovian treatment of intensional predicates, this would mean that the intensional affix is interpreted as a relation between an individual and a second order property. Consequently, it would not be possible to interpret the incorporated noun as a predicate modifier in the way presented in the LF under (131). Of course, under a Montagovian view, it would be possible to say that the noun incorporated by an intensional affix is reconstructed and interpreted in its D-structural position, because raising this reconstructed NP at LF would be semantically vacuous. If Bittner adopted Zimmermann's treatment — like I do —, a noun incorporated by an intensional affix would be interpreted as a property, while a noun incorporated by an extensional affix would be interpreted as a predicate modifier. Moreover, only the remnant NP of the latter would be interpreted as an existential quantifier. The remnant of the former would be a predicate modifier.

In sum, whatever approach to intensional verbs Bittner adopts, both options give rise to a situation in which West Greenlandic nouns incorporated by an extensional verb and those incorporated by an intensional verb receive different interpretations. In contrast, my approach interprets all incorporated nouns in a uniform way.

7 The anaphoric potential of predicative indefinites

There is one more aspect of West Greenlandic incorporated nouns that I want to account for in this chapter. It is the possibility of picking up the referent restricted by an incorporated noun with a pronominal constituent. I repeat some of the examples given in chapter 2.

(133) Suulut   timmisartu-liur-p-u-q.

Søren.ABS   airplane-made-IND-[-tr]-3SG

Suluusa-qar-p-u-q   aquute-qar-llu-ni-lu.   [Sadock (1980): 311]

wing-have-IND-[-tr]-3SG   rudder-have-INF-3SG.PROX-and

"Søren made an airplane$_i$. It$_i$ has wings and it$_i$ has a rudder."

(134) Erneq-taar-p-u-t   atser-lu-gu-lu

son-get.a.new-IND-[-tr]-3PL   name-INF-3SG-and

     Mala-mik.   [Sadock (1986): 23]

     Mala-INST

"They had a son$_i$ and they called him$_i$ Maala."

(135) Aani   qimmi-qar-p-u-q.

A.ABS   dog-have-IND-[-tr]-3SG

Miki-mik   ati-qar-p-u-q.   [Bittner (1994): 67]

M.-INST   name-have-IND-[-tr]-3SG

"Aani has a dog$_i$. It$_i$ is called Miki."

In chapter 4, section 1.2.2, I criticized the widespread view that the discourse transparency of West Greenlandic incorporated nouns is a direct mirror of the syntactic fact that these nouns are the head of a base generated phrase. Rather, examples like (136) illustrate that it is related to the accessibility of a discourse referent, if one believes in discourse semantic binding [Kamp (1981), Heim (1982), Groenendijk and Stokhof (1991)].

(136) Aani   qimmi-qa-nngi-l-a-q.

       A.ABS   dog-have-NEG-IND-[-tr]-3SG

       Miki-mik   ati-qar-p-u-q.   [fw]

       M.-INST   name-have-IND-[-tr]-3SG

       "Aani doesn't have a dog$_i$. # It$_i$ is called Miki."

A first question to be answered is how the present semantic analysis of West Greenlandic incorporated nouns as predicative indefinites can be extended in such a way that it also covers the discourse transparency of these nouns. In addition, we are confronted with the question of why West Greenlandic incorporated nouns are discourse transparent, whereas nouns that are part of a German or English compound are not [Postal (1969)].

(137) Johann ist Buchhändler. Es ist im Angebot.

       "John is a book$_i$ dealer. # It$_i$ (= the book) is on sale."

(138) Carol bought cat food. It turned out soon that it didn't like it.

       "Carol bought cat$_i$ food. # It turned out soon that it$_i$ (= the cat) didn't
       like it."

In this section, I first discuss how my proposal of semantic incorporation relates to the Kamp-Heim treatment of the discourse transparency of indefinites. Next, I turn to the question of which words are anaphoric islands and which aren't.

7.1 Semantic incorporation in a discourse semantic framework

The above West Greenlandic examples (133) through (135) are very reminiscent of the use of English indefinites as intersentential antecedents [Sadock (1980), Van Geenhoven (1992)]. The discourse transparency of indefinites gave rise to the idea that an indefinite introduces a novel variable, and that this variable can antecede a pronominal expression [Kamp (1981), Heim (1982)].

(139) Frederik has *a horse. It* is very nice.

"Frederik has a horse$_i$. It$_i$ is very nice."

In the first section of this chapter, I suggested that if we integrate the semantic incorporation proposal into a discourse semantic framework, we can capture the discourse transparency of West Greenlandic incorporated nouns and of any other predicative indefinite in terms of semantic binding. In that section, I also mentioned that there are two routes one can take, a strictly compositional route and a representational one. However, I will not discuss which is the better way to go since for the above examples the choice is not relevant. A compromise that fits this compositionally oriented chapter well is Rooth (1987), a compositional translation of the Kamp-Heim approach. More precisely, it is a translation of Heim's (1982) File Change Semantics, her semantic version of the indefinites-are-variables idea. The idea is that the meaning of a sentence is captured in terms of its potential of changing the context. From a formal perspective this means that the meaning of a sentence is regarded as a set of pairs of assignment functions, an input and and output function, assigning variables to indices. Depending on whether its output function is or is not identical to its input function, a sentence did not or did change the context in which it occurs.

In light of a shortened version of Sadock's example (133), I illustrate how a discourse semantic analysis captures the discourse transparency of the incorporated nouns involved.

(140) Suulut   timmisartu-liur$_i$-p-u-q.   Suluusa-qar-p-u-q$_i$.

S.ABS   airplane-make-IND-[-tr]-3SG   wing-have-IND-[-tr]-3SG

"Søren made$_i$ an airplane. It$_i$ (= the airplane) has wings."

The indices in italics added to (140) are mine. The index on the agreement morpheme $-q_i$ indicates that this morpheme has pronominal force. The index on the incorporating verbal affix $-liur_i-$ indicates that from the perspective of semantic incorporation it is not the incorporated noun but rather the semantically incorporating verb which introduces a novel discourse referent. This is clearly distinct from the Kamp-Heim approach in which it are indefinites, that is, nominal expressions, which introduce a novel discourse referent. In terms of changing the context, this means that a semantically incorporating verb changes an input context [i.e., a variable assignment function g] into an output context [i.e., a variable assignment function g'] by assigning a novel variable to a syntactic index. Note again the relevance of my claim that noun incorporating configurations are syntactically transparent [see chapter 4]. If they weren't, there would be no straightforward way to syntactically differentiate the incorporated noun from the incorporating verb so that we could assign a syntactic index to the latter.

Using the notation of Rooth (1987), we can write down the context change potential of $-liur_i-$ ("to make") as follows:

(141) $\| \text{liur}_i \| = \{ <g \; x \; P \; g' > \mid \exists y \; [\; <x,y> \in F(\text{make}) \land g' = g \cup \{<i \; y>\}$
$\land <g \; y \; g' > \in P \;] \}$

The context change potential of -liur_i- ("to make") is defined as a set of quadruples consisting of an input function g, an object-level variable x, which is the verb's first argument, a property-level variable P, which is the verb's second argument, and an output function g'. For each such quadruple there is an object y that has P as a property and to which x stands in the *MAKE* relation. Moreover, the output g' differs from the input g in that it assigns y to the index i on -liur_i-. In other words, it adds a discourse referent to the existing context.

Next, the meaning of the incorporated airplane is not very interesting from a context change perspective. It does not introduce a discourse referent.[29] This means that it will not change the context and, hence, the input g and the output g' are identical.

(142) $\| \text{timmisartu} \| = \{ <g \; y \; g' > \mid y \in F(\text{airplane}) \land g' = g \}$

The meaning of the complex verb "airplane-make" results from applying (141) to (142):

(143) $\| \text{timmisartu-liur}_i \| = \{ <g \; x \; g' > \mid \exists y \; [\; <x,y> \in F(\text{make}) \land y \in$
$F(\text{airplane}) \land g' = g \cup \{<i \; y>\}] \}$

The context change potential of the whole first sentence in (140) is then represented in (144).[30]

(144) $\| \textit{Suulut timmisartu-liur}_i \| = \{ <g \; g' > \mid \exists y \; [\; <s,y> \in F(\text{make}) \land y \in$
$F(\text{airplane}) \land g' = g \cup \{<i \; y>\}] \}$

Now, we move on to the second sentence in (140) which contains a pronominal element realized as the third singular Subject agreement morpheme -q_i. As a pronoun, it will be assigned the meaning in (145) which says that the discourse semantic function of a pronominal element is to assign an index a familiar variable, namely, y.

(145) $\| -q_i \| = \{ <g \; y \; g' > \mid g'(i) = y \land g = g' \}$

The meaning of the whole piece of discourse under (140) is now captured as in (146). Note that the incorporated noun *suluusa*- ("wing") and the affixal verb -*qar*- ("to have") are interpreted as a predicative indefinite and a semantically incorporating verb as well.

---

[29] Of course, one could say that like any nominal it introduces a property- or kind-level referent. Below we will see that this additional machinery is useful when dealing with property and kind anaphora.

[30] For the sake of not creating additional questions at this point, I represent names as constants here.

(146) ‖ *Suulut timmisartu-liur$_i$-p-u-q. Suluusa-qar$_k$-p-u-q$_i$.* ‖ =

$\{<g\ g'' > \mid \exists y\ \exists z\ [\ <s,y> \in F(make) \wedge y \in F(airplane) \wedge z \in$
$F(wing) \wedge <y,z> \in F(have) \wedge g'' = g \cup \{<i\ y>, <k\ z>\}\ ]\ \}$

Informally, (146) says that the combination of the two sentences under (140) changes the original context in such a way that in the first part a novel discourse referent y is being introduced of which it is said that it is an airplane made by Suulut and, in the second part, that this referent has wings.

What is interesting about this example is that the number of the discourse referent introduced by an incorporating verb remains unspecified until the pronominal element enters the scene. In this respect, West Greenlandic incorporated nouns are clearly different from phrasal predicative indefinites. For example, the NP *a horse* in (139) is singular, and it is the indefinite itself, which introduces the number of the verb's internal argument.[31] The following example illustrates how a plural pronoun, the Subject agreement morpheme *-t*, fixes the plurality of the incorporating verb's argument.

(147) Aani   qimmi-qar-p-u-q.   Kusana-q-a-a-t.   [fw]

A.ABS   dog-have-IND-[-tr]-3SG   nice.very-be-IND-[-tr]-3PL

"Aani has$_i$ dogs. They$_i$ are very nice."

Finally, what about the following example?

(148) Aani   qimmi-qa-nngi-l-a-q.

A.ABS   dog-have-NEG-IND-[-tr]-3SG

Miki-mik   ati-qar-p-u-q.   [fw]

M.-INST   name-have-IND-[-tr]-3SG

"Aani doesn't have$_i$ a dog. # Its$_i$ name is Miki."

From the present perspective, the fact that the discourse referent of which the incorporated noun *qimmi-* ("dog") holds cannot antecede the pronoun in the second sentence under (148) simply follows from the fact that this referent is embedded under negation [see chapter 3, section 1.2].

7.2 Which words are anaphoric islands?

Postal (1969) observed that the components of English compounds are anaphoric islands. They cannot serve as the antecedent of a pronoun.

---

[31] Note in this respect that the English bare plural does not always fix the number of the referent introduced by a semantically incorporating verb. When we ask (i), (ii) is a felicitous answer.

(i)   Did you eat apples?
(ii)   Yes, one.

Obviously, the same holds for compounds in languages closely related to English.

(149) Johann ist Buchhändler. Es ist im Angebot.

"John is a book$_i$ dealer. # It$_i$ (= the book) is on sale."

(150) Carol bought cat food. It turned out soon that it didn't like it.

"Carol bought cat$_i$ food. # It turned out soon that it$_i$ (= the cat) didn't like it."

At first sight, these data are in striking contrast with the West Greenlandic data, where it is possible to pick up the referent of an incorporated noun. In the morphosyntactic literature on noun incorporation, this often leads to the conclusion that English compounds are lexical in nature and noun incorporating configurations syntactic. This lexical–syntactic distinction is supposed to explain the difference in discourse behaviour of the respective incorporated nouns. However, stipulating a division of labour between two components of the grammar is in itself not very explanatory. It does not answer the question of what exactly the discourse transparency of West Greenlandic incorporated nouns amounts to, as we just did. Nor does it answer the question of why lexicalized material is discourse opaque. Moreover, it may give rise to a syntactization of the phenomena involved which simply misses the point. For instance, Baker (1988) argues that the discourse transparency of incorporated nouns is a consequence of them being the head of a D-structural phrase. However, there is no reason to believe that there is a one-to-one relation between being a semantically accessible antecedent and being a phrase.

My answer to the question of why lexicalized material is discourse opaque and of what exactly the lexicon–syntax division amounts to follows a suggestion of Zimmermann (p.c.). It simply says that the existential quantification involved in the semantic interpretation of parts of lexicalizations is always static, whereas the one that comes with parts of syntactic constructs is dynamic. Hence, the boundary between the syntactic and the lexical component of a grammar does not mirror the boundary between phrase and word structure. Rather, it recapitulates the semantic distinction of whether an expression is interpretable in a dynamic way or not.[32]

Finally, in contrast to the English and German examples given so far Ward, Sproat and McKoon (1991) provide a number of examples in which a part of a compound apparently antecedes a pronoun. Here are some of their examples.

---

[32] In this book, I do not further elaborate this suggestion. But see Van Geenhoven (1997).

(151) Museum visitors can see through its (= the museum's) big windows the 900-year-old Tower of London and the modern office blocks of the city financial district.

(152) Bush supporters would stay home figuring he (= Bush)'d already won.

(153) At the same time as coffee beans were introduced, the Arabs made changes in the coffee preparations that greatly improved its (= coffee's) taste.

With respect to the first of these examples, I am not convinced that it is indeed the compound part *museum* that provides us with an accessible antecedent. The reason is that this sentence is clearly taken from a larger context (e.g. a museum brochure or a newspaper article) and it is very probably the case that at some point in this larger context the relevant antecedent, a particular museum, has been mentioned explicitly. The second example illustrates the case in which a compound contains a proper name. Under the view advocated here that names are presuppositional, the fact that a pronoun can refer to a morphologically embedded proper name is not a surprise. In the third example, the pronoun does not refer to an object-level but rather to a kind-level entity. It is a well-known feature of kinds that they ignore quantificational and modal embeddings [Krifka et al. (1995)]. In fact, Postal's claim that words are anaphoric islands has be to made more specific in the sense that words are nonkind anaphoric islands. The parts of the nominalizations that I used to illustrate the discourse opacity of embedded words in (149) and in (150) can introduce a kind- or property-level antecedent [see fn. 29]. This is illustrated for *cat* in *cat food* in (154) and (155), respectively.

(154) Carol always buys high quality *cat* food because she thinks it is good for *their* health.

(155) Carol often buys *cat* food so I guess she has *one*.

7.3 Summary

We have seen that as long as the discourse referent of which a predicative indefinite holds is not semantically embedded, it can antecede a pronoun. The novelty of the present approach is that this referent is introduced by a verb that incorporates the predicative indefinite, rather than by the indefinite itself. The fact that nouns embedded in an English compound cannot antecede a non-kind anaphoric expression is explained as the consequence of their static interpretation. This may be only a partial explanation of the compound facts, but a full explanation would require yet another chapter.

8 Chapter summary

In this chapter, I have expounded and illustrated semantic incorporation as a uniform account of the semantic behaviour of a (modified) West Greenlandic incorporated noun, a West Germanic bare plural and a German "split" Object. The basic idea behind my proposal is that these narrow indefinites are predicates of a referent that is introduced by a semantically incorporating predicate. In other words, like the Kamp-Heim approach, a predicative indefinite does not have quantificational force, but unlike this approach, a predicative indefinite does not introduce a novel variable.

I dealt with the discourse transparency of West Greenlandic incorporated nouns and with the question of which words are anaphoric islands. Although it is the incorporating verb and not its indefinite argument which introduces a novel discourse referent this does not prohibit this referent from being able to antecede a pronoun.

Finally, this chapter has also shown that a syntactic analysis which simply regards noun incorporating configurations as syntactically base generated constructions delivers an appropriate input for their (discourse) semantic interpretation. The syntactic transparency of noun incorporating constructions is semantically relevant in at least the following three cases. The semantic interpretation of incorporated *wh*-elements and of intensional external modifiers, as well as the interpretation of incorporating verbs as discourse referent introducers.

6

The Scope of Indefinites

0 Introduction

The goal of this final chapter is to develop a general strategy to account for the different readings (scope, partitivity) an indefinite description can get, on the one hand, and to integrate semantic incorporation into this strategy, on the other. Whereas the previous chapter was primarily concerned with the question of why particular indefinites never reach non-narrow scope positions, this chapter answers the additional questions of how other indefinites reach non-narrow scope positions and which indefinites can be interpreted in a partitive way.

Focusing my attention to indefinites in Object position, I start from a basic distinction between predicative and free variable indefinites. I furthermore suggest that the default interpretation of an indefinite which is ambiguous between the two readings is that of a predicative indefinite. We have seen that the inherently narrow scope of predicative indefinites is determined through semantic incorporation. Their discourse referents are introduced by the verb. Here, I argue that the introduction of free variable indefinites is determined through accommodation, a mechanism to repair the context of utterance. Both mechanisms meet the requirement stated by Abusch (1994) that the restriction contributed by an indefinite has to be taken into account in the latter's binding procedure [see chapter 3, section 3]. I close the chapter with a discussion of partitivity. I argue that only those nominal expressions which introduce a (bound) variable themselves are appropriate candidates for a partitive interpretation because this variable is needed to create the membership relation.

This chapter contains four sections. In the first section, I outline the background of my proposal. The second section presents the role of the accommodation mechanism in van der Sandt's (1992) presupposition theory. With van der Sandt's accommodation strategy in mind, the third section illustrates how this repair mechanism successfully determines the "scope" of free variable indefinites. In the fourth section, I discuss partitive readings of indefinites, and I provide an answer to the question of why West Greenlandic incorporated nouns in particular, and predicative indefinites in general, do not receive a partitive interpretation.

Before I open this chapter, I should mention the following with respect to the framework used. In chapter 5, I decided to present predicative indefinites in a type-driven system for methodological reasons. That is, this system was used only to show the reader how semantic incorporation works. At the same time, I pointed out in the previous chapter that in order to grasp the discourse transparency of predicative indefinites, it is useful to integrate semantic incorporation into a discourse semantic framework. In this chapter, my aim is to present semantic incorporation as a subtheory of a larger approach to indefinite descriptions in which van der Sandt's notion of accommodation plays a crucial role. Given that this notion of accommodation can be characterized in a representational framework only, this chapter uses a DRT-style semantics to represent the interpretation of indefinite descriptions. To some readers, this switch from one framework to another may come across as a conceptual switch that he or she may not want to follow. The author, however, always tries to keep in mind that a framework is nothing but a device. Moreover, this chapter aims to present the characteristics of a larger approach to indefinites in such a way that it makes clear how my proposal differs from existing DRT approaches. It does not present an elaborated formalization of these characteristics.

1 The trigger of the accommodation proposal

It is a well-known puzzle in the literature on the English partitive construction that although a "specific" indefinite can be embedded into a partitive construction, as illustrated in (1), this clearly violates Jackendoff's (1977) PARTITIVE CONSTRAINT. This constraint says that the complement NP of the partitive preposition *of* has to be a definite NP, as illustrated in (2).

(1)   John was one of *several students* who arrived late. [Ladusaw (1982): 240]

(2)   John was one of *the students* who arrived late.

Whereas "specific" indefinites and definites can show up in a partitive *of*-phrase, a bare plural cannot.

(3)   * John was one of *students* who arrived late.

The above data illustrate that "specific" indefinite and definite descriptions have something in common that an English bare plural lacks. Following Heim (1982), the definite description in (2) is an anaphoric expression. As we will spell out in more detail below, these can either find a straightforward antecedent or create their own antecedent through the accommodation of their descriptive content [Lewis (1979), van der Sandt (1992)]. I will argue that those indefinites that can be embedded in a partitive construction are free variable expressions and that their "existential closure" is the result of accommodation.

    My claim that free variable indefinites are accommodated should not be misunderstood in such a way that I regard these indefinites as presuppositions. In contrast to definite descriptions, "specific" indefinites are not presuppositional, that is, they are not anaphoric expressions. This can be easily illustrated through the following pair of examples:

(4)   A man$_i$ entered the bar. The man$_i$ ordered a beer.

(5)   A man$_i$ entered the bar. # A man$_i$ who just entered ordered a beer.

A definite needs an antecedent as its binder. Either it finds this antecedent — as in (4) — or it creates an antecedent by means of accommodation [see section 2 below].[1]   (5) shows that an indefinite is not an anaphoric expression. That is, it cannot be set equal to a potential antecedent.

My proposal that some indefinites are *free* variable expressions does not only find empirical support in examples like (1). Unlike standard DRT approaches, Abusch's (1994) approach to indefinites makes the same claim: indefinites and their variables are stored in a U-set until the latter is bound through her rule of EXISTENTIAL CLOSURE. As an alternative, I propose that the introduction of a free variable indefinite's discourse referent is determined through the mechanism of accommodation.

2 Accommodation and presupposition projection

When I claim that accommodation determines the introduction of free variable indefinites, I have a particular view of presupposition projection in mind. It is van der Sandt's (1992) view that presupposition projection is not a matter of contextual satisfaction [Karttunen (1973), Heim (1983)], but rather a matter of anaphora resolution.

In this section, I first discuss van der Sandt's idea that presuppositions are anaphoric expressions. Next, I show which role accommodation plays in his approach.

2.1 Van der Sandt: Presupposition as anaphora

... presuppositional expressions are claimed to be anaphoric expressions, which have internal structure and semantic content. In fact, they only differ from pronouns ... in that they have more descriptive content. It is this fact which enables them to create an antecedent in case discourse does not provide one. If their capacity to accommodate is taken into account, they can be treated by basically the same mechanism which handles the resolution of pronouns [van der Sandt (1992): 333].

A nice way in which van der Sandt makes his idea that presuppositional expressions are anaphors transparent is by relating prototypical examples of anaphoric relations which a discourse semantic framework should be able to deal with [see (6)], to some of Karttunen's (1973) examples that illustrate the need for presupposition projection [see (7)].

---

[1] Originally, Lewis (1979) defines accommodation as a rule for adding existential presuppositions to the common ground. Since Heim (1983), this term has been used as the label of the strategy to determine the interpretation of a presuppositional expression. The position such an expression reaches through Heimian accommodation (global and local) is not necessarily the position achieved by Lewisian accommodation (global only).

(6)   a.   John owns a donkey. He beats it.

        b.   If John owns a donkey, he beats it.

(7)   a.   Jack has children and all of Jack's children (= them) are bald.

        b.   If Jack has children, then all of Jack's children (= them) are bald.

Each of these examples provides us with an overt antecedent — *a donkey* in (6) and *children* in (7) — with which the definite pronouns in (6a) and (6b) and the definite descriptions in (7a) and (7b) can be identified, respectively. However, if no such overt antecedent is available, only those anaphoric expressions which bear descriptive content will get an interpretation. This is illustrated in the following minimal pair.

(8)   If Jack is bald, then *they* (= ?) are bald.

(9)   If Jack is bald, then all of *Jack's children* (= the children Jack has) are bald.

At this point, a crucial capacity of presuppositional phrases comes into play, which is their capacity to be accommodated. Whereas the discourses in (6) and (7) already contain the relevant antecedents, in (8) and (9) this is not the case. In this case, the discourse context has to be adjusted or "repaired." Accommodation, that is, adding information to the context is a mechanism which fulfills exactly this requirement.[2]

2.2 The resolution of presuppositions

Van der Sandt regards anaphora resolution as a pre-interpretive process. Here, I will point out various strategies to resolve a presupposition together with some constraints on these strategies.

2.2.1 Direct anaphoric linking

A definite description — like any other presuppositional expression — comes with an anaphoric binding instruction.[3] That is, it comes with a free variable together with the instruction to identify this variable with an

---

[2] The context can be repaired in different ways, namely appropriate and less appropriate ways. For this reason, accommodation has been defined in different ways and from different theoretical perspectives. In Heim (1983), we find an accommodation strategy within the traditional view of presupposition projection, i.e., the view of contextual satisfaction. Van der Sandt shows that both this strategy and the theory of contextual satisfaction are wrong. One basic mistake is that presuppositional satisfaction is defined in terms of entailment. For a detailed discussion see van der Sandt (1992): 9-17.

[3] Of course, this only holds for a subset of definites. We also find those that denote kinds, as in (i), or that have a functional reading, as in (ii). I restrict my attention to anaphoric definites.

(i)   The duck is a fascinating animal.
(ii)   Today I will take the bus.

antecedent. In order to fulfill this binding instruction in the interpretation procedure, the interpreter first checks whether there is an accessible antecedent to which the definite NP can be set equal. In (10) and (11), there are such antecedents.

(10)   John has a child. The child is happy.

"John has a child x. x is happy."

(11)   If John has a child, the child is happy.

"If John has a child x, x is happy."

2.2.2 Top-level accommodation

In example (9), however, direct anaphoric binding of a presuppositional expression was not possible. I repeat it here.

(12)   If Jack is bald, then all of *Jack's children* are bald.

We have to adjust the discourse context by setting up a representation in which the presupposition *Jack has children* triggered by the definite description *Jack's children* is accommodated to the highest level. This we call top-level or global accommodation.

(12)   GLOBAL   "Jack has children x. If Jack is bald, then all of x are bald."

In this way, we establish a discourse referent, namely *children*, with which the anaphoric expression *Jack's children* is identified.

The claim that the default option for the accommodation of the presuppositional content of a definite description which is part of the consequent of an implication, is top-level accommodation goes against the more widespread view that the presuppositional content of such a definite description is made dependent on the antecedent of that implication [Heim (1983)]. The latter view is part of a theory of presupposition projection as contextual satisfaction, a treatment in which the presupposition of a sentence is computed on the basis of a set of update rules [see fn. 2]. Van der Sandt shows that making the presuppositional content of *Jack's children* in (12) dependent on the *if*-clause *if Jack is bald* gives us a presupposition, namely (13), which is too weak.

(13)   "If Jack is bald, then Jack has children."

(13) is too weak because it cannot capture the possibility of continuing (12) with the following piece of discourse:

(14)   *They* look very much like Jack.

The plural pronoun in (14) requires a set of children as its antecedent, and (13) — as opposed to (12 GLOBAL) — does not provide such a set.

2.2.3 Trapping

Accommodation to the highest level, which is the default case, can be blocked by "trapping." A case in point is (15).

(15)   Every man loves *his wife*.

In order to resolve the complex anaphoric expression *his wife*, we need to resolve the embedded anaphor *his* first. Because we do not want to be left with a free variable in the final semantic representation of (15), we bind this pronoun to the quantifier *every*. This means that we cannot accommodate the complete description *his wife* to any level higher than the level at which the pronoun *his* is bound. The "highest" interpretation of *his wife* in (15) is what I call its relational reading, and it results from its intermediate accommodation into the restrictor of the *every* quantifier.[4]

(15)   RELAT   "Every man who has a wife *i* loves *i*."

Through the intermediate accommodation of a presupposition in the scope of a quantifier, the latter's domain becomes more restricted.

Intermediate accommodation does not necessarily give rise to relational readings. In the following example, there are two suitable intermediate accommodation positions for the definite description *his wife* that is in the restrictor of the embedded quantifier. The first position is the restrictor of the embedding quantifier, the second one is the "highest" position in the scope of this quantifier.

(16)   Every man danced with every woman who likes his wife.

    RELAT   "Every man who has a wife *w* danced with every woman
    who likes *w*."

    INTERM   "For every man *m* there is a wife *w* and *m* danced with
    every woman who likes *w*."

2.2.4 Local accommodation

The way I have presented accommodation so far may lead to the impression that van der Sandt only uses global (top-level) and intermediate accommodation. That is, it may appear as if the examples discussed in the previous subsections have a global, a relational or an intermediate reading only. However, these readings are only one part of the interpretation picture. For instance, (15) also has a reading that is the result of local accommodation.

(15)   LOCAL   "Every man *m* has a wife *w* and *m* loves *w*."

---

[4] Of course, it is possible to understand the definite pronoun in a deictic way as well.

Some people defend the view that the local interpretation of *his wife* in (15) is its primary and only interpretation. For instance, Beaver (1994) claims that its above relational reading does not exist. His argument is based on the fact that a sentence like (17) is contradictory.

(17)   # Few of the 15 team members and none of the 5 cheerleaders can drive but every team member will come to the match with her car.

According to Beaver, van der Sandt cannot account for this contradiction since his theory predicts the following intermediate reading of (17).

(17)   RELAT   "Few of the 15 team members and none of the 5 cheerleaders can drive but every team member who has a car c will come to the match with c."

Van der Sandt (p.c.) points out that Beaver overlooks an essential part of his approach, and that his theory does not predict (17 RELAT). Beaver overlooks the fact that the quantifier *every team member* itself comes with a presupposition, namely, its domain of quantification. Given that van der Sandt adopts an on-line strategy of anaphora resolution, the latter presupposition is resolved before the presupposition *her car* enters the scene. (18) is the paraphrase of this intermediate step in the interpretation of (17).

(18)   # Few of the 15 team members and none of the 5 cheerleaders can drive but every team member (= those who can drive and those who cannot drive) will come to the match with her car.

Every's domain named by *team member* is identified with the set of team members which we know from the first part of the sentence, and of which we know that the majority of its elements cannot drive. What happens if one now tries to resolve *her car*? The presence of the pronoun *her* requires that the whole presupposition *her car* is located at the level at which this pronoun is bound, namely, at the level of the quantifier *every team member*. However, the intermediate position is not a suitable accommodation position for *her car* because it is simply not compatible to say of a group that they all come with their car if one already knows that the majority of this group cannot drive. In other words, if a presupposition in the scope of a quantifier cannot globally accommodate because it contains a pronoun, it is still possible that independent reasons do not allow us to accommodate it into the restrictor of that quantifier either. One such reason is that this position is already occupied.

Note also in this respect that a sentence like (16), repeated here as (19), does not allow the local accommodation option. The presupposition *his wife* has to escape its embedded position, and the only option available is intermediate accommodation.[5] This yields the relational and the intermediate reading.

(19)   Every man danced with every woman who likes his wife.

> LOCAL   # "Every man m danced with every woman for whom there is a wife w of m and who likes w."
>
> RELAT   "Every man who has a wife w danced with every woman who likes w."
>
> INTERM   "For every man m there is a wife w such that m danced with every woman who likes w."

2.2.5 Pragmatic ambiguity

The next example of van der Sandt illustrates how the treatment of a definite description that is in the consequent of an implication can give rise to an ambiguity. The ambiguity follows because we can either accommodate the presupposition of the definite in a global way, namely, at the top level, or we can bind it to a referent in the antecedent of the same implication.

(20)   If John has sons, his children will be happy.

> GLOBAL   "John has children c and if John has sons, c will be happy."
>
> BIND   "If John has sons s, s will be happy."

According to (20 GLOBAL) John has children. The presupposition *his children* is accommodated to the highest level establishing a set of children of which John is the proud father. On this reading, (20) means that John has children and that depending on whether there are boys among them, all of his children will be happy. According to (20 BIND), John may have no children at all. The presupposition *his children* is directly bound to the indefinite *sons* which is part of the conditional's antecedent and, therefore, no accommodation takes place.

2.2.6 Bridging effects

The following constraint on accommodation is not discussed in van der Sandt (1992) but I think it is of equal importance as the trapping constraint. I call it the bridging constraint and as an illustration, I take the following example.

---

[5] The local accommodation of *his wife* requires that we interpret *his wife* as *a wife of his*. This, and I believe that most people agree, is not possible.

(21)   Each choreographer believes that it would be damaging for a dancer of
      his to quit the company.   [Abusch (1994): 92]

We are interested in the definite description *the company*. If we
accommodate it to the top level, we get the following input for the
interpretation.

(21)   GLOBAL   "There is a company c and each choreographer k believes
                 that it would be damaging for a dancer of k to quit c."

There are two other readings possible as well, namely, the reading where we
are only talking about the choreographers who have a company, and the
reading where for each choreographer there is a different company. To get
these readings, we either accommodate the definite description to the
restrictor of the *each* quantifier, or to the "highest" position in the scope of
that quantifier. Implicitly, this "constrained" accommodation is the result of
trapping, since we interpret *the company* as *his company*.

(21)   RELAT   "Each choreographer k who has a company c believes that
              it would be damaging for a dancer of k to quit c."

     INTERM   "Each choreographer k has a company c and k believes
              that it would be damaging for a dancer of k to quit c."

The origin of this ambiguity is a conceptual one: the ambiguity follows
because we can think of one company having more than one choreographer
— as in (21 GLOBAL) —, of each choreographer having a company — as in
(21 INTERM) —, or of those choreographers who have a company — as and
(21 RELAT). In the latter two cases, we *bridge* a choreographer with a
company. Bridging gives rise to implicit trapping. Whereas in the case of
trapping a free variable is in the descriptive content of a presupposition, the
result of conceptual bridging is to smuggle a free variable into the
presupposition's descriptive material. Note that to reach a bridging effect
the descriptive content of the nominal expressions plays an important role.
Consider the following example.

(22)   Each landlord cuts the lawn reluctantly.

In (22), the relational reading appears to be the preferred reading. It is easy
to think of landlords with a house that has its own lawn. We thus bridge a
landlord with a house that has a lawn, and we interpret (22) as (22 RELAT).
The global reading seems rather strange at first. It presupposes that there is
only one house with a lawn. This is possible if we are talking about some
apartment complex with one lawn.

(22)   RELAT   "Each landlord cuts *his* lawn reluctantly."

                 = "Each landlord who has a house with a lawn y, cuts y
                 reluctantly."

GLOBAL   "There is a lawn y and each landlord cuts y reluctantly."

= "There is (a house with) a lawn y and each landlord cuts y reluctantly."

2.3 Summary

In this section, I discussed the role of the accommodation mechanism and the constraints on this repair mechanism within van der Sandt's view that presuppositions are anaphoric expressions.

For the sake of completeness, I should mention that van der Sandt's approach has been implemented into a version of DRT. In van der Sandt and Geurts (1991) anaphoric expressions are processed in two stages and in a bottom-up fashion. In the first stage, anaphoric expressions are awaiting their integration into a DRS while they are encoded in a separate DRS, namely, the A-structure ["A" stands for "anaphor"]. In the second stage, the anaphors are either bound to an antecedent or accommodated at an appropriate level of representation thereby establishing their own antecedent. With the help of example (23), I give a short illustration of this two-stage procedure.

(23)   Max didn't like the cat.

(24a) represents the DRS of (23) that we gain through a construction algorithm. This DRS is incomplete since it contains two more free variables that have been introduced by the presuppositions *Max* and *the cat*.

(24)   a.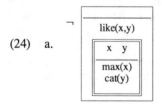

The presuppositions are stored in the double-boxed A-structure. The accommodation of the material in the A-structure transforms (24a) into the DRS under (24b). As soon as the A-structure is empty, the DRS is complete. That is, (24b) is equivalent to (24c) and can be interpreted according to the DRS verification definitions given in Kamp and Reyle (1993).

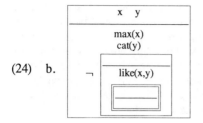

(24)   b.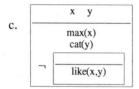

The idea behind this two-step pre-interpretive processing is that the semantic representation that we construct from a sentence containing anaphoric expressions is not interpretable. What van der Sandt and Geurts suggest is that we transform a semantic representation — be it an LF or a DRS — by means of accommodation so that as a result we get an interpretable representation.

3 Incorporating and accommodating indefinites

So far, we have seen that in van der Sandt's theory the purpose of accommodating a definite description is to establish an antecedent for anaphoric binding. In this section, I return to my proposal that accommodation applies also as a pre-interpretive mechanism to those indefinite descriptions that come with a free variable. In other words, whereas a semantically incorporating verb delivers the discourse referent of a predicative indefinite, the purpose of accommodating a free variable indefinite is to locate the position at which the latter's discourse referent is introduced. Thus, as opposed to standard DRT an indefinite does not automatically introduce a discourse referent into the discourse universe of the DRS into which it is integrated as a restriction of this referent.

In the first part of this section, I show how I capture the ambiguity of indefinites that show up in the scope of a quantifier at LF. This involves those indefinites that one finds in sentences like *every man loves a woman, every student is reading a book*. Whereas the narrow reading is said to be the result of semantic incorporation, the wide reading results from accommodating the indefinite's descriptive content. The second part focuses on indefinites that are in the scope or in the restrictor of an embedded quantifier. These are the cases discussed in Abusch (1994) [see chapter 3, section 3]. What is interesting is that the different cases of presupposition resolution for which either global (top-level) or intermediate accommodation is used [see section 2], appear to be very similar to Abusch's cases where a maximal reading or an intermediate reading of an indefinite is expected. I revisit Abusch's data to illustrate these parallels. In the third section, I discuss what it means for an indefinite to accommodate.

3.1 *Every man loves a woman*

How does the present approach deal with the often discussed ambiguity of example (25)?

(25)   Every man loves a woman.

        NARROW   "For every man m there is a woman w and m loves w."

        WIDE   "There is a particular woman w and every man loves w."

Here is my strategy. On the one hand, I regard the narrow reading of this sentence as the result of semantic incorporation. The indefinite *a woman* is interpreted as a predicate that is absorbed by the verb *to love* as the predicate of its internal argument's variable. On this reading, the verb is interpreted as an extensional, incorporating verb. On the other hand, I take the wide reading of (25) to be the result of global accommodation. In this case, the indefinite *a woman* is interpreted as a free variable expression and the verb *to love* as a two-place predicate. In sum, the following tripartite structure schemata underly these two readings.

(A1)   Quant[restr ...][nucl ... **indefinite** ...]

(B1)   Quant[restr ...][nucl ... **indefinite(x)**...]

If the matrix verb is an extensional verb, the predicative indefinite in (A1) will be incorporated as the predicate of this verb's internal argument's variable. This verb also delivers the existential interpretation of this variable. The result of this process is exemplified in (C1).

(C1)   Quant[restr ...] $\exists x$ [nucl ... **indefinite(x)** ...]

The free variable indefinite in (B1) reaches a maximal position through the global accommodation of its descriptive content. The "transformation" from (B1) into (D1) is triggered by the fact that (B1) is not interpretable because the variable x is free. The default way of doing so is by accommodation it in a global way, that is, by assigning it an existential interpretation at the highest position possible. Or, in DRT terms, by introducing x into the top-level discourse universe.

(D1) $\exists x$ **indefinite(x)** ... Quant[restr ...][nucl ... **x** ...]

Many people have a preference for interpreting (25) in the narrow way. They have a harder time to derive the wide reading. I suggest that within the present approach to indefinites it is possible to capture this preference. What we need to add is the following slogan:

(26)　ACCOMMODATION CONDITION [AC]

> Unless there is sufficient evidence for an indefinite to be accommodated, it is semantically incorporated.

AC says that an indefinite is primarily understood as a predicate, and that semantic incorporation is the default operation applied to an indefinite description. It also says that for an indefinite to be accommodated, that is, to be a free variable expression, we need additional support. This claim immediately raises the difficult question of what counts as additional support. I do not intend to answer it exhaustively. Rather, I wish to point out some features of a nominal expression that may give rise to its interpretation as a predicative or as a free variable indefinite.

One such feature is case marking. In chapter 4, we saw that in many languages the interpretation of an Object NP depends on the case it bears. I repeat the examples for West Greenlandic.

(27)　a.　Jaaku　*arna-mik*　　　tuqut-si-v-u-q.　　　　[Bittner (1988): 5]

　　　　　J.ABS　woman-INST.SG　kill-AP-IND-[-tr]-3SG

　　　　　"Jacob killed a woman."

　　　b.　Jaaku-p　*arnaq*　　　tuqut-p-a-a.

　　　　　J.-ERG　woman.ABS.SG　kill-IND-[+tr]-3SG.3SG

　　　　　"Jacob killed the/a particular woman."

The ABSOLUTIVE constituent *arnaq* ("woman") can either get a definite or a "specific" indefinite interpretation. The fact that in West Greenlandic a strong Case Object can get both interpretations seems to support the present proposal that definites and indefinites can undergo one and the same pre-interpretive process. Note that the adjective *particular* used in the English paraphrase of (27b) does not necessarily trigger a free variable interpretation. It also can be used to describe a particular kind. This is illustrated by the following example in which *a particular saw* easily gets a de dicto reading.

(28)　To carve figures in this piece of wood, I need a particular saw.

Yet another piece of evidence for a free variable interpretation of an indefinite is the determiner used. For instance, it is a known fact about the English plural determiner *some* that it cannot get a narrow scope reading with respect to negation.

(29)   John didn't eat some apples.

      NARROW   # "It is not the case that John ate apples."

      WIDE   "There are some apples that John didn't eat."

This means in the present theoretical perspective that indefinites with *some* cannot be semantically incorporated. As such, this determiner must be lexically marked as not semantically incorporatable. The same holds for its Dutch and German counterparts, *enkele* and *einige*.

(30)   * Jan   heeft   niet   enkele   appels   gegeten.

      J.   has   not   some   apples   eaten

(31)   * Johann   hat   nicht   einige   Äpfel   gegessen.

      J.   has   not   some   apples   eaten

In these languages, negation takes scope to its right. Hence, (30) and (31) are ungrammatical because the only interpretation they can get is that of a narrow indefinite.

    Apart from the presence of strong Case in determinerless languages and the lexical marking of particular determiners in languages with determiners, discourse can give us an additional clue that an indefinite has to be accommodated. As an illustration, I borrow the following example from Dayal (p.c.):

(32)   John ate everything his mother gave for lunch but he didn't eat an apple and a pear.

Finally, focus can help us to decide whether an indefinite receives a free variable interpretation.

(33)   Daß die meisten Franzosen EINEN Film besonders mögen, liegt wohl daran, daß Cathérine Deneuve die Hauptdarstellerin ist.

    "The fact that most Frenchmen like one movie particularly is related to the fact that Cathérine Deneuve plays the leading part."

Focusing the indefinite determiner *einen* ("a") can give rise to a wide scope reading with respect to the quantifier *die meisten Franzosen* ("most Frenchmen"), which means that it is globally accommodated. When this focus is not present, the indefinite is interpreted as a predicate that is semantically incorporated by the verb *mögen* ("to like").

    In the previous section, we saw that there are different options for the accommodation of presuppositions, namely, global, intermediate and local accommodation, and that global accommodation was the default option. I suggest that the default accommodation option of free variable indefinites is global accommodation as well. The question that arises is whether the other options, namely, intermediate and local accommodation, are also used in the present context.

The local accommodation of the free variable indefinite in our scheme (B1) gives rise to a local or *in situ* existential interpretation. That is, the result of local accommodation is the same as the above reached through semantic incorporation in (C1). Since the latter process is regarded as the default binding mechanism of an indefinite, local accommodation appears to be a redundant operation for a sentence like (25).[6]

What about the intermediate accommodation option? With respect to the resolution of presuppositions, we saw that intermediate accommodation applies if global accommodation is constrained. One constraint that gives rise to intermediate accommodation is trapping, which is activated through the presence of a pronoun in the descriptive content of a presupposition. The intermediate accommodation of a presupposition can then restrict a quantifier's domain [see (15 RELAT)]. The question we have to address here is whether an indefinite that is in the scope of a quantifier and whose descriptive material contains a pronoun can restrict the domain of that quantifier as well. The following examples show that it cannot: such an indefinite lacks a relational reading.

(34)   Every man danced with a woman he really liked.

    NARROW   "Every man really liked a woman x and danced with x."

    RELAT   # "Every man who really liked a woman x danced with x."

(35)   Every singer chose a song he had practiced the day before.

    NARROW   "Every singer had practiced a song x the day before and chose x."

    RELAT   # "Every singer who had practiced a song x the day before chose x."

I believe that the primary and only reading of (34) and (35) is the narrow reading, in which case the indefinite is interpreted as an incorporated predicate. If the indefinite is interpreted as a free variable, it is locally accommodated and this yields — redundantly — a narrow reading as well. How can we explain the fact that a free variable indefinite that contains a pronoun does not allow a relational reading, although its definite counterpart easily can?

(36)   Every singer chose the song he had practiced the day before.

    RELAT   "Every singer who had practiced a song x the day before chose x."

---

[6] The local accommodation of indefinites is probably not redundant in general because there are situations in which an indefinite with narrowest scope can, for some reason or other, NOT be semantically incorporated. Relevant cases are indefinites with nonincorporatable determiners, as discussed in this section, which may still get narrow readings with respect to operators other than negation. See section 4.2.2 below on *some*.

I suggest that a free variable indefinite's inability of receiving a relational reading is related to the fact that such an indefinite is not anaphoric. In section 1, I already illustrated its inability of being bound to an accessible antecedent through example (5). The relational reading of the definite description in (36) follows because the description as a whole is an anaphoric expression and therefore it is preferably bound at the *same* level at which the anaphoric expression it contains is bound. As a result, the definite description restricts the quantifier's domain. The indefinite descriptions in (34) and (35) lack a relational reading because these descriptions are not anaphoric. It is not because they contain an anaphoric expression that they themselves become anaphoric. As a consequence, they cannot restrict a domain of quantification and, hence, there is no reason to bind them at the level at which the anaphoric expression they contain is bound.

3.2 Abusch's data revisited

In chapter 3, I concluded that from Abusch's discussion of the scope properties of indefinites we can draw two important observations [see chapter 3, section 3.3]. On the one hand, she shows that an intermediate reading of an indefinite is neither the narrowing of a wide scope reading, nor the strengthening of a narrow scope one: it is a logically independent reading. On the other hand, she points out why an account à la Heim (1982) fails to capture the correct truth conditions of a sentence containing an intermediate indefinite description: the restriction of an indefinite is forced to be interpreted *in situ*, regardless of whether the latter's variable is interpreted *in situ* or not. Abusch argues that an adequate mechanism to determine the scope of an indefinite has to meet the requirement that an indefinite's descriptive material shows up at the same level at which that indefinite's variable is bound. Abusch's U-set storage mechanism meets this requirement. In other words, the descriptive content of an indefinite becomes a DRS condition of that DRS into whose universe the indefinite's discourse referent has been introduced.

In chapter 3, I pointed out that Abusch's proposal gives rise to a set of shortcomings and problems [see chapter 3, section 3.4]. She defines a mechanism that serves no other purpose than that of determining the scope of indefinites. The proposal also fails to see an important link between the resolution of presuppositions and the scope determination of indefinites. Moreover, her proposal does not mirror the preferences people often have when interpreting an indefinite description. In addition, the U-set mechanism lacks a way of blocking non-narrow readings of bare plural NPs. And finally, to deal with indefinites in sentence initial *if*-clauses Abusch still makes use of the notion of "referential indefinite." The purpose of this section is to show that we can solve these problems if we determine the scope of an indefinite either by means of semantic incorporation or through accommodation.

Abusch's data differ from the *every man loves a woman* kind of data in the following way. She examines indefinites that appear in the restrictor of a quantifier, which itself is embedded either in the scope, or in the restrictor of yet another quantifier. The basic LF schemata of her data are the following.

(A2)   Quant[restr ...][nucl ... Quant[restr ... **indefinite(x)** ...][nucl ...]]

(A3)   Quant[restr ... Quant[restr ... **indefinite(x)** ...][nucl ...]][nucl ...]

(A2) and (A3) show that Abusch always interprets indefinite descriptions as free variables. She then computes the independent existing maximal, intermediate and narrow reading, respectively. If an indefinite is interpreted in situ, its variable is unselectively bound by the lowest c-commanding quantifier. This provides the narrow reading of the indefinites in (A2) and (A3), as captured in (B2) and (B3), respectively.

(B2)   Quant[restr ...][nucl ... Quant x[restr ... **indefinite(x)** ...][nucl ...]]

(B3)   Quant[restr ... Quant x[restr ... **indefinite(x)** ...][nucl ...]][nucl ...]

In order to account for the intermediate and the maximal readings, the U-set mechanism makes it possible to shift the free variable together with its descriptive content to a higher quantificational level. These "shifts" are captured in (C2) and (C3), and (D2) and (D3), representing the intermediate readings and the maximal readings of (A2) and (A3), respectively.

(C2)   Quant[restr ...][nucl ... $\exists$x **indef.(x)** ... Quant[restr ... x ...][nucl ...]]

(C3)   Quant x[restr ... **indef.(x)** ... Quant[restr ... x ...][nucl ...]][nucl ...]

(D2) $\exists$x **indef.(x)** ... Quant[restr ...][nucl ... Quant[restr ... x ...][nucl ...]]

(D3) $\exists$x **indef.(x)** ... Quant[restr ... Quant[restr ... x ...][nucl ...]][nucl ...]

I now return to my critical comments on Abusch U-set mechanism made in chapter 3. I argue that the "shifts" in (C2) and (C3), and (D2) and (D3) are the result of intermediate and global accommodation instead, and that the in situ interpretations (B2) and (B3) result from the semantic incorporation of the indefinites involved.

3.2.1 Predicting the preferences

According to Abusch's account, the indefinite NP *a proposal* in the sentence below can either get a narrow, an intermediate or a wide scope reading. Her account predicts that there is no preference.

(37)   Every professor invited each committee member who accepted a
       proposal.

   NARROW   "Every professor invited each committee member who
             accepted a proposal."

   INTERM   "For every professor x there is a proposal p such that x
             invited each committee member who accepted p."

   WIDE   "There is a particular proposal p and every professor
             invited each committee member who accepted p."

But is this really the case? Many people have to invest some extra brain
work to get the wide reading, and even more extra work to compute the
intermediate reading. If they do not get the narrow reading, they prefer the
maximal reading. And if they think long enough about the example, they
are able to establish a link between each of the professors mentioned in the
example and some proposal they made respectively. In other words, the
narrow reading appears to be the default reading. Next, we get the maximal
reading. The intermediate reading appears to be the less preferred one.
These predictions are built into the approach of indefinite descriptions
developed in this book. In section 3.1, I proposed that in addition to the
distinction between predicative and free variable indefinites we need the
slogan AC, repeated here:

(26)   ACCOMMODATION CONDITION [AC]

       Unless there is sufficient evidence for an indefinite to be
       accommodated, it is semantically incorporated.

AC captures that indefinites are preferably understood as predicative material
that is absorbed by an incorporating verb in the way discussed in chapter 5.
For our example (37) this means that its narrow reading is the consequence
of interpreting *a proposal* as a predicative indefinite and *to accept* as a
semantically incorporating verb.

     The above slogan furthermore captures that, as a secondary reading, an
indefinite comes with a free variable that receives its existential force
through accommodation. We said that global accommodation is the default
accommodation operation for a presupposition that does not find an
antecedent, as well as for the introduction of a free variable indefinite's
discourse referent. This predicts that next to its primary narrow reading our
indefinite in (37) is likely to get a maximal reading. This prediction fits our
intuitions.

     The intermediate and tertiary reading of *a proposal* in (37) is the result
of intermediate accommodation. In the following two subsections, I
suggest that the intermediate reading of indefinite descriptions is the result
of trapping and bridging.

For the sake of fairness, one must mention that it is possible to build the distinction between predicative and free variable indefinites into Abusch's proposal. This, I believe, would improve the U-set mechanism, but the undesirable situation that one has a separate mechanism for determining the scope of indefinites remains.

3.2.2 Presuppositions determine the scope of an indefinite

In chapter 3, I pointed out that Abusch rejects the option of replacing her U-set mechanism by some mechanism used for the projection of presuppositions. The examples supporting her rejection illustrate cases in which the indefinite is contained in a presuppositional phrase, for example, the complement of a factive verb or the restrictor of a quantifier. However, what she does not take into account is the fact that an indefinite NP's scope position is sometimes fixed by virtue of containing — and not of being contained in — a phrase which is presuppositional, that is, an anaphoric expression. Many of her "intermediate reading" examples are exactly of this kind.

(38)   Every professor rewarded every student who read a book *he* had recommended.

　　　NARROW   "Every professor p rewarded every student who read a book p had recommended."

　　　INTERM   "For every professor p there is a book b that p had recommended such that p rewarded every student who read b."

(39)   Every professor got a headache whenever a student *he* hated was in class.

　　　NARROW   "Every professor p got a headache whenever there was a student whom p hated in class."

　　　INTERM   "For every professor p there is a student s whom p hated such that p got a headache whenever s was in class."

I claim that, on the one hand, the narrow readings of the indefinites in these examples are the consequence of semantic incorporation, whereas, on the other hand, the intermediate reading of the same indefinites are the result of accommodation constrained by trapping.[7] If they are not understood as semantically incorporated predicates, that is, in a narrow way, the indefinites in (38) and (39) are understood as free variable expressions. These

---

[7] If the pronoun is bound to the lowest quantifier, (38) has a secondary narrow reading.

NARR2   "Every professor rewarded every student s who read an arbitrary book s had recommended."

obligatorily get the intermediate reading since otherwise the definite pronouns they contain would remain free.[8] In other words, (38) and (39) illustrate that the constraint on accommodation dubbed "trapping" by van der Sandt (1992) also applies to indefinites. If a free variable expression contains an anaphoric expression, the latter has to be resolved first.

Note again that the resolution of a pronoun does not give rise to a relational reading of the free variable indefinite of which it is a part. Free variable indefinites are not anaphoric expressions. Hence, they cannot accommodate into the restrictor of a quantifier if they are not already part of it.[9]

(38) Every professor rewarded every student who read a book *he* had recommended.

> RELAT   # "Every professor who had recommended a book *b* rewarded every student who read *b*."

(39) Every professor got a headache whenever a student *he* hated was in class.

> RELAT   # "Every professor who hated a student *s* got a headache whenever *s* was in class."

3.2.3 Bridging effects

The indefinite NP *a book that was deemed pornographic* in the following example has at least three possible interpretations.

(40) Each author in this room despises everyone who laughs about a book that was deemed pornographic.

> NARROW   "Each author in this room despises everyone who laughs about any book that was deemed pornographic."

> INTERM   "For each author *a* in this room there is a book *b* that was deemed pornographic such that *a* despises everyone who laughs about *b*."

---

[8] Of course, it is possible to understand the definite pronouns in these indefinite NPs deictically.

[9] If an indefinite is embedded in the restrictor of an embedded quantifier already, it is of course possible to accommodate this indefinite to the restrictor of the embedding quantifier. A case in point is the following example taken from Abusch (1994).

(i) Every person who likes everyone who likes a cat, likes the cat.
  NARR "Every person who likes everyone who likes a cat *c*, likes *c*."
  RELAT "For every person for whom there is a cat *c* and who likes everyone who likes *c*, likes *c*."
  WIDE "There is a cat *c* and every person who likes everyone who likes *c*, likes *c*."

WIDE   "There is a book b that was deemed pornographic such that each author in this room despises everyone who laughs about b."

First, the narrow reading is the result of semantic incorporation. Secondly, the wide reading is a matter of global accommodation. Thirdly, the intermediate reading is possible because one can easily draw a conceptual link between authors and books they write. Again, we encounter a constraint on accommodation of indefinites that we encountered in the context of the accommodation of presuppositions as well, namely, the bridging constraint [see section 2.2.5]. If we replace the NP *each author* — as in (41) —, the intermediate reading is nearly unavailable.

(41)   Each cleaning lady in this building despises everyone who laughs about a book that was deemed pornographic.

For me it is harder to link a cleaning lady with an allegedly pornographic book and, hence, harder to get the intermediate reading. This means that what Abusch's mechanism computes is sometimes hardly available. In other words, her compositional account does not match our intuitions. The bridging account given here does capture the fact that in order to get the intermediate reading of some indefinites, one needs to do some extra thinking.

3.2.4 Bare plurals

Although some readers may not be convinced by the idea that the interpretation procedure of indefinite descriptions has to mirror the order of the preferred readings, I believe that these readers are convinced that such an interpretation procedure has to block impossible readings. Abusch does not discuss these cases and it is unclear to me how the U-set mechanism prevents that the bare plurals in (42) and (43) receive a wide or an intermediate interpretation.

(42)   Each author in this room despises everyone who laughs about books.

NARROW "Every author in this room despises everyone who laughs about any book."

INTERM # "For every author a in this room there are books b such that a despises everyone who laughs about b."

WIDE   # "There are books b such that every author in this room despises everyone who laughs about b."

(43)   Each author in this room despises everyone who laughs about books
         that were deemed pornographic.

>   NARROW   "Every author in this room despises everyone who laughs
>   about books that were deemed pornographic."

>   INTERM   # "For every author a in this room there are books b that
>   were deemed pornographic such that a despises everyone
>   who laughs about b."

>   WIDE   # "There are books b that were deemed pornographic such
>   that every author in this room despises everyone who
>   laughs about b."

In my approach, the narrow scope effect of bare plurals is not a surprise. It
simply follows from the idea that bare plurals are inherently predicative
indefinites and therefore necessarily incorporate. Accommodation cannot
apply to such indefinites. A secondary and a tertiary reading do not exist,
since English bare plurals never translate as free variable expressions.

3.2.5 Indefinites in sentence initial scope islands

We have arrived at the conclusion that intermediate readings are the result of
(implicit) trapping, which is a constraint on default top-level
accommodation. With this in mind, I now turn to yet another, but as we
will see below only apparent, problem that shows up in Abusch (1994).

At the end of her paper, Abusch mentions that for some unclear reason
an indefinite in a sentence-initial *if*-clause does not get an intermediate
reading. Unfortunately, she doesn't give examples of this sort herself so I
assume (44) is a case in point.

(44)   If a student in the syntax class cheats on the exam, every professor
         gets angry.

According to Abusch sentences like (44) do not have an intermediate reading
although they have a maximal one.

>   (44) INTERM   # "For every professor p there is a student s, such that
>   always if s cheats on the exam, p gets angry."

>   WIDE   "There is a particular student s and every professor gets
>   always if s cheats on the exam, angry."

Her interpretive U-set mechanism, by which the free variable that comes
with an indefinite is bound, cannot deal with those examples where an
indefinite lacks the intermediate scope reading. It generates all readings
without exception. For this reason, she proposes to maintain "the concept
of referential indefinites [Abusch (1994): 134]." However, this proposal
does not bring us any further. If we call the indefinite *a student* in the

above example a referential indefinite to capture its maximal scope reading, how do we account for its narrow reading?

(44)　NARROW　"Every professor gets, always if there is a student who cheats on the exam, angry."

Moreover, I believe that the source of why (44) lacks an intermediate reading lies exactly in the fact that the *if*-clause is being topicalized. I show that if we take this surface syntactic fact into account the U-set mechanism predicts the nonexistence of the intermediate reading for (44). Here is how.

First, the above reading paraphrases of (44) take the universal quantifier which binds professors as the higher quantifier and the universal quantifier which has the topicalized *if*-clause in its restrictor as the lower quantifier. This in itself doesn't seem to be a point since in predicate logic (45a) and (45b) are equivalent.

(45)　a.　$\forall x\ [\ P(x) \rightarrow \forall y\ [\ Q(y) \rightarrow R(x,y)\ ]$

　　　b.　$\forall y\ [\ Q(y) \rightarrow \forall x\ [\ P(x) \rightarrow R(x,y)\ ]$

Indeed, for the wide as well as for the narrow reading the order in which the universal quantifiers occur does not play a role. (44 WIDE) and (44 NARROW) are equivalent to the paraphrases (44 WIDE') and (44 NARROW'), respectively.

(44)　WIDE'　"There is a student *s* in the syntax class and always if *s* cheats on the exam, every professor gets angry."

　　　NARROW'　"Always if there is a student in the syntax class who cheats on the exam every professor gets angry."

However, when we derive the intermediate reading the order does play a role. Remember that Abusch's U-set mechanism works bottom up. If we apply the U-set mechanism to the LF which is based on the surface structure of (44), namely (46), the free variable and the restrictive content of the indefinite *a student* are processed after the quantifier *every professor* has been processed.

(46)

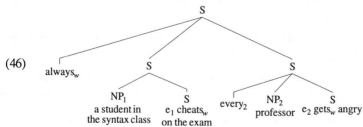

In contrast, if we apply the U-set mechanism to the LF in which the topicalization is made unvisible, as in (47), the possibility of processing *a student* before *every professor* is processed still exists.

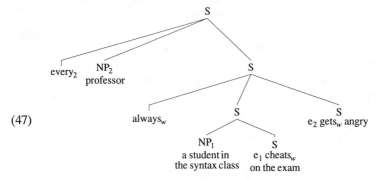

(47)

In other words, the U-set mechanism doesn't allow an interaction between the free material that is in the restrictor of a higher quantifier, with the material that is in the restrictor of a lower quantifier if the latter is in the former's scope. This means that if the surface order of the constituents is respected at LF, the U-set mechanism in fact predicts that there is no intermediate reading for (44). Hence, the need for the notion of "referential" indefinite vanishes.

There was one more issue related to the readings of indefinites in sentence-initial *if*-clauses. In chapter 3, I pointed out that if such an indefinite contains a pronoun, it is possible to assign it an intermediate reading. Abusch's observation that such readings do not exist is thus incorrect. (48), (49) and (50) are illustrations of this case.

(48)   If a student of *his* cheats on the exam, every professor gets angry.

(49)   If a horse from *his* team were in bad condition, every coachman would cancel a race.

(50)   If a horse on which *he* took a chance won, every gambler would be happy.

Apparently, the presence of the pronoun forces the lower universal quantifier to raise because an LF of these examples based on their surface structure would leave us with a free pronoun.

Within the current incorporation–accommodation proposal, we explain why the indefinite in (44) has a narrow and a wide, but lacks an intermediate reading as follows. If the narrow scope of an indefinite is the consequence of semantic incorporation, the existence of the narrow reading of *a student* in (44) is not a surprise. If the other scope readings are the result of accommodation and top-level accommodation is the default operation, the maximal reading of this indefinite is not a surprise either. Finally, given that we take the surface structure of (44) as the input for DRS construction we can explain the fact that (44) lacks an intermediate reading in a way similar to my above explanation in terms of the U-set mechanism. Accommodation is an upward movement and, hence, there is no way to reach a situation in which the indefinite *a student* lands in the restrictor of the lower universal quantifier. To account for the intermediate reading of the indefinites in (48) through (50), we have to assume that an operation like QUANTIFIER RAISING applies to the lower quantifier in order to bind the pronouns in the descriptive content of the respective indefinites.

3.2.6 Summary

In this section, I have revisited some of the data from Abusch (1994) that illustrate cases of indefinites with wide and intermediate readings. As opposed to Abusch, who develops a separate U-set mechanism for determining the scope of an indefinite, I defend the view that we do not need a separate mechanism for this job. Rather, the narrow scope of an indefinite is argued to be a direct consequence of semantic incorporation, and non-narrow readings are determined by the accommodation of their descriptive content.

3.3 What does it mean for an indefinite to accommodate?

Abusch's answer to the question of why a Heimian approach cannot deal with intermediate readings of indefinites is that the restriction of an indefinite becomes a conjunct in the interpretation of the clause in which it immediately occurs. Very much like Abusch, I need

> a mechanism which preserves the restrictions on free variables corresponding to indefinites, ... [Abusch (1994): 108].

Unlike Abusch, I use a pre-interpretive mechanism we already have: accommodation. Unlike Abusch, I let this mechanism only apply to the indefinites which really need it, namely those that leave us with an uninterpretable LF. The predicative indefinites are not involved at all.

Very much like Abusch, I rethink the concept of EXISTENTIAL CLOSURE in Heim's syntactic system and of its counterpart in Kamp's DRT, namely, the introduction of a discourse referent. In the latter approach, an indefinite does not simply contributes a restriction over a variable, rather, it simultaneously introduces this variable into the discourse universe of the same DRS of which its restriction becomes a part [see chapter 3, section 1.1]. In this way, the system ensures the interpretability of an indefinite. But in this way, the system also blocks the way towards an interpretation of nonlocal readings of indefinites. Therefore I suggest that we free an indefinite from this discourse-referent-introduction task and that we associate this task with other sources. On the one hand, a semantically incorporating verb takes care of the introduction of a predicative indefinite's discourse referent. In this way, we get narrow scope and other desirable effects for free as outlined in detail in chapter 5. On the other hand, a free variable indefinite's discourse referent is not introduced by means of a linguistic expression: it is introduced into the right discourse universe as part of a pre-interpretive process, namely, accommodation.

Usually, indefinites are associated with assertion and definites with presupposition. According to Lewis (1979), accommodation takes care of the salience of the latter if needed. As Lewis notes, indefinites are "idioms of existential quantification" and

> ... they [indefinites, VVG] may raise the salience of particular individuals in such a way as to pave the way for referring expressions that follow [Lewis (1979): 180].

In other words, indefinites cannot trigger accommodation. This, I believe is a wrong conclusion and I propose to widen the range of the accommodation mechanism to cover some indefinites as well. Here is why and how.

Even though indefinites shouldn't be called presuppositions in the strict sense in which we have been using this term, namely, as anaphoric expression, there is something presuppositional about some of them. This can be illustrated by the negation-survival test used to distinguish presuppositions from assertions. Let us look again at Rullmann's (1989) observation about a difference between nonspecific and specific indefinite Subjects in Dutch [see chapter 5, section, 4.4]. If the indefinite is interpreted in a specific way, the existential *er* ("there") is dropped.

(51) dat er een student bij mij op bezoek zal komen.

   that there a student at me on visit will come

   i. "Any student will visit me."

   ii. # "There is a student and (s)he will visit me."

(52) dat een student bij mij op bezoek zal komen.[10]

   that a student at me on visit will come

   i. # "Any student will visit me."

   ii. "There is a student and (s)he will visit me."

(52) entails that there is a student. When we embed (52) in a negative context, as in (53), the sentence still entails that there is a student. This indicates that the indefinite is not used as an assertion.

---

[10] Under a kind-contrastive reading, in which case the noun *student* needs focus, *een student* in (52) can get a nonspecific interpretation. I ignore this special case here.

(53)   Het is niet het geval dat een student bij mij op bezoek zou komen.

"It is not the case that a student will visit me."

So, the proposition *there is a student* in (52ii) has to become part of the common ground.

Becoming part of the common ground is done through accommodation. When in van der Sandt's (1992) system accommodation is used as a pre-interpretive mechanism for the interpretation of a definite, its job is to add a proposition to the common ground. As a consequence, the anaphora resolution instruction that comes with a definite can be followed up: the definite gets an antecedent. When we use accommodation for the interpretation of a free variable indefinite, it basically performs the same action. By adding its descriptive content in the form of a proposition to the common ground, an indefinite's free variable automatically gets an existential interpretation. The only difference is that accommodation does not have anaphora resolution as its goal. Rather, its goal is to let an indefinite be an idiom of existential quantification. Thus, if one departs from the assumption that indefinites "introduce" a discourse referent, that is, are a priori associated with local EXISTENTIAL CLOSURE — and Abusch (1994) has successfully argued that we have to depart from this assumption if we want to cover the full range of scope readings of indefinites —, one novel way to introduce the discourse referent of an indefinite is by letting accommodation do this job.

At first sight, my view may appear incompatible with the NOVELTY CONDITION. In chapter 3, I made use of Heim's syntactic formulation.

NOVELTY CONDITION   [Heim (1982): 151]

An NP must not have the same index as an NP to its left.

In discourse semantic terms this condition says that an indefinite never comes with an instruction for anaphora resolution. Nothing in the present approach requires the opposite to be true.

Yet another consequence of my approach may cause some readers to raise their eyebrows. If some indefinites and definites give rise to an existential presupposition, the propositions in which they occur will end up having the same truth conditions. So, as the proposal stands now, the following two sentences will get the same truth conditions.

(54)   Max didn't like some neighbour's cats who had made scratches on his door.

(55)   Max didn't like the neighbour's cats who had made scratches on his door.

This in itself is not an optimal situation, but I don't think that we have to conclude from it that we shouldn't say that free variable indefinites give rise to an existential presupposition. Maybe the fact that (54) and (55) end up with the same truth conditions does not lie in the fact that under its specific reading the indefinite in (54) is being misrepresented as an existential presupposition trigger, but rather in the fact that the current presupposition projection machinery does not deliver satisfactory, or better, complete representations for the interpretation of the definite in (55). In fact, the latter view we find in Krahmer (1995). He argues that just saying that definites trigger existential presuppositions is too weak to capture their meaning. According to Krahmer, definites do not only presuppose existence, they also presuppose determinedness, a term that he defines as familiarity (or, later on, as the more flexible notion of salience [Lewis (1979)]).[11] If we adopt Krahmer's view, we can say that free variable indefinites only trigger an existential presupposition. Unlike definites, they cannot trigger a determinedness presupposition.

In sum, the point in which I deviate from a traditional Lewisian view on accommodation is that it does not only apply when we are dealing with expressions that require an antecedent in a conversation. This repair mechanism applies to any nominal expression whose discourse referent is not introduced by any other means. It applies to any representation which leaves us with free and thus uninterpretable information and transforms such an incomplete semantic representation into an interpretable semantic representation.

As an illustration, I go through the different readings of the following example:

(56) Each author in this room despises every publisher who would not
      publish a book that was deemed pornographic.

For its narrowest interpretation, the indefinite *a book that was deemed pornographic* is interpreted as a property that is absorbed as the predicate of the internal argument's variable of the verb *to publish*. As such, it automatically ends up in the scope of the negation operator triggered by *not* [see chapter 5, section 4].

(56) NARROW "Each author in this room despises every publisher who
            would not publish any book that was deemed
            pornographic."

To receive its non-narrow readings, the indefinite *a book that was deemed pornographic* is interpreted as a free variable expression. Adding the material of a free variable indefinite to the A-structure which is the collector for anaphoric expressions in van der Sandt and Geurts (1991) is surely

---

[11] Krahmer defines familiarity in such a way that it covers both uniqueness and anaphoricity, two basic properties of definite descriptions. (5) has already shown that the latter isn't a property of free variable indefinites. The unacceptability of Krahmer's example (i) shows that uniqueness isn't either.

(i)   # A tallest Frenchman would like to have a new XXXXL T-shirt. [Krahmer(1995):157]

inappropriate because we do not want to say that free variable indefinites are anaphoric [see section 2.3]. Instead, one could create an F-structure — "F" stands for "free" — which fulfils the same function as van der Sandt and Geurts' A-structure. It contains the material that awaits its introduction into some appropriate discourse universe and, if necessary, its resolution as an anaphoric expression. Thus, unlike their A-structure my F-structure collects all the free material. Moreover, if a free variable is introduced by an anaphoric expression, it has to be identified as such. One way of doing this is by saying that it does not only trigger an existential presupposition but also a determinedness presupposition in the sense of Krahmer (1995). Free variable indefinites never come with an anaphora resolution instruction. Hence, they never trigger a determinedness presupposition. The elaboration of a formal framework with an F-structure is beyond the scope of this study.

(57) gives the representation of (56) with the indefinite interpreted as a free variable expression. The latter material is in the double-boxed F-structure.[12]

(57)

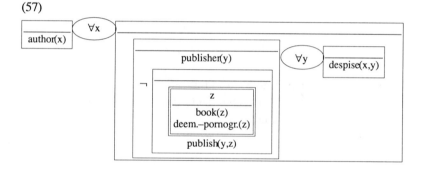

To this incomplete DRS the accommodation mechanism applies thereby emptying the F-structure and yielding an interpretable DRS. The material in the double box in (57) is either accommodated at the highest level or at

---

[12] For the sake of comparison, I give the LF corresponding to this incomplete DRS in (i) and Abusch's (1994) "φ:U" representation in (ii) [see chapter 3, section 3].

(i) ∀x[author(x)][∀y[publisher(y) ∧ ¬[book(z) ∧ deemed-pornogr.(z) ∧ publish(y,z)]] [despise(x,y)]]

(ii) ∀x[author(x)][∀y[publisher(y) ∧ ¬[publish(y,z)]] [despise(x,y)]] : {<z, book(z) ∧ deemed-pornogr.(z)>}

z is free in both representations. In the LF under (ii), the U-set contains the indefinite's descriptive material together with this free variable z. Abusch's interpretive rules bind the variable at the right location and ensure that the descriptive content lands at the same site at which this variable is bound. Note that the U-set mechanism contains exactly the same material which is in the F-structure in (57).

an intermediate level. The resulting wide, intermediate and relational readings are visualized in the respective DRSs.

(56) WIDE "There is a book z that was deemed pornographic and each author in this room despises every publisher who would not publish z."

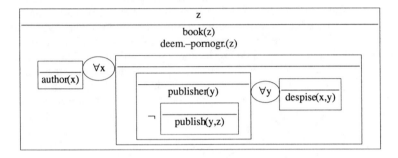

(56) INTERM "For each author x in this room there is a book z that was deemed pornographic and x despises every publisher who would not publish z."

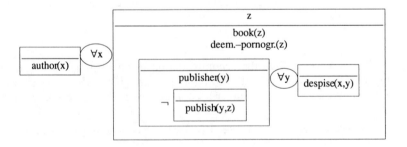

(56) RELAT "Each author in this room despises every publisher for whom there is a book z that was deemed pornographic and who would not publish z."

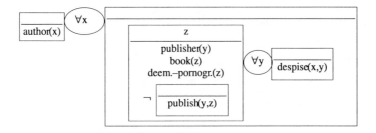

The effect of Heim's text-level EXISTENTIAL CLOSURE RULE probably comes closest to the top-level accommodation of indefinites which is taken to be the default option of accommodation. A case in point is the DRS under the wide reading of (56).

As I illustrated in the previous section, the accommodation of indefinites underlies the same constraints as the accommodation of definites, namely trapping and bridging. Within the current proposal, the INTERM and RELAT reading of (56) each result from intermediate accommodation. There is no counterpart of intermediate accommodation in Heim's system, which is exactly the gap pointed out by Abusch (1994).

Finally, local accommodation is an available option but it mostly gives rise to readings that are equivalent to the readings resulting from semantic incorporation [see (56 NARROW)]. These are the cases covered by Heim's VP-level EXISTENTIAL CLOSURE.

3.4 Summary

In this section, I defended the proposal that semantic incorporation and accommodation determine the interpretation of predicative and free variable indefinites, respectively. As such, both mechanisms take over the discourse-referent-introduction task, a task which in Kamp's DRT is associated with the semantic force of an indefinite itself and which is ruled through EXISTENTIAL CLOSURE in Heim's syntactic approach. Basically, the accommodation of indefinite descriptions underlies the same restrictions as the accommodation of definites. The basic property that a free variable indefinite does not share with the latter is determinedness in the sense of Krahmer (1995).

4 Partitivity

With the assumptions about indefinites made so far, I am now in a position to account for yet another meaning aspect of indefinites often addressed throughout this book. It is the ability of some indefinites, and the inability of others, of receiving a partitive interpretation.

In chapter 2, section 3.2, I pointed out that West Greenlandic numeral-noun incorporating configurations lack a partitive reading. The same holds for German split topics.

(58)   Jensi   marlun-nik   manni-tu-ssa-a-q.   [fw]

     J.-ABS   two-INST.PL   egg-eat-FUT-IND.[-tr]-3SG

     # "Jensi will eat two of the eggs."

(59)   Fragen   hat   Johann   sieben   richtig   beantwortet.

     questions   has   J.   seven   correctly   answered

     # "Of the questions, John has answered seven correctly."

With regard to the West Greenlandic data, I said in chapter 4, section 1.2.2, that Baker's (1988) analysis of noun incorporation cannot account for why the D-structural NP, of which an incorporated noun is assumed to be the head, lacks a partitive reading. In general, NPs often receive such an interpretation.

The prerequisites for arriving at an explanation for why some indefinites do and others don't get a partitive reading are the following. We have to know more about partitivity and the semantic wellformedness of overt partitives in the first place. For this purpose, I discuss the PARTITIVE CONSTRAINT [Jackendoff (1977)] and I propose a novel formulation of this constraint. Secondly, I argue that covert partitives are either quantifiers or free variable expressions. Furthermore, these covert partitives trigger the presupposition of a set of which the bound variable of a quantifier, or the free variable of an indefinite is an element. Predicative indefinites never come with a variable, and as such they lack the trigger of the membership relation. This explains their lack of a partitive interpretation.

4.1 Overt partitivity: The PARTITIVE CONSTRAINT revisited

In English, an overt partitive expression is usually of the form DET-of-NP.[13]

(60)   one of the horses

(61)   [NP [NP one *e*] [PP of the horses]] [14]

---

[13] I do not discuss group partitives. See Abbott (1996) for a discussion of some of these cases.

(i)   one of the team
(ii)   one of every group

Neither do I intend to analyze the following kind of measure phrases.

(iii)   one liter of red wine
(iv)   half a bottle of wine

The semantic wellformedness of English partitives has been widely discussed in the literature [Ladusaw (1982), Hoeksema (1983b, 1996), Wilkinson (1996), Abbott (1996)]. A requirement that any analysis of this construction has to meet is explaining why particular partitives are well-formed, whereas others aren't. In particular, it has to account for which NPs are allowed in the complement position of the embedded PP.

(62)   one of the horses

(63)   one of them

(64)   * one of the horse

(65)   (*) one of several horses in the meadow

(66)   * one of horses

(67)   * one of most horses

Jackendoff's (1977) PARTITIVE CONSTRAINT accounts for some of the above ungrammatical partitive NPs in a syntactic way. It says that the complement NP of the partitive preposition *of* has to be a definite NP. On top of that, the latter has to be plural. This morphosyntactic constraint accounts for the ungrammaticality of those partitive constructions in which either a singular definite — as in (64) —, an indefinite — as in (65) —, a bare plural — as in (66) —, or a quantificational NP — as in (67) — is embedded. However, the wellformedness of an English partitive is not a purely syntactic matter since Jackendoff's constraint does not explain why (65) can be grammatical when the indefinite is interpreted specifically.

In the first section of this chapter, I indicated that the wellformedness of a partitive expression is determined by means of a constraint on the meaning of the embedded NP. That is, I suggested that the NP in the complement of a partitive has to translate as a free variable expression. Before I get to my own proposal, I discuss the problems of the semantic translation of the PARTITIVE CONSTRAINT that we find in Barwise and Cooper (1981).[15]

4.1.1 Barwise and Cooper's (1981) PARTITIVE CONSTRAINT

Barwise and Cooper (1981) give a direct semantic translation of Jackendoff's PARTITIVE CONSTRAINT within the theory of generalized quantifiers. Following the requirement that the embedded NP in a partitive construction

---

[14] I do not discuss the proper syntactic analysis of partitive constructions [Hoeksema (1983b)]. One of the main reasons that I adopt the analysis shown in (61), where the PP is adjoined to a headless NP, is that one can easily extract partitive *of*-phrases. This is illustrated in (i).

(i)   Of the horses, John had taken one.

[15] Other attempts to reduce the wellformedness of a partitive construction to its compositional meaning based on Barwise's and Cooper's translation are Ladusaw (1982), Hoeksema (1983b) and Wilkinson (1996).

is definite, it says that the NP complement of the partitive preposition *of* has to denote a proper principal filter. A proper principal filter is a particular type of principal filter (type $<<e,t>,t>$), namely, one that has a nonempty generator set. In their view, definite NPs exactly fit this semantic type. On top of that, the plurality requirement on the embedded NP is stated as the requirement that the cardinality of the generator set of the proper principal filter is equal to or greater than two. With these semantic constraints, the partitive preposition *of* is interpreted as a function that maps the NP denotation of its right argument into a common noun denotation (type $<e,t>$). The latter can then combine with a determiner (type $<<e,t>,<<e,t>,t>>$).

(68)

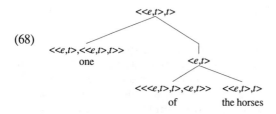

However, this approach to the semantic wellformedness of partitive NPs has at least three shortcomings.

First, it has already been noticed by Ladusaw (1982) that we need a pragmatic treatment of those partitive constructions in which a specific indefinite NP has been embedded. Indefinite NPs are not proper principal filters, and therefore Ladusaw's examples (69) and (70) are clear counterexamples to the above formulation of the PARTITIVE CONSTRAINT.[16]

(69)   That book could belong to one of *three people*.

(70)   John was one of *several students who arrived late*.

The NPs in the *of*-phrases are clearly not definite but, as Ladusaw points out, the reason that these indefinite NPs can occur in the partitive *of*-phrase is related to the fact that they are to a certain degree specific. *Three people* in (69) and *several students who arrived late* in (70) are used to refer to a particular group of individuals that the speaker has in mind.

Secondly, if the meaning of the partitive preposition *of* is regarded as a function which maps the meaning of its right argument into the domain of its left argument, we need to assign yet another meaning to the same preposition in the following "nonstandard" partitive NP.

(71)   two horses of those in the meadow

---

[16] Counterexamples like Ladusaw's have brought Jackendoff's PARTITIVE CONSTRAINT into discredit with many semanticists. Abbott (1996) even proposes to dismiss this constraint.

In (71), it is not the left argument of *of* which is a nonheaded NP but rather its right argument. The following interpretation picture shows that this *of* has another meaning than Barwise and Cooper's type reducing *of* in "standard" partitives in (68).

(72)

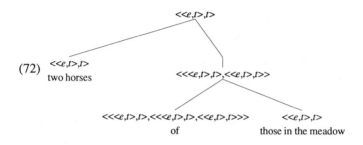

We would have to conclude that partitive *of* is semantically ambiguous although (71) and its "standard" counterpart under (73) have one and the same meaning.

(73)   two of those horses on the meadow.

Thirdly, according to Barwise and Cooper (1981) a partitive NP is interpreted as a quantifier. Diesing (1992) and de Hoop (1992) defend a similar view [see chapter 3, section 2.3.2 and chapter 4, section 2.3.2]. I question whether partitivity itself forces us to interpret every nominal expression with a partitive interpretation as a quantifier. What gives rise to this question is the observation that some partitive NPs can escape scope islands, whereas others cannot. When we contrast (74) with (75), only the former can — in addition to its narrow reading — get an intermediate and a maximal reading, whereas the latter cannot.

(74)   Every gambler will be happy, if one of the horses wins.

NARROW   "Every gambler will, if any h' of the horses h wins, be happy."

INTERM   "For every gambler g there is one h' of the horses h such that g will be happy if h' wins."

WIDE   "There is one h' of the horses h and every gambler will be happy if h' wins."

(75)   Every gambler will be happy, if each of the horses wins.

NARROW   "Every gambler will , if each of the horses wins, be happy."

This indicates that Farkas' (1981), Ruys' (1992) and Abusch's (1994) observation that indefinites but not genuine quantifiers can escape scope islands also holds of partitives with an indefinite determiner but not of those with a quantificational determiner.

4.1.2 A novel interpretation of the PARTITIVE CONSTRAINT

To get rid of the above shortcomings, I capture the semantic wellformedness of an overt partitive phrase as follows. In the representation which is the input for semantic interpretation the complement of the partitive preposition *of* always comes with a variable.

(76)   PARTITIVE CONSTRAINT [PC]

> The complement constituent in a partitive construction has to translate as a nonatomic variable.

The requirement that the NP embedded in the *of*-phrase of a partitive construction be a variable accounts for the fact that free variable indefinites as well as definites are acceptable in this position. In contrast, I pointed out in section 1 that embedding a predicative indefinite into a partitive construction gives rise to ungrammaticality. I repeat the examples here.

(77)   John was one of *several students* who arrived late.

(78)   John was one of *the students* who arrived late.

(79)   * John was one of *students* who arrived late.

Secondly, I take partitive *of* to denote the membership relation ($\in$) regardless of whether it shows up in a standard or in a nonstandard partitive construction [see example (71) versus (73)]. The membership meaning of *of* is fully compatible with the requirement in PC that the complement constituent is a nonatomic variable.

In addition to PC, I draw a distinction between indefinite and quantificational partitives. This enables us to account for the distinct scope behaviour of indefinite partitives and quantificational partitives, as illustrated in (74) and (75). I assume that only those partitive phrases headed by a genuine quantificational determiner denote the quantifier type $<<e,t>,t>$, whereas those headed by a numeral determiner are indefinites. Below, I will argue that indefinite partitives are either interpreted as predicative or as free variable indefinites. Like nonpartitive indefinites, the former receive their existential interpretation through semantic incorporation, and the latter through accommodation.

In the light of the following example containing the quantificational partitive *each of the cookies*, I give a first illustration of my proposal. (81) represents the incomplete DRS of (80), whose F-structure contains the material awaiting its resolution. Accommodation yields (82), a complete DRS which is the input for semantic interpretation.

(80)   Each of the cookies tasted fine.

(81)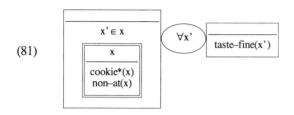

(82)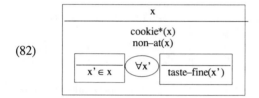

I close this section with the representation of Ladusaw's example (70), repeated here as (83). Accommodating the material in (84)'s F-structure transforms (84) into (85), a complete DRS.

(83)   John was one of several students who arrived late.

(84)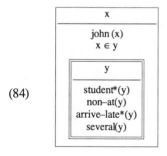

(85)

x   y
john (x)
x ∈ y
student*(y)
several(y)
non–at(y)
arrive–late*(y)

4.1.3 The interpretation of indefinite partitives

In the literature, partitive NPs are usually classified as "strong" NPs, that is, as genuine quantificational expressions [Barwise and Cooper (1981), Diesing (1992), de Hoop (1992), et al.]. Against this standard view, I claim that in the class of indefinite overt partitives, we have those that receive a predicative and those that receive a free variable interpretation. What is the evidence supporting this claim?

I already mentioned in section 4.1.1 that the fact that particular partitive phrases can escape scope islands is a good reason to believe that not every partitive phrase is a genuine quantifier [see example (74)]. However, it does not suffice to distinguish free variable indefinite partitives from quantificational partitives. I propose that we additionally need the notion of a predicative partitive phrase, and here are some arguments supporting this proposal.

First, (86) shows in the most obvious way that the partitive NP *one of the students who organized the party* is interpreted as a predicate.

(86)   Mia is one of the students who organized the party.

(86) says that Mia has the property of being a member of a familiar set of students.

Secondly, I argued that the existential predicate is an inherently semantically incorporating verb [chapter 5, section 3.2]. My view that an overt partitive can receive a predicative interpretation straightforwardly captures the fact that the existential predicate can combine with a partitive NP. Here are two examples taken from McNally (1992) which illustrate this point.

(87)   This time, there were none of the objections they had encountered on
        other occasions.   [McNally (1992): 8]

(88)   There were many of the same people at both events. [McNally (1992): 8]

Also in chapter 5, we concluded that intensional predicates incorporate a property as their internal argument. The following example shows that these predicates easily combine with a partitive phrase without losing their intensional meaning.

(89)   To open this beer bottle, I need one of your keys.

(90)   Jim was looking for one of the teachers to explain his absence.

In (89), I am happy with any of the keys mentioned to open the beer bottle, not only with a particular one of them. What I need is the property of being a member of a familiar set of keys. In (90), Jim is not necessarily looking for a particular teacher, either. Rather, he is looking for a property, namely, the property of belonging to a familiar set of teachers.[17]

And finally, in chapter 4 I gave two West Greenlandic examples from Bittner (1994) illustrating that in this language the de dicto – de re distinction is realized as a weak–strong Case distinction. I repeat the examples here.

(91)   a. *Atuartu-t   ila-an-nik*

            student-ERG.PL   part-3PL.SG-INST.PL

            ikiu-i-sariaqar-p-u-nga.   [Bittner (1994): 138]

            help-AP-must-IND-[-tr]-1SG

            "I must help one of the students, any one will do."

        b. *Atuartu-t   ila-a-t*

            student-ERG.PL   part-3PL.SG-ABS.PL

            ikiur-tariaqar-p-a-ra.   [Bittner (1994): 138]

            help-must-IND-[+tr]-1SG.3SG

            "There is one of the students that I must help."

I pointed out that these examples do not fit in a theory which unambiguously interprets partitive phrases as genuine quantifiers [see chapter 4, section 2.3.2]. I suggest that the weak Case (= INSTRUMENTAL) partitive in (91a) is interpreted as a property, the property of being a member of an existentially presupposed set of students. Its strong Case (= ABSOLUTIVE) counterpart in (91b) is interpreted as a free variable indefinite whose variable belongs to an existentially presupposed set of students. Whereas the former is semantically incorporated by the predicate *to help*, the latter receives its existential interpretation through accommodation.

In light of the ambiguity of example (92), I now show how my analysis strictly separates the treatment of partitivity from the determination of the scope of a partitive phrase.

---

[17] Even hard core Montagovians who follow Moltmann's (1997) view that only verbs of resemblance take a property as their argument should agree that (i) has a de dicto reading. See Van Geenhoven and McNally (1997) for a discussion of *to look like*.

(i)   Tom looks like one of these basketball players who only care about fancy cars.

(92)   John didn't play one of the variations.

    NARROW   "It is not the case that John played any of the variations."

    WIDE   "There is one of the variations that John didn't play."

For its narrow reading, the partitive phrase *one of the variations* is interpreted as a property that is absorbed by the incorporating meaning of *to play*. Note that this property contains a free variable, which is the translation of the presupposition *the variations*. First, we construct the incomplete DRS under (93), which is then transformed into the complete DRS under (94) by means of accommodation.

(93)

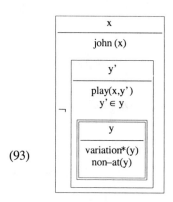

(94)

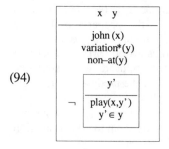

For the wide reading of (92), that is, the case in which the partitive phrase *one of the variations* does not care about the negation operator, *one of the variations* is translated into a free variable expression. Again, the descriptive content which holds for this variable contains the presuppositional NP *the variations*. (95) is the incomplete DRS which serves as the input of the wide reading of (92). The resolution of *the variations* and the accommodation of the whole indefinite partitive transforms the incomplete DRS (95) into the complete and interpretable DRS (96).

(95)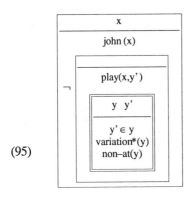

(96)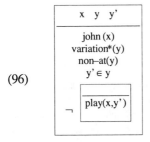

To some readers it may appear as if my claim that an incorporating verb and the accommodation of a free variable indefinite are subject to the NOVELTY CONDITION [see chapter 5, section 1 and this chapter, section 3.1] is not compatible with my claims that the former can absorb a overt partitive, and that the latter can be either an overt or covert partitive. This apparent incompatibility arises because it seems to be conceptually strange to say of a variable that it is novel if one knows that its referent is a member of a presupposed set. However, there is nothing in my first claim that prevents me from making the second one. To say that a variable must be novel is not incompatible with the claim that through predication over this variable the variable is interpreted as a member of a presupposed set.

4.2 Covert partitivity

In the previous section, we captured the semantic wellformedness of an overt partitive construction. As a next step towards our account for why the predicative indefinites in the examples (58) and (59) lack a partitive interpretation, we have to figure out which nominal expressions can receive a partitive interpretation, that is, which nominals are covert partitives. The answer to this question provides us with an explanation for why predicative indefinites are not interpreted in a partitive way.

4.2.1 Nominal expressions with a partitive interpretation

It is a widely accepted assumption that quantificational NPs presuppose their domain of quantification. Phrased differently, we can assume that quantifiers are covert partitive expressions. For example, *each cat in the room* means *each of the cats in the room*, *most dogs on the lawn* means *most of the dogs on the lawn*. If a quantifier NP is interpreted, it will be treated as if it were an overt partitive.

(97)   Every cellist arrived late.

(98)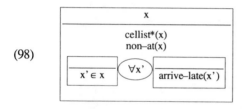

Indefinite descriptions can receive a partitive interpretation as well. For example, *one cellist* can means *one of the cellists*. But, as opposed to the genuine quantifier, an indefinite does not necessarily get a partitive interpretation. *One cellist* will be interpreted in a partitive way if there is an obvious context to do so. For example, if a group of cellists has been mentioned before to which this one cellist somehow belongs. Also focusing *one* gives rise to the presupposition that there is such a group.

(99)   One cellist arrived late.

(100)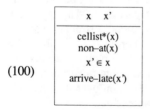

The DRS under (100) shows that the variable which comes with the indefinite *one cellist* is said to be the member of a presupposed set of cellists.

4.2.2 Predicative indefinites lack a partitive interpretation

By now it should be fairly clear why the numeral–noun configurations in the above examples (58) and (59) do not receive a partitive interpretation. Because they are predicative indefinites, they simply lack a variable which stands in the membership relation to some presupposed set. This explanation is not contradictory to my claim that overt partitives can receive a predicative interpretation, and that these overtly partitive indefinites can be semantically incorporated [see section 4.1.3]. In chapter 4, section 2.3.2, I already discussed the fact that predicative indefinites receive a partitive interpretation only if they are overtly marked as such. A predicative indefinite is semantically interpreted in a partitive way only if this indefinite's descriptive content contains the partitive relation, that is, if it is an explicit partitive construction. It does not contain the required power to trigger this membership relation by itself.[18]

At this point, I want to return to Diesing's example (101).

(101) Every cellist played some variations.

How does the present approach account for the different readings of the indefinite *some variations* in this sentence? First of all, the indefinite determiner can be either interpreted as *SM* or as nonincorporatable *some*. Under the former interpretation, *some variations* is interpreted as a predicate that is semantically incorporated by the verb *to play*. The result is a narrow reading with respect to the quantifier *every cellist*. Under the latter interpretation, there are four more options left. If for some contextual reason, the variable introduced by *some variations* can be interpreted as being a member of a familiar set of variations, this variable can be either globally or locally accommodated. The resulting readings are the wide partitive and the narrow partitive — or what Diesing calls "narrow presuppositional" — reading, respectively. If there is no reason to think of

---

[18] Rullmann (1989) defends a similar view that only specific indefinites can be interpreted as what he calls "concealed" partitives. An anonymous reviewer gives (i) as a counterexample to our common view:

(i)   Every student who brought records to the party played a record of the teacher's choice.

When the indefinite *a record of the teacher's choice* has narrow scope with respect to the quantifier *every student who brought records to the party* it can be understood as one of records that was brought by some student. Still, I take this possible partitive interpretation to be a pragmatic side effect and as such it is not part of the semantic representation of (i) that is composed from the meanings of (i)'s parts. In other words, when an indefinite is interpreted as a predicate and the verb as a semantically incorporating verb, nothing in the semantic representation of either is responsible for, or triggers, a membership relation.

the variable introduced by *some variations* as a member of a presupposed set, this variable will still be either globally or locally accommodated. The resulting readings are a wide and a narrow nonpartitive reading, respectively.

4.3 Summary

In this section, I have first discussed the semantic wellformedness of overt partitive expressions. This I took as the basis for the interpretation of covert partitives and for the explanation of why predicative indefinites lack a partitive interpretation. Only those nominal expressions whose meaning contains a variable can receive a partitive interpretation. The presence of this variable is crucial for creating a membership relation between this variable and some presupposed set. Finally, I have shown that unlike Diesing (1992) my treatment of partitivity is strictly separated from determining the scope of a (c)overt partitive.

5 Chapter summary

In this final chapter, I have presented my proposal that predicative indefinites receive their interpretation through semantic incorporation as a fundamental part of a larger approach to the interpretation of indefinite descriptions. I argued that the predicative interpretation is the default way to interpret an indefinite description, and that its secondary interpretation is that of a free variable expression. Moreover, a discourse referent restricted by a predicative indefinite is introduced through a semantically incorporating verb. A discourse referent that comes with a free variable indefinite is introduced through accommodation.

I examined how accommodation has been used within the theory of presupposition projection presented in van der Sandt (1992). Next, I discussed how the mechanism of accommodation determines the scope position of a free variable indefinite. The main advantage of the present accommodation approach is that we only need one mechanism to deal with two phenomena — the scope determination of indefinites and the resolution of presuppositions — that have been treated separately so far. Another advantage is that it predicts which scope reading is possible or preferred to another one.

Finally, I discussed the role of partitivity in the interpretation of indefinite descriptions. I concluded that free variable indefinites, but not predicative indefinites, can be semantically interpreted in a partitive way, unless the latter are overt partitive constructions.

7

Summary and Open Ends

The contributions made in this book can be summarized as follows. My primary goal was to gain a better understanding of the meaning of noun incorporation in West Greenlandic. I believe that with my approach of semantic incorporation, in which incorporated nouns are regarded as predicative indefinites which can only be absorbed by semantically incorporating verbs, we successfully reached this goal. Furthermore, my view that West Greenlandic incorporated nouns are indefinite descriptions of a special sort made it possible to embed the semantic analysis of these nouns into a theory of indefinite descriptions. This theory is based on the distinction between predicative and free variable indefinites and on the presence of two interpretive processing principles, namely semantic incorporation and accommodation. I have shown in chapters 5 and 6 that my approach is capable of answering some of the questions any theory of indefinites should be able to answer. First of all, it answers the question of why particular indefinites do not reach non-narrow scope positions. Secondly, it answers the question of how other indefinites receive non-narrow interpretations. Thirdly, it answers the question of which indefinites receive a partitive interpretation and which don't.

It was my secondary goal to figure out whether and how the meaning aspects of West Greenlandic noun incorporating configurations are represented in the syntactic representations of these configurations. In chapter 4, I defended the view that noun incorporation is a syntactically base generated construction. Chapter 5 has shown that this analysis serves as an appropriate input for the semantic interpretation of incorporated nouns and their external modifiers.

This book leaves many questions also unanswered. In closing, I wish to point out some of them as interesting issues for future research in this area.

First, my study focuses on the semantic incorporation of predicative Objects. Even though I have not investigated this question in an exhaustive fashion, I strongly believe that semantic incorporation can be extended to cover grammatical relations other than Direct Objects. In chapter 5, I have briefly raised the question of how predicative Subjects could be interpreted on the basis of semantic incorporation. In Van Geenhoven (1998), I show how this can be done for predicative Indirect Objects.

Secondly, we have seen that many semantically incorporating verbs have a nonincorporating counterpart. The question of whether the link between them is a matter of lexical type shifting or whether it comes into existence during the semantic interpretation has been addressed, but again not exhaustively answered, in this book. I believe that the lexicon lists those verbs that are either strictly semantically incorporating, for instance the existential predicate, or strictly nonincorporating, for instance individual-level predicates. For verbs capable of taking both guises, we can assume that one appearance is derived from the other. Still, deriving the semantically incorporating version of a verb from its nonincorporating counterpart should not be a matter of semantically nonvacuous type shifting, which takes place during the semantic interpretation. Rather, this semantic derivation must be contributed by some (implicit) linguistic element. A case in point is the antipassive morpheme in West Greenlandic.

A third issue that has been left unaddressed in this book is the interaction between semantic incorporation and focus semantics. Again, this is an open field for future research, some of which has already been built upon by Cohen and Erteschik-Shir (1997).

Fourthly, with semantic incorporation we are able to give a novel definition of the commonly used semantic notion of "weak quantifier." In the present approach, a weak quantifier is a semantically incorporated indefinite. With this in mind and building on insights from Ladusaw (1994), McNally and Van Geenhoven (1997) present a novel cross-linguistic definition of the semantic weak–strong distinction in the class of nominal expressions. Whereas weak nominals are property denoting, strong nominals come with or bind a discourse referent. It is also within this research that we must examine generic interpretations of indefinites, yet another issue largely ignored in this book.

Finally, the presentation of my view that semantic incorporation is a subtheory of a larger theory of indefinites has not extended beyond an informal discussion of the supportive arguments. A fully formalized presentation of my incorporation–accommodation proposal to determine the scope of indefinites may provide further conclusive evidence that these arguments are sound.

References

Abbott, Barbara. 1996. Doing Without a Partitive Constraint. In Jacob Hoeksema, ed. , 1996, 25-56.

Abusch, Dorit. 1994. The Scope of Indefinites. *Natural Language Semantics* 2, 83-135.

Anderson, Stephen R. 1992. *A-Morphous Morphology*. Cambridge: Cambridge University Press.

Bach, Emmon. 1983. On the Relationship Between Word-Grammar and Phrase-Grammar. *Natural Language and Linguistic Theory* 1, 65-89.

Bäuerle, Rainer, Christoph Schwarze and Arnim von Stechow. eds. 1983. *Meaning, Use and Interpretation of Language*. Berlin: de Gruyter.

Baker, Mark C. 1988. *Incorporation: a Theory of Grammatical Function Changing*. Chicago: University of Chicago Press.

Baker, Mark C. 1995. Lexical and Nonlexical Noun Incorporation. In Urs Egli, Peter Pause, Christoph Schwarze, Arnim von Stechow and Götz Wienold, eds., 1995, *The Lexicon and the Organization of Language*, 3-33. Amsterdam: Benjamins.

Barwise, John and Robin Cooper. 1981. Generalized Quantifiers and Natural Language. *Linguistics and Philosophy* 4, 159-219.

Beaver, David. 1994. Accommodating Topics. In Rob van der Sandt and Peter Bosch, eds., 1994, *Focus and Natural Language Processing Vol. 3*, 439-448. Heidelberg: IBM Deutschland.

Beck, Sigrid. 1996. Quantified Structures as Barriers for LF Movement. *Natural Language Semantics* 4, 1-56.

Belletti, Adriana. 1988. The Case of Unaccusatives. *Linguistic Inquiry* 19, 1-34.

Bittner, Maria. 1988. *Canonical and Noncanonical Argument Expressions*. Doctoral dissertation, University of Texas, Austin.

Bittner, Maria. 1994. *Case, Scope and Binding*. Dordrecht: Kluwer.

Bok-Bennema, Reineke. 1991. *Case and Agreement in Inuit*. Doctoral dissertation, Katholieke Universiteit Brabant, Tilburg.

Bresnan, Joan. 1978. A Realistic Transformational Grammar. In Morris Halle, Joan Bresnan and George A. Miller, eds., 1978, *Linguistic Theory and Psychological Reality*, 1-59. Cambridge, Mass.: MIT Press.

Butt, Miriam. 1993. Specificity in Hindi/Urdu. In Katherine Beals, Gina Cooke, David Kathman, Sotaro Kita, Karl-Erik McCullough and David Testen, eds.,

1993, *Papers from the 29th regional meeting of the Chicago Linguistics Society*, Vol.1, 89-103.

Carlson, Gregory N. 1977. *Reference to Kinds in English*. Doctoral dissertation, University of Massachusetts, Amherst. Published 1980. New York: Garland.

Carlson, Gregory N. and Francis J. Pelletier. eds. 1995. *The Generic Book*. Chicago: University of Chicago Press.

Chierchia, Gennaro. 1984. *Topics in the Syntax and Semantics of Infinitives and Gerunds*. Doctoral dissertation, University of Massachusetts, Amherst. Published 1989. New York: Garland.

Chierchia, Gennaro. 1995. *Dynamics of Meaning*. Chicago: University of Chicago Press.

Chomsky, Noam. 1972. Remarks on Nominalization. In Noam Chomsky, ed., 1972, *Studies on Semantics in Generative Grammar*, 11-61. The Hague - Paris: Mouton

Chomsky, Noam. 1981. *Lectures on Government and Binding*. Dordrecht: Foris.

Cohen, Ariel and Nomi Erteschik-Shir (1997) Topic, Focus and the Interpretation of Bare Plurals. In Paul Dekker, Martin Stokhof en Yde Venema, eds., 1997, *Proceedings of the 11th Amsterdam colloquium*, 31-36. Amsterdam.

Cresswell, Max and Arnim von Stechow. 1982. De Re Belief Generalized. *Linguistics and Philosophy* 5, 503-535.

de Hoop, Helen. 1992. *Case Configuration and NP Interpretation*. Doctoral dissertation, RijksUniversiteit Groningen. Published 1996. New York: Garland.

Diesing, Molly. 1992. *Indefinites*. Cambridge, Mass.: MIT Press.

Di Sciullo, Anna-Maria and Edwin Williams. 1987. *On the Definition of Word*. Cambridge, Mass.: MIT Press.

Doron, Edit. 1993. The Discourse Function of Appositives. *Proceedings of IATL*, 53-65.

Dowty, David. 1979. *Word Meaning and Montague Grammar*. Dordrecht: Reidel.

Dowty, David. 1981. Quantification and the Lexicon: a Reply to Fodor & Fodor. In Michael Moortgat, Harry van der Hulst and Teun Hoekstra, eds., 1981, *The Scope of Lexical Rules*, 79-106. Dordrecht: Foris.

Dowty, David. 1994. The Role of Negative Polarity and Concord Marking in Natural Language Reasoning. In Mandy Harvey and Lynn Santelmann, eds., 1994, *Proceedings of the 4th conference on Semantics and Linguistic Theory*, 114-144. Ithaca: CLC Publications, Cornell University.

Enç, Mürvet. 1991.The Semantics of Specificity. *Linguistic Inquiry* 22, 1-25.

Evans, Gareth. 1980. Pronouns. *Linguistic Inquiry* 11, 337-362.

Fanselow, Gisbert. 1988. Aufspaltung von NPen und das Problem der "freien" Wortstellung. *Linguistische Berichte* 114, 91-112.

Fanselow, Gisbert. 1993. The Return of the Base Generators. In Werner Abraham, ed., *Groninger Arbeiten zur Germanistischen Linguistik* 36, 1-74. Groningen.

Farkas, Donka. 1981. Quantifier Scope and Syntactic Islands. In Roberta Hendrick, Carrie Masek and Mary F. Miller, eds., 1981, *Papers from the 17th regional meeting of the Chicago Linguistics Society*, 59-66.

Fodor, Janet and Ivan Sag. 1982. Referential and Quantificational Indefinites. *Linguistics and Philosophy* 5, 355-394.

Fortescue, Michael. 1984. *West Greenlandic*. London: Croom Helm.

Gallin, Daniel. 1975. *Intensional and Higher Order Modal Logic: with Applications to Montague Semantics*. Amsterdam: North Holland.

Geach, Peter T. 1962. *Reference and Generality*. Ithaca: Cornell University Press.

Groenendijk, Jeroen, Dik de Jongh and Martin Stokhof. eds. 1987. *Studies in Discourse Representation Theory and the Theory of Generalized Quantifiers*. Dordrecht: Foris.

Groenendijk, Jeroen and Martin Stokhof. 1990. Dynamic Montague Grammar. In Laszlo Kálmán and Laszlo Pólos, eds., 1990, *Papers from the Second Symposium on Logic and Language*, 3-48. Budapest: Akadémiai Kiadó.

Groenendijk, Jeroen and Martin Stokhof. 1991. Dynamic Predicate Logic. *Linguistics and Philosophy* 14, 39-100.

Heim, Irene. 1982. *The Semantics of Definite and Indefinite Noun Phrases*. Doctoral dissertation, University of Massachusetts, Amherst. Published 1984. New York: Garland.

Heim, Irene. 1983. On the Projection Problem for Presuppositions. *Proceedings of the 2nd West Coast Conference on Formal Linguistics*, 114-126.

Heim, Irene. 1987. Where Does the Definiteness Restriction Apply? Evidence from the Definiteness of Variables. In Eric Reuland and Alice ter Meulen, eds., 1987, 21-42.

Heim, Irene. 1990. E-Type and Donkey Anaphora. *Linguistics and Philosophy* 13, 137-177.

Hoeksema, Jacob. 1983a. Plurality and Conjunction. In Alice ter Meulen, ed., 1983, *Studies in Model-Theoretic Semantics*, 63-84. Dordrecht: Foris.

Hoeksema, Jacob. 1983b. Partitives. Manuscript, RijksUniversiteit Groningen.

Hoeksema, Jacob. ed. 1996. *Partitives: Studies on the Syntax and Semantica of Partitive and Related Constructions*. Berlin: Mouton de Gruyter.

Huang, C.-T. James. 1982. *Logical Relations in Chinese and the Theory of Grammar*, Doctoral dissertation, MIT, Cambridge, Mass.

Jackendoff, Ray. 1977. *X' Syntax: A Study of Phrase Structure*. Cambridge, Mass.: MIT Press.

Jacobs, Joachim. 1982. *Syntax und Semantik der Negation im Deutschen*. München: Fink Verlag.

Jacobs, Joachim, Arnim von Stechow, Wolfgang Sternefeld and Theo Vennemann. eds. 1993. *Syntax. An International Handbook of Contemporary Research*. Berlin: de Gruyter.

Kadmon, Nirit. 1987. *On Unique and Non-Unique Reference and Asymmetric Quantification*. Doctoral dissertation, University of Massachusetts, Amherst.

Kamp, Hans. 1981. A Theory of Truth and Semantic Interpretation. In Jeroen Groenendijk, Theo Jansen and Martin Stokhof, eds., 1981, *Formal Methods in the Study of Language*, 277-322. Amsterdam: Mathematisch Centrum.

Kamp, Hans und Uwe Reyle. 1993. *From Discourse to Logic*. Dordrecht: Kluwer.

Karttunen, Lauri. 1973. Presuppositions of Compound Sentences. *Linguistic Inquiry* 4, 167-193.

Karttunen, Lauri. 1977. Syntax and Semantics of Questions. *Linguistics and Philosophy* 1, 3-44.

Keenan, Edward. 1987. A Semantic Definition of "Indefinite NP". In Eric Reuland and Alice ter Meulen, eds., 1987, 286-318.

Klein, Ewan. 1980. Determiners and the Category Q. Manuscript, University of Sussex.

Klein, Ewan and Ivan Sag. 1985. Type-Driven Translation. *Linguistics and Philosophy* 8, 163-197.

Kornfilt, Jaklin. 1990. Naked Partitive Phrases in Turkish. Manuscript, Syracuse University.

Krahmer, Emil. 1995. *Discourse and Presupposition*. Doctoral dissertation, Katholieke Universiteit Brabant, Tilburg.

Kratzer, Angelika. 1980. Die Analyse des bloßen Plurals bei Gregory Carlson. *Linguistische Berichte* 70/80, 47-50.

Kratzer, Angelika. 1988. Stage-Level and Individual-Level Predicates. In Manfred Krifka, ed., 1988, *Genericity in Natural Language*, SNS-Bericht 88-42, Universität Tübingen, 247-284. Reprinted in Gregory N. Carlson and Francis J. Pelletier, eds., 1995, 125-175.

Kratzer, Angelika. 1994. *The Event Argument and the Semantics of Voice*. Book manuscript, University of Massachusetts, Amherst.

Krifka, Manfred. 1992. Thematic Roles as Links between Nominal Reference and Temporal Constitution. In Ivan Sag and Anna Szabolsci, eds., 1992, *Lexical Matters*, 29-54. Stanford: CSLI Publications.

Krifka, Manfred, Francis J. Pelletier, Gregory N. Carlson, Alice ter Meulen, Godehard Link and Gennaro Chierchia. 1995. *Genericity: an Introduction*. In Gregory N. Carlson and Francis J. Pelletier, eds., 1995, 1-124.

Ladusaw, William. 1982. Semantic Constraints on the English Partitive Construction. *Proceedings of the 1st West Coast Conference on Formal Linguistics*, 231-242.

Ladusaw, William. 1992. Expressing Negation. In Chris Barker and David Dowty, eds., 1992, *Proceedings of the 2nd conference on Semantics and Linguistic Theory*, 237-259. Columbus: Ohio State University.

Ladusaw, William. 1994. Thetic and Categorical, Stage and Individual, Weak and Strong. In Mandy Harvey and Lynn Santelmann, eds., 1994, *Proceedings of the 4th conference on Semantics and Linguistic Theory*, 220-229. Ithaca: CLC Publications, Cornell University.

Lewis, David. 1975. Adverbs of Quantification. In Edward Keenan, ed., 1975, *Formal Semantics of Natural Language*, 3-15. Cambridge: Cambridge University Press.

Lewis, David. 1979. Score Keeping in a Language Game. In Rainer Bäuerle, Urs Egli and Arnim von Stechow, eds., 1979, *Semantics from Different Points of View*, 172-187. Berlin: Springer Verlag.

Link, Godehard. 1983. The Logical Analysis of Plurals and Mass Terms: a Lattice Theoretical Approach. In Rainer Bäuerle, Christoph Schwarze and Arnim von Stechow, eds., 1983, 303-323.

Marantz, Alec. 1984. *On the Nature of Grammatical Relations*. Cambridge, Mass.: MIT Press.

McNally, Louise. 1992. *An Interpretation for the English Existential Construction*, Doctoral dissertation, University of California, Santa Cruz. Published 1997 as *A Semantics for the English Existential Construction*. New York: Garland.

McNally, Louise. 1995. Bare Plurals in Spanish are Interpreted as Properties. In Glyn Morrill and Richard Oehrle, eds., 1995, *Formal Grammar*, 197-222. Barcelona: Universitat Politécnica de Catalunya.

McNally, Louise. to appear. Existential Sentences without Existential Quantification. *Linguistics and Philosophy*.

McNally, Louise and Veerle Van Geenhoven. 1997. Redefining the Weak/Strong Distinction. Paper read at the Colloque de Syntaxe et Sémantique 2, Université de Paris 7, Paris. Manuscript, Universitat Pompeu Fabra, Barcelona.

Milsark, Gary. 1974. *Existential Sentences in English*. Doctoral dissertation, MIT, Cambridge, Mass.

Milsark, Gary. 1977. Towards an Explanation of Certain Peculiarities in the Existential Construction in English. *Linguistic Analysis* 3, 1-30.

Mithun, Marianne. 1984. The Evolution of Noun Incorporation. *Language* 60, 847-894.

Mohanan, Tara. 1995. Wordhood and Lexicality: Noun Incorporation in Hindi. *Natural Language and Linguistic Theory* 13, 75-134.

Moltmann, Friederike. 1997. Intensional Verbs and Quantifiers. *Natural Language Semantics* 5, 1-52.

Montague, Richard. 1974. *Formal Philosophy: Collected Papers of Richard Montague, Edited and with an Introduction by Richmond H. Thomason*. New Haven: Yale University Press.

Neale, Stephen. 1990. *Descriptions*. Cambridge, Mass.: MIT Press.

Neeleman, Ad. 1994. *Complex Predicates*. Doctoral dissertation, RijksUniversiteit Utrecht.

Partee, Barbara. 1987. Noun Phrase Interpretation and Type-Shifting Principles. In Jeroen Groenendijk, Dik de Jongh and Martin Stokhof, eds., 1987, 115-143.

Partee, Barbara and Mats Rooth. 1983. Generalized Conjunction and Type Ambiguity. In Rainer Bäuerle, Christoph Schwarze and Arnim von Stechow, eds., 1983, 361-383.

Pollock, Jean-Yves. 1989. Verb Movement, Universal Grammar and the Structure of IP. *Linguistic Inquiry* 20, 365-424.

Postal, Paul. 1969. Anaphoric Islands. *Papers from the 5th regional meeting of the Chicago Linguistics Society*, 205-239.

Reinhart, Tanya. 1997. Quantifier Scope: How Labor is Divided between QR and Choice Functions. *Linguistics and Philosophy* 20, 335-397.

Reuland, Eric and Alice ter Meulen. eds. 1987. *The Representation of (In)definiteness*. Cambridge, Mass.: MIT Press.

Rischel, Jørgen. 1971. Some Characteristics of Noun Phrases in West Greenlandic. *Acta Linguistica Hofniensia* 12, 213-245.

Rooth, Mats. 1987. Noun Phrase Interpretation in Montague Grammar, File Change Semantics, and Situation Semantics. In Peter Gärdenfors, ed., 1987, *Generalized Quantifiers*, 237-268. Dordrecht: Reidel.

Rooth, Mats. 1995. Indefinites, Adverbs of Quantification and Focus. In Gregory N. Carlson and Francis J. Pelletier, eds., 1995, 265-299.

Rosen, Sarah. 1989. Two Types of Noun Incorporation. *Language* 65, 294-317.

Rouveret, Alain and Jean-Roger Vergnaud. 1980. Specifying Reference to the Subject: French Causatives and Conditions and Representations. *Linguistic Inquiry* 11, 97-202.

Rullmann, Hotze. 1989. Indefinite Subjects in Dutch. Manuscript, University of Massachusetts, Amherst.

Rullmann, Hotze. 1995. *Maximality in the Semantics of Wh-Constructions*. Doctoral dissertation, University of Massachusetts, Amherst.

Ruys, Eduard. 1992. *The Scope of Indefinites*. Doctoral dissertation, RijksUniversiteit Utrecht.

Ruys, Eduard. 1995. Weak Cross-over as a Scope Phenomenon. Manuscript, RijksUniversiteit Utrecht.

Sadock, Jerrold. 1980. Noun Incorporation in Greenlandic, A Case of Syntactic Word Formation. *Language* 56, 300-319.

Sadock, Jerrold. 1986. Some Notes on Noun Incorporation. *Language* 62, 19-31.

Sadock, Jerrold. 1991. *Autolexical Syntax*. Chicago: University of Chicago Press.

Schwarz, Bernhard. 1992. Noun Phrase Split in German. Manuscript, University of Massachusetts, Amherst.

Sells, Peter. 1994. Sub-Phrasal Syntax in Korean. *Journal of the Linguistic Society of Korea* 30, 351-386.

Szabolsci, Anna. 1986. Indefinites in Complex Predicates. *Theoretical Linguistic Research* 2, 47-83.

van der Sandt, Rob. 1992. Presupposition Projection and Anaphora Resolution. *Journal of Semantics* 9, 333-377.

van der Sandt, Rob and Bart Geurts. 1991. Presupposition, Anaphora and Lexical Content. Institut für Wissensbasierte Systeme, Report 185. Stuttgart: IBM Deutschland.

Van Geenhoven, Veerle. 1992. Noun Incorporation from a Semantic Point of View. In Laura A. Buszard-Welcher, Lionel Wee and William Weigel, eds.,

1992, *Proceedings of the 18th annual meeting of the Berkeley Linguistics Society*, 453-467.

Van Geenhoven, Veerle. 1995. Semantic Incorporation: a Uniform Semantics of West Greenlandic Noun Incorporation and West Germanic Bare Plural Configurations. In Audra Dainora, Rachel Hemphill, Barbara Luka, Barbara Need and Sheri Pargman, eds., 1995, *Papers from the 31st regional meeting of the Chicago Linguistics Society*, 171-186.

Van Geenhoven, Veerle. 1997. A Semantic Analysis of External Possessors in West Greenlandic Noun Incorporating Constructions. Paper read at the Conference on External Possession and Related Noun Incorporation, University of Oregon, Eugene. Manuscript, MPI, Nijmegen.

Van Geenhoven, Veerle. 1998. On the Argument Structure of some Noun Incorporating Verbs in West Greenlandic. In Miriam Butt and Wilhelm Geuder, eds., 1998, *The Projection of Arguments: Lexical and Compositional Factors*, 225-263. Stanford: CSLI Publications.

Van Geenhoven, Veerle and Louise McNally. 1997. De Dicto Readings via Semantic Incorporation. Paper read at the Texas Linguistic Society Conference on the Syntax and Semantics of Predication, University of Texas, Austin. Manuscript, MPI, Nijmegen.

van Riemsdijk, Henk. 1987. Movement and Regeneration. In Paola Beninça, ed., 1987, *Dialect Variation and the Theory of Grammar*, 105-136. Dordrecht: Foris.

von Stechow, Arnim. 1993. Die Aufgaben der Syntax. In Joachim Jacobs, Arnim von Stechow, Wolfgang Sternefeld and Theo Vennemann, eds., 1993, 1-88.

Ward, Gregory, Richard Sproat and Gail McKoon. 1991. A Pragmatic Analysis of So-called Anaphoric Islands. *Language* 67, 439-473.

Weir, Carl E. 1986. *English Gerundive Constructions*. Doctoral dissertation, University of Texas, Austin.

Wilkinson, Karina. 1996. Bare Plurals, Plural Pronouns and the Partitive Constraint. In Jacob Hoeksema, ed., 1996, 209-230.

Williams, Edwin. 1983. Semantic vs. Syntactic Categories. *Linguistics and Philosophy* 6, 423-446.

Winter, Yoad. 1997. Choice Functions and the Scopal Semantics of Indefinites. *Linguistics and Philosophy* 20, 398-466.

Woodbury, Hanni. 1975. Onondaga Noun Incorporation: Some Notes on the Interdependence of Syntax and Semantics. *International Journal of American Languages* 41, 10-20.

Zimmermann, Thomas Ede. 1993. On the Proper Treatment of Opacity in Certain Verbs. *Natural Language Semantics* 1, 149-179.

Zucchi, Alessandro and Michael White. 1996. Twigs, Sequences and the Temporal Constitution of Predicates. In Teresa Galloway and Justin Spence, eds., 1996, *Proceedings of the 6th conference on Semantics and Linguistic Theory*, 329-346. Ithaca: CLC Publications, Cornell University.